Locked out: Understanding and tackling school exclusion in Australia and Aotearoa New Zealand

Locked out: Understanding and tackling school exclusion in Australia and Aotearoa New Zealand

Edited by Patty Towl and Sheryl Hemphill

NZCER PRESS
New Zealand Council for Educational Research
PO Box 3237
Wellington
New Zealand

© Authors, 2016

ISBN 978-1-927231-73-9

This book is not a photocopiable master.
No part of the publication may be copied, stored or communicated
in any form by any means (paper or digital), including recording
or storing in an electronic retrieval system, without the written
permission of the publisher.
Education institutions that hold a current licence with Copyright
Licensing New Zealand may copy from this book in strict accordance
with the terms of the CLNZ Licence.

A catalogue record for this book is available from the National Library
of New Zealand

Designed by Smartwork Creative Ltd

Contents

Foreword — vii
Megan Mitchell, National Children's Commissioner, Australia

Foreword — x
Judge Andrew Becroft, Principal Youth Court Judge for Aotearoa New Zealand: Te Kaiwhakawā Matua o Te Kooti Taiohi

Introduction — 1
Patty Towl and Sheryl Hemphill

Part One: Talking about exclusion

Chapter 1 The right to education: Advocacy in school exclusion contexts — 11
Janis Carroll-Lind

Chapter 2 'The kid with ADHD who fished up the land of the kiwi' and other stories from exclusion to inclusion: Human rights, disability and education in the post Disability Convention world — 31
Paul Gibson, Disability Rights Commissioner, New Zealand Human Rights Commission

Chapter 3 Is internal suspension associated with better student outcomes than external suspension? — 47
Sheryl Hemphill, Jess Heerde and Barbara McMorris

Chapter 4 What results from psychological questionnaires? — 71
Tim Corcoran

Part Two: Resolving school exclusion contexts

Chapter 5 A way forward? Finding room for flexible behaviour management approaches in inflexible school structures — 91
Sheryl Hemphill, Sarah Drew, David Broderick, Lynn Gillam and Lyndal Bond

Chapter 6 The relationship between the compulsory school experience and youth offending — 114
Alison Sutherland

Chapter 7 Writing the wrong: Using restorative practices to address student behaviour — 135
Michelle Kehoe, Sheryl Hemphill and David Broderick

Chapter 8 A stitch in time: Clues to mending the home–school relationship after a crisis event 153
Patty Towl

Chapter 9 The McAuley Champagnat Program: A community response to a local problem 174
Kevin Quin and Katrina Mohammed

Chapter 10 Outside in: One school's endeavours to keep disadvantaged young people in school and engaged 196
Margaret Callingham

Chapter 11 The Ministry of Education's Behaviour Crisis Response Service: Helping educational facilities to manage crisis situations and keep students engaged in learning 216
Mike Crosby, Grant Malins and Terry Carter

Chapter 12 Narrative therapy as a guide for responding to unacceptable actions 236
Donald McMennamin

Chapter 13 Conclusions 257
Sheryl Hemphill and Patty Towl

About the authors 261

Index 268

Foreword

Megan Mitchell, National Children's Commissioner, Australia

By reconceptualising school exclusion as a rights issue, *Locked Out: Understanding and Tackling School Exclusion in Australia and Aotearoa New Zealand* is a much welcome departure from punitive disciplinary approaches that are so often harmful to children and young people. This book offers us a unique chance to reimagine school practices within the framework of children's inalienable right to education, and all other rights that extend from that vital starting point.

Australia and New Zealand share many things in common, including a commitment to children's rights and experiences of school exclusion. Both countries have ratified the United Nations Convention on the Rights of the Child—Australia in 1990 and New Zealand in 1993—which asserts that children have a right to education and that school disciplinary measures must respect the dignity of the child and conform to the Convention as a whole.[1]

Education is both a human right in itself and a crucial means of realising other human rights.[2] In my role as Australia's first National Children's Commissioner, I have found—and this book confirms this—that disengagement through suspensions, expulsion and other forms of school exclusion can have far-reaching implications for the rights and wellbeing of children and young people. There are often immediate negative impacts on children's health and safety, as well as lifelong damage to their developmental trajectory and ability to participate fully in society. For example, long-term unemployment is acknowledged in this book as having a significant relationship with school exclusion.

School exclusion can also entrench the very social and behavioural problems it is trying to address. As the authors and contributors identify, being excluded from school has been linked to low school achievement, antisocial behaviour, substance abuse and youth crime. The age at which children and young people are most likely to be excluded from school overlaps with crucial stages in adolescent brain development.

The research presented in this book is vital for understanding how we can develop more effective forms of school intervention that address the learning and emotional needs of children at this age.

As noted by the authors, schools have a unique opportunity to interrupt patterns of behaviour through early identification and well-timed intervention. We know that schools are crucial to the development of children's physical, intellectual, emotional and mental wellbeing. Today's generation of young people is exposed to a range of complex stressors that, as adults, we need to understand much better if we are to help young people to successfully navigate their school years and beyond.

This book demonstrates that school exclusion is also a condition of inequality, which disproportionately affects children who already face disadvantage, such as through poverty, ethnicity and disability. For example, in Australia higher rates of school exclusion of Aboriginal and Torres Strait Islander children are linked to patterns of social exclusion and disenfranchisement across the generations. In the New Zealand context, the writers identify that Māori and Pasifika students continue to incur higher rates of exclusion, which are linked to long-standing socioeconomic factors. In both New Zealand and Australia, human rights and discrimination bodies have recorded high numbers of complaints combining the ground of disability and the area of education.

From a rights-based perspective, we have a duty to direct education towards the development of every child's unique personality, abilities and learning needs, and to ensure that education is culturally appropriate.[3] The first step to achieving this is listening to the views and experiences of children themselves, who, after all, are the experts in their own lives. In fact, the right of children to be heard and taken seriously is a principle that underpins the Convention in its entirety. More specifically, children have the right to be heard "in any judicial and administrative proceedings affecting the child, either directly, or through a representative or an appropriate body."[4]

Many schools have made steps to develop mechanisms that enable children to participate in the policies and decision-making processes that affect them. However, significant gaps remain, especially for children under 15 years of age.[5] Ignoring the experiences of children and young people will invariably lead to interventions that just don't work for them, whereas privileging the voice of children sends a powerful message about their worth and also acts as a strong safeguarding measure against abuse and exploitation.

The solutions discussed in this book, such as restorative justice and narrative therapy, share a common focus on the involvement of children in school disciplinary proceedings as part of the process of learning and experiencing the realisation of rights.[6] These options will require specific engagement skills, the provision of adequate information and support for children to participate meaningfully, and, in some instances, additional or different resources.

This book makes it clear that school environments need to better reflect children's connection to their community, including their parents and carers. School environments also need to foster greater connection between students, peers and educators. School connectedness has been shown to have a positive effect on school attendance, academic achievement, and the mental and physical health of children. There is also a correlation between high levels of connectedness and a reduced likelihood of engaging in risky behaviour as an adolescent. I have visited many schools around Australia and it is clear the moment you walk in the gates which schools have achieved this connectedness, and there is a palpable difference in the behaviour and attitudes of the students in those schools, right across the student body.

I look forward to the new ideas and innovations in school practices that will no doubt stem from this excellent work, and I congratulate the authors and the contributors for bringing the issue of school exclusion to light and showing a way forward.

Notes

1 *Convention on the Rights of the Child*, 1989, article 28.
2 This is recognised by the Committee on Economic, Social and Cultural Rights in *General Comment 13, The Right to Education*, UN Doc E/C.12/1999/10 (1999), para 1.
3 *Convention on the Rights of the Child*, 1989, article 29.
4 *Convention on the Rights of the Child*, 1989, article 12.
5 This was observed by the Committee on the Rights of the Child in its *Concluding Observations on Australia* on 15 June 2012. www2.ohchr.org/english/bodies/crc/docs/co/CRC_C_AUS_CO_4.pdf
6 These approaches are in line with those promoted by the Committee on the Rights of the Child in *General Comment 13, The Aims of Education*, UN Doc CRC/GC/2001/1 (2001), para 8.

Foreword

Judge Andrew Becroft, Principal Youth Court Judge for Aotearoa New Zealand: Te Kaiwhakawā Matua o Te Kooti Taiohi

> "If you are planning for a year, sow rice; if you are planning for a decade, plant trees; if you are planning for a lifetime, educate children." (*Chinese proverb*)

If there is a central message to this challenging book, it is that keeping young people in school, rather than excluding them, is of pivotal importance to our community's long-term health. This is a message that resonates with all those involved in youth justice. It is music to our ears, especially those involved at the coal face who each day deal with our most challenging and problematic young people. This is because most serious young offenders are not engaged in education. They have drifted out of the formal education system, often in their early teenage years, having been the recipient of a series of failed school-based interventions. Then they typically move through successive programmes aimed at curbing their behaviour. All too often they end up before the Youth Court.

That is why it is not so unusual that a Youth Court judge would write a foreword to a book such as this. Youth Court judges have a significant interest in our education system. There is also a statutory mandate to address the causes underlying a child's or young person's offending. Of course there is no magic bullet to reduce youth offending. But if there were, it would be to keep every young person meaningfully involved in education—preferably mainstream education—for as long as possible. Nowadays, all those involved in the youth justice community accept that educational involvement is one of the most significant protective factors in a young person's life. It builds resilience. Re-engagement in education is probably the most effective response that the youth justice system can make to repetitive youth offending.

It is perhaps worth unpacking my perspective in more detail. In

New Zealand, most youth offenders do not come to court and are dealt with effectively by the police in the local community. For most of these young people, educational disengagement is not the issue. However, about 20 percent of youth offenders are charged and brought to court. Most are what are known, according to the jargon, as "life course persistent offenders" or "early onset offenders". They make up probably only 10 to 15 percent of all youth offenders, but they might be responsible for up to 50 percent of youth offending in their area. They come with an alarming cocktail of characteristics which are often referred to as co-morbid, or co-occurring and inter-related.

- About 81 percent are male, although the number of young women who are offending is increasing, especially for violent offending. Young women present with a range of issues that differ from those of young men, making engagement more difficult and time consuming to address.
- A number of youth offenders (estimated at 10 to 15 percent), both male and female, are already parents of children themselves. In many cases they are the subject of government intervention regarding the care and protection of their children.
- Up to 70 to 80 percent of young offenders have alcohol or drug issues. The drugs of choice are mainly alcohol (beer and Ready to Drink beverages (RTDs)) and cannabis. Many young people before the Youth Court started their drug use before 10 years of age.
- Crucially for the purposes of this book, up to 70 percent of youth offenders are estimated not to be engaged with school or even enrolled at a secondary school. They have usually been excluded or simply drifted out of education. Non-enrolment rather than truancy is the key problem.
- Most have experienced family dysfunction and disadvantage and are transient and violent. They also lack positive role models.
- Many have some form of psychological disorder, especially conduct disorder, and display little remorse or empathy.
- Many have a neuro-disability. No prevalence study on this issue has been undertaken in New Zealand, but it is unlikely that the rate here would differ significantly from those found in a study carried out by

the Office of the Children's Commission for England and Wales. The study undertook an "extensive structured literature review … chosen to provide extensive coverage of a variety of relevant academic disciplines" (Hughes et al, 2012, p.20). The review found that young people held in custody had significantly higher rates of neuro-disability than young people in the general population across all neurodevelopmental disorders. Young people in custody, for example, are eight times more likely to have autistic spectrum disorder and twice as likely to have traumatic brain injury. More than one in three young people in custody are also likely to have a learning or communication disability

- Māori, the indigenous population of Aotearoa New Zealand, are over-represented among youth offenders. They make up 24 percent of the 10–16-year-old population, yet they comprise 61 percent of court appearances nationally, and in some North Island courts the appearance rate is significantly higher. The disproportion of Māori representation in the Youth Court is getting worse, not better (an increase from 44 percent in 2005 to 61 percent in 2014).
- Child, Youth and Family records show that 73 percent of youth justice clients are known for care and protection concerns.

This is a rather depressing and bleak analysis. However, it does indicate the significant number of young offenders who are not engaged in education in any form and the likelihood that they have other co-occurring problems. It also serves to emphasise the size of the problem that will face some secondary schools in retaining young people with these sorts of challenges. They represent some of the most damaged and challenging young people in the country.

I do not wish to be misunderstood. In some cases it seems to me that exclusion from school may well be inevitable in the interests of the greater majority of students. But the message of this book is that such a step must be a last resort, and in fact may apply to many fewer children and young people than previously thought. In this respect, it has long been suggested that schools in the future may well become 'social service hubs', where co-located expert services provide input and assistance to the school's most problematic and damaged pupils.

There is every reason to think that the young people in the education system who are most at risk of exclusion display many of the characteristics identified and described above. This book addresses these issues very frankly and brings a message of hope. The practical initiatives collected in Part Two of the book focus on endeavours that are being used in Aotearoa New Zealand and Australia to keep challenging young people engaged in school. Especially encouraging are the efforts described that aim to include indigenous young people, who are just as disproportionately represented in the school disengagement statistics as they are in the youth justice statistics.

There is also an interesting chapter on the use of restorative justice. This will resonate with all New Zealanders involved in the youth justice system, given the use of the Family Group Conference as the key decision-making mechanism for all those young people who appear in our courts. Family Group Conferences are practised in a restorative justice way and are often hailed as the first comprehensive (and probably only) example of restorative justice being incorporated into a country's legal system. The use of restorative justice in secondary schools in Aotearoa New Zealand is already well advanced and proving very successful. There are other New Zealand government initiatives, such as Positive Behaviour for Learning initiative (PB4L), which are also bearing fruit in terms of providing a school-wide approach to improving responses to challenging behaviour.

I could go on. The point is that significant strides are clearly being made by schools to involve difficult and problematic students. The message of this book is that more needs to be done and can be done. Indeed, there is another interesting chapter which flips conventional wisdom on its head and talks about how schools can change to deal with difficult young pupils rather than seeing the solution as a matter of fixing the pupils. In this way, school disengagement is seen as the school's issue rather than the young person's problem: what has the school done to alienate the young person? This all represents a different paradigm and constitutes challenging new thinking.

From the Youth Court's perspective there have already been significant changes in the attitudes of Aotearoa New Zealand secondary schools to retaining their most difficult young people. Increasingly it seems to be accepted that excluding or expelling a problem does not solve that problem for the community: it only relocates it. There has been a sea change in the attitude of most schools, and we see the benefits in youth justice. Youth Court numbers have halved in the last 5 years. The rates of appearances in court have reduced dramatically. It is difficult to isolate a single factor, but the view of most is that the increased commitment by the Ministry of Education and schools around Aotearoa New Zealand to retaining students within the school community has been a significant contributing factor. Long may this continue. And improve.

I conclude with a challenge through the lens of a Youth Court judge. Schools are the community's ultimate—and certainly its first-line—'crime fighters'. Schools that engage and involve as many young people as possible, and for whom exclusions/expulsions are a rarity, provide an enormous service to the justice system and their country. Their efforts bring down the crime rate. Schools are not usually cast in this role. The language of crime fighting is seldom attributed to the educational community. But it should be. Young people who are no longer locked out of school and who are able to access some form of meaningful educational/vocational training are unlikely to become adult criminals.

All those in education will find this book interesting and challenging. But it is also a message of practical hope for the wider community, and, in particular, the youth justice community, which relies so much on successful educational engagement. The words of this whakataukī (Māori proverb), with which I conclude, perhaps put it best:

> Māmā kē te tohutohu tamariki, i te whakatika pakeke.
> (It is better to train up a child than to try to repair an adult.)

References

Hughes, N. Williams, H., Chitsabesa, P. Davies, R. & Mounce, L. (2012). *Nobody Made the Connection: The Prevalence of Neurodisability in Young People Who offend.* United Kingdom. The Office of the Children's Commissioner.

Introduction

Patty Towl and Sheryl Hemphill

School exclusion is a legal process that removes a child from school, on either a short- or long-term basis. It is a world-wide practice, common to many school jurisdictions similar to Australia's and Aotearoa New Zealand's. It is a process with many competing pressures. While school communities argue that excluding students is necessary to maintain school safety, extensive research shows that being excluded from school is linked to low school achievement (Fergusson, Swain-Campbell, & Horwood, 2002) and youth offending (Sutherland, 2007), antisocial behaviour (Hemphill, Toumbourou, Herrenkohl, McMorris, & Catalano, 2006), and substance use (Hemphill, Heerde, Herrenkohl, Toumbourou, & Catalano, 2012). Furthermore, statistics reveal that school exclusion disproportionately affects children from identified at-risk groups (e.g. low-income, indigenous Australian, Māori and Pasifika children, and children with disabilities) (Grant, 2004).

It would be easy, therefore, to label school exclusion practices as socially unjust. The practice continues, however, which suggests that school communities—like most communities—perceive a need for a point at which decisions about membership are made. The authors in this book respect the right of schools to make these decisions but question the wisdom of using a practice that excludes a child from school without resolution. The purpose of this book is to present the issues relating to school exclusion and then suggest processes and programmes that might help retain students in school.

There is a second stage to any decision to exclude, which involves deciding how to return the child to school. We put forward research-based evidence and practices designed to support those who resolve crisis situations with young people and seek to retain students in mainstream education. An alternative view of any school exclusion event is that it provides an opportunity to re-engage the child with school. Any school exclusion can be a sentinel point, where authentic conversations can occur among those who have a stake in keeping that particular child in lifelong, high-quality education (Towl, 2013).

Research shows that excluding a child from school affects a wide range of practitioners who work to reduce poor life outcomes for young people. The authors in this volume, therefore, are drawn from health, justice and education. Those who read this book will not all be school-based practitioners, but also youth and health workers, school trustees, youth aid and community workers, and policy analysts—anyone, that is, who is looking for reliable local research to support their practice, and for practical solutions that will work in local situations.

Definitions and statistics: Aotearoa New Zealand and Australia

In Aotearoa New Zealand the legislation that sets the parameters for school exclusion can be found in the Education Act 1989, sections 13–19. The school principal has the absolute right to send students home under these provisions, but except in the case of stand-down (see definition below) the responsibility for deciding the circumstances under which the student may return to school is the responsibility of the school's board of trustees, a group of elected parents.

There are four types of school exclusion: stand-down, suspension, exclusion, and expulsion. Stand-down is similar to the practice of short-term suspension in Australia. It is the least serious of the exclusion provisions available to principals. Principals may stand down a student for up to 5 days in a term and 10 days in any school year. Any further incidents that may prompt an exclusion event must become a suspension. Once the principal suspends the student, the board of trustees must meet within 7 days and may decide to return the student to school with or without restrictions. Trustees also have the absolute right to exclude or—if the student is over 16 years of age—expel the student. Parents may appeal the board's decision, but only through judicial review. In Aotearoa New Zealand about 3 percent of the school population is stood down each year. Students are rarely suspended without having been stood down at some time, and among the children who are stood down about 25 percent are suspended. Of those suspensions, about 25 percent again end in exclusion or expulsion.

In Australia, the legislation for school exclusion is determined separately by each state – there is no federal government legislation. Since the authors of all of the chapters on Australia reside in Victoria, the legislation in Victoria will be described here. Ministerial Order Number 184 sets out the grounds for suspension and expulsion in government schools (these are the two types of exclusion described in the Ministerial Order). Only the principal of the school can suspend or expel a student from that school (this authority cannot be delegated to anyone else). A student can be suspended from school for up to 5 days at any one time, and for up to 15 days in any school year (unless approval is obtained from the regional director in the school's area). A student who has been suspended for 15 days in the school year does not automatically become expelled. When a student is suspended for 3 days or fewer, meaningful school work must be provided to them, and when a student is suspended for more than 3 days, a Student Absence Learning Plan and Return to School Plan must be completed. Students can lodge an appeal against a decision to expel them through the Secretary of the Department of Education and Training. In Victoria the rates of exclusion from school each year are not publically reported. It is therefore difficult to provide an indication of how many students in Victoria are excluded from school. Research on a state-representative sample of Victorian students suggests that in Years 7 and 9 suspension rates are approximately 11 percent for boys and 6 percent for girls (Hemphill et al., 2006).

New knowledge, organisation and major themes
This is the first book to describe the Aotearoa New Zealand and Australian context for the practice of school exclusion. It provides accessible, locally based research and practical responses for practitioners who

work with exclusion and excluded young people. Although this volume establishes school exclusion as a condition of poverty, ethnicity, and social and educational disadvantage, it also presents a way forward to significantly reduce school exclusion in all its forms.

The volume is divided into two parts. The first, shorter, part establishes the context for school exclusion in Australia and Aotearoa New Zealand. Writers in this section outline school exclusion in its local context. Authors present up-to-date, locally based research and comment on the effects of school exclusion on children and young people in this part of the world. Themes addressed highlight the negative aspects of school exclusion for local children. It is made clear that school exclusion is a rights issue, one that influences negatively and disproportionately the potential for children from identified at-risk communities to participate as valued members of society, both at and beyond school. In addition, Part One promotes the voices of excluded children, their parents and those who speak for them—a hidden aspect of most exclusion events (Towl, 2013). Supported by up-to-date research, this part provides evidence of the consequences to young people of school exclusion, and supplies details of the real experiences of real children.

Part One begins with Janis Carroll-Lind describing the context of school exclusion in Aotearoa New Zealand. Dr Caroll-Lind, through her experience working for the Office of the Commissioner for Children, introduces one of the key themes of this volume: student rights and advocacy in the exclusion environment. The second contributor, Paul Gibson, the New Zealand Disability Rights Commissioner, raises an important issue: the vulnerability to being suspended from school for children with disabilities and special education needs. Paul argues that when we exclude children because of difference, we reduce the richness of our culture. In the third chapter, Sheryl Hemphill, Jess Heerde and Barbara McMorris introduce another major theme of the volume: being suspended from school has serious consequences for young people, in both the immediate and the long term, and these consequences affect not only the child and family but also the wider community. Drs Hemphill, Heerde and McMorris draw on data from the Victorian arm of the International Youth Development Study to suggest implications for school management of young people at risk of suspension. Finally,

Tim Corcoran, a psychologist with extensive experience in schools and the prison service, questions the current trend in market-centred school contexts of too much reliance on psychological testing when making decisions about young people.

The second part of the book provides a number of examples of research-based interventions that are not resource heavy and appear to be effective for all children, regardless of social background. These suggested interventions are practical and applicable to most situations. Their key messages promote early intervention, flexible approaches, robust communication and maintaining school connectedness. Practitioners who work in exclusion and with excluded children, both in school and in the community, should find suggestions and programmes in this section that are clearly described and easily uplifted and administered. Practitioners could use the changes to practice described in this part to make a difference to children and reduce the number of excluded young people in their community.

The first four contributors to Part Two write about initiating flexible alternative approaches to resolving school exclusion within inflexible and often punitive school structures. Sheryl Hemphill, Sarah Drew, David Broderick, Lynn Gillam and Lyndal Bond present both student and school staff perspectives on school suspension. Hemphill et al. present the barriers to and opportunities for moving schools from punitive to preventive behaviour management strategies. In Chapter 6 Alison Sutherland presents the school estrangement factors that, if linked with already-existing family-based risk factors, can combine to put young people not only at risk of exclusion but also of youth offending. Dr Sutherland suggests some school protocols and practices that work to reduce the potential cumulative effect of inflexible school and negative home-based factors. Michelle Kehoe, Sheryl Hemphill and David Broderick show how restoratives practices work positively in different situations. Kehoe et al. suggest that whole-school approaches to restorative practices improve communication across the school and increase the students' potential to think reflectively. In Chapter 8 Patty Towl argues the case for early intervention from the first stand-down event. Dr Towl explains that there are clear actions that schools can take and protocols schools can follow to enhance the potential for an enduring return to school.

The final four contributors provide a selection of ways in which flexible options for resolution can and do work within existing structures. Kevin Quin, a psychologist, and Katrina Mohamed, a Gooreng Gooreng woman and journalist, write about the success excluded indigenous Australian youth can achieve through an alternative education facility which specifically recognises and caters for their needs. Kevin and Katrina present a clear picture of the multifaceted nature of successful alternative education provision. Margaret Callingham, an ex-teacher and principal, shows how programmes responsive to the individual needs of excluded children can successfully retain young people in mainstream education. She provides detailed examples of how flexibility in programming works effectively for excluded children in a school in a disadvantaged neighbourhood. Mike Crosby, Grant Malins and Terry Carter comprise the Ministry of Education Behaviour Crisis Response Service for the Northern Region of Aotearoa New Zealand. Their chapter describes how this initiative works to resolve school crises for children with severe and challenging behaviour in mainstream education. Finally in Part Two, Donald McMenamin, a school counsellor, describes the theory and practice of re-authoring school identity stories through narrative therapy. Through examples of counselling practice, Dr McMenamin shows how young, excluded and marginalised young people can learn to express their school identity in positive and appropriate ways.

References

Fergusson, D., Swain-Campbell, N., & Horwood, L. J. (2002). Outcomes of leaving school without formal educational qualifications. *New Zealand Journal of Educational Studies, 37*(1), 39–55.

Grant, P. (2004, 2 August). Suspended students lack basic rights. *New Zealand Herald*.

Hemphill, S. A., Heerde, J. A., Herrenkohl, T. I., Toumbourou, J. W., & Catalano, R. F. (2012). The impact of school suspension on student tobacco use: A longitudinal study in Victoria, Australia, and Washington State, United States. *Health Education & Behavior, 39*, 45–56.

Hemphill, S. A., Toumbourou, J. W., Herrenkohl, T. I., McMorris, B. J., & Catalano, R. F. (2006). The effect of school suspensions and arrests on subsequent adolescent antisocial behavior in Australia and the United States. *Journal of Adolescent Health, 39*, 736–744.

Sutherland, A. (2007). *Classroom to prison cell.* Wanganui, NZ: Stead & Daughters.

Towl, P. (2013). Making opportunity from disappointment: Students, parents and teachers talk about stand-down. *New Zealand Journal of Educational Studies, 48*(1), 127–139.

Notes

1 *Convention on the Rights of the Child,* 1989, article 28
2 This is recognised by the Committee on Economic, Social and Cultural Rights in *General Comment 13, The Right to Education,* UN Doc E/C.12/1999/10, (1999), para 1.
3 *Convention on the Rights of the Child,* 1989, article 29.
4 *Convention on the Rights of the Child,* 1989, article 12.
5 This was observed by the Committee on the Rights of the Child in its Concluding Observations on Australia on 15 June 2012.
6 These approaches are in line with those promoted by the UN Committee on the Rights of the Child in *General Comment 13, The Aims of Education,* UN Doc CRC/GC/2001/1 (2001), para 8.

PART ONE: TALKING ABOUT EXCLUSION

Chapter 1 The right to education: Advocacy in school exclusion contexts

Janis Carroll-Lind

Key points

1. Educational advocacy involves advancing the interests, rights and welfare of students.
2. All students have the right to be included at school.
3. To ensure that students' rights are upheld within the context of school exclusion, schools are required to manage the procedural issues involving paramountcy and natural justice.
4. Schools play a key role in engaging restoratively with challenging behaviours to interrupt the pathway of youth offending.

Introduction

Advocacy in an educational context involves the recognition of basic rights, which includes the right to education. The right to education also recognises students' rights to have disciplinary matters dealt with according to the principles of natural justice. In Aotearoa New Zealand there is a range of legislation and regulations that give effect to students' rights to education, yet complaints to the Office of the Children's Commissioner (OCC) confirm that some students continue to be denied access to or full participation in an inclusive education. With its statutory responsibility to be an independent advocate for children and young people, OCC endeavours to:

- provide positive outcomes for schools and students by maintaining students within the education system
- reduce barriers to learning that are created by conflict between schools, students, and parents and families
- improve relationships between the early childhood and school sectors and their communities.

The use of an advocate introduces a new relationship into the traditional home–school relationship in exclusion events. This chapter draws on some of those advocacy cases while navigating the competing rights of students, their parents and schools when making educational decisions that affect their futures.

Before reading this chapter, think about where you stand on the following issues.

- A student should be sent home for not wearing his or her school uniform.
- A student with special needs does not have the right to go on the class camp.
- A student with special needs can only attend school during the time (s)he has a teacher aide allocated.
- A student whose parents do not pay the school donation should be suspended until the fee is paid.
- Any student who assaults another student should be stood down, no matter what the circumstances.
- Young people who commit serious crimes at school (e.g. assault) should be treated the same as adults.
- A student should be stood down after refusing to submit to drug testing.
- If suspected of having a communicable disease, a student may be prevented from attending school.
- A suspended student should be allowed to return to school to sit exams.

The New Zealand education system must ensure that all children and young people receive equal opportunities in realising their right to education, as enshrined by Article 28 of the United Nations Convention on the Rights of the Child. New Zealand has a range of

- policy (e.g. Special Education, 2000 [Ministry of Education, 1996]; National Education Goals [amended 2004]; Success for All—Every School, Every Child [Ministry of Education, 2011])
- legislation (e.g. the Education Act 1989; the Education Amendment Act 2013; the Human Rights Act 1993), and
- human rights conventions (e.g. the United Nations 1948 Universal Declaration of Human Rights and the 1989 Convention on the Rights of the Child)

that aim to increase the presence, participation and achievement of all students within an inclusive education system. Section 8 of the Education Act 1989 demonstrates how rights are positioned within the law: people who have special educational needs (whether because of disability or otherwise) have the same rights to enrol and receive education at state schools as people who do not.

Clearly, students in this country have the right to high-quality education that meets their specific needs as learners. Schools have both a legal responsibility under the Education Act 1989 and an ethical obligation under the Human Rights Act 1993 to cater for all their students, and the role of school boards of trustees is to ensure that all of the policies, procedures and practices that relate to their students are in place in their school and are applied without discrimination.

Inclusion is also a key principle of *The New Zealand Curriculum* (Ministry of Education, 2007):

> The Curriculum is non-sexist, non-racist, and non-discriminatory; it ensures that students' identities, languages, abilities and talents are recognised and affirmed and that their learning needs are addressed.
> (p. 9)

Booth and Ainscow (2011) define inclusion as the process of increasing the presence, participation and achievement of all students in schools, with particular reference to those groups of students who are at risk of exclusion, marginalisation and underachievement. This involves restructuring the cultures, policies and practices, and minimising the barriers in schools, so that they respond to the diversity of students in their communities (Booth & Ainscow, 2011). Successfully including learners may require making changes and modifications in the content, approaches, structures and strategies used. Improving schools in this way enables the building of relationships within and beyond schools and fosters a shared concern for "how people learn together, how they treat one another and how they learn to live within a common world" (Ainscow, Booth, & Dyson, 2006, p. 1).

There are no legitimate reasons to separate children for their education. Inclusive education is a human right and all children have the right to learn together. Children belong together—with advantages and benefits for everyone. They should not be devalued or discriminated against by being excluded or sent away because of their learning or behaviour difficulty (CSIE, n.d.). Academic and behavioural difficulties are both problems of learning (Prochnow & Johansen, 2013).

Inclusive education celebrates diversity and, as documented in New Zealand's best evidence synthesis for teaching diverse students (Alton-Lee, 2003), the concept of diversity rejects the notion of 'normal', 'other' or 'minority groups of children', but instead views diversity and difference as being central to the learning and development of children and central to the focus of quality teaching. Hence, government strategies aim to support diverse learners to achieve educational success. Building on its predecessor (*Ka Hikitia—Managing for Success 2008–2012*), *Ka Hikitia—Accelerating Success 2013–2017* sets the strategic pathway for improving how the education system performs for Māori students (Ministry of Education, 2013b). Similarly, the Pasifika Education Plan aims to raise Pasifika students' participation, engagement and achievement (Ministry of Education, 2013a). Other recent responses to improving the outcomes of diverse learners include the Positive Behaviour for Learning Action Plan, the Youth Guarantee Programme, and the requirement for registered teacher involvement in the provision of alternative education (Carroll-Lind, 2011).

Yet, despite the policy, legislation and human rights conventions, disparities in access, participation and achievement continue to be a major concern, with strong forces of exclusion working against inclusion to exclude and marginalise some students from and within school

(Kearney, 2013). Students with challenging behaviours are often considered to be the most difficult to include (Prochnow & Johansen, 2013). The New Zealand reviews of special education (Ministry of Education, 2010), alternative education (Education Review Office, 2011) and complaints received by OCC support this view. The following discussion explains the role of OCC and its function as an advocate in school exclusion contexts.

Office of the Children's Commissioner

The role of the Children's Commissioner was established in the 1989 Children, Young Persons and Their Families Act as part of a worldwide move towards having commissioners or ombudsmen for children. In 2003 the Children's Commissioner's Act was passed, setting out the Commissioner's powers and functions in a stand-alone statute. It encompasses all children and young people up to 18 years of age and is not restricted to those who are subject to the provisions of the Children, Young Persons, and their Families Act 1989. The Children's Commissioner's Act 2003 retains the monitoring and review functions in relation to Child, Youth, and Family, the Aotearoa New Zealand government agency that has legal powers to intervene to protect children. However, the 2003 Act requires the Commissioner to take cognisance of the diversity of children in New Zealand, with the statutory right to investigate any matters affecting children and young people (unless the issue is before the courts). Under the Children's Commissioner's Act, the Commissioner can require information from agencies if it concerns the interests, rights or welfare of a child or children. In addition, the Crown Entity Act 2004 means that in the core functions of advocacy, monitoring or investigative matters, the Commissioner must, by law, form a view independently of the government.

A key part of the Commissioner's role is to promote the participation of children and young people in decision making affecting them. At any one time 10 young people, aged between 12 and 17 years, are appointed to OCC's Young People's Reference Group. They come from diverse backgrounds and represent rural and urban communities. Their role is to give advice to the Commissioner, assist in the strategic direction of the office, assist in the achievement of office goals, facilitate consultation with children and young people, and inform the Children's Commissioner of regional issues. They speak out on issues that are important to them (Young People's Reference Group, 2011).

In its advocacy role for children and young people, OCC endeavours to:

- provide positive outcomes for schools and students by maintaining students within the education system
- reduce barriers to learning that are created by conflict between schools, students, and parents and whānau[1]
- improve relationships between the early childhood and school sectors and their communities.

Students with disabilities, in particular, experience barriers to their learning that in many cases have resulted in exclusion from school. OCC has provided advocacy support for students with disabilities in the following scenarios. Although just a snapshot of the requests fielded by OCC, they give a good indication of the experiences of many students requiring advocacy support and are applicable to both primary and secondary students.

- Attendance was restricted because of a lack of support. Students are only allowed to be at school when support is available
- Parents were asked to contribute financially to their children's teacher aide hours
- Students were sent home whenever they "misbehaved".
- One student with autism missed a whole term of school because he hit the new taxi driver (who had not been advised by the taxi company always to drive the same route to school).
- Full-time teacher aide funding for a specific student was used to pay for a remedial teacher to do literacy work with other groups of students (and not the student for whom the funding was granted).
- Parents were told their daughter would be excluded unless she always used her wheelchair during school times (against her physiotherapist's advice).
- Students were refused enrolment or excluded unless they gained Ongoing Resourcing Scheme (ORS) funding.

Limiting students' attendance at school is a common form of marginalisation. For example, OCC has supported students who were only allowed at school during the hours funded by a teacher aide; told they could only attend 4 days a week; or sent home over the lunch break (which prevented their mothers, in most cases, from being employed outside the home). One student experienced a very slow transition into his new school after exclusion from his previous school (i.e. 1 hour a day in the school library for over a term).

Another common form of advocacy undertaken by OCC is in response to parents, students, principals and other professionals seeking advice and advocacy for students when there are issues of concern with their education that have escalated to the stand-down, suspension, exclusion or expulsion of those students. OCC funded the Wellington Community Law Centre to provide a guide to parents and caregivers (*Schools and the Right to Discipline*) about legal issues in Aotearoa New Zealand schools, and this chapter draws on the advice contained in that publication (see Darlow, 2011).

Stand-downs, suspensions, exclusions and expulsions

A stand-down is the short-term, formal removal of a student from school by the principal (or acting principal) for a specified period (up to 10 days) because of (1) continual disobedience (regular or deliberate non-compliance or disregard of school rules) or (2) gross misconduct (serious misbehaviour that is striking and reprehensible to a high degree). The behaviour must be a dangerous example to others, or harmful (or likely to cause harm) to themselves or others. Students can be stood down more than once, but this cannot total more than 5 days in a school term or 10 days in a school year (Darlow, 2011).

Suspension is the formal removal of a student from school. While initiated by the principal (or acting principal), the suspension meeting is held—and the outcome decided—by the board of trustees. The board of trustees may choose to lift the suspension or extend the suspension (with or without conditions), or they may exclude or expel the student. Exclusion is the formal removal from school of students less than 16 years old. A board of trustees can only exclude a student if the behaviour warrants the most serious of responses. The excluded student must enrol at another school and the principal is required to help with these arrangements. If a new school cannot be found after 10 days, the principal must inform the Ministry of Education so that the Ministry can then help to place the student. Expulsion is the formal removal from school of students aged 16 years and older. The expelled student may seek enrolment at a school elsewhere, but the principal and Ministry of Education are not required to help the student to find a new school (Darlow, 2011).

Section 13 of the Education Act 1989 states that the purpose of the legislation regarding stand-downs, suspensions, exclusions and expulsions is to provide a range of responses for cases of varying degrees of seriousness, minimise the disruption to a student's attendance at school and facilitate the return of the student to school when that is appropriate, and ensure individual cases are dealt with in accordance with the principles of natural justice. Exclusions and expulsions are for the most serious cases only. Relevant sections of the Education Act include:

- Section 3: Right to Education
- Section 60A: National Education Guidelines
- Section 77: Right to Counselling
- Section 77: Obligation to Parents
- Section 13C: Natural Justice.

The Education Amendment Act 2013, passed on 12 June 2013, sets out changes to the law governing expulsion and exclusion of students and attendance at school. The Amendment Act provisions relating to new search and retention powers came into effect on 1 January 2014, following the development of rules and guidelines on searches and the surrender and retention of property, in consultation with the education sector.

The Ministry of Education's website includes an excellent guidelines document for principals and boards of trustees, which describes the legislation and processes for stand-downs, suspensions, exclusions and expulsions, and has information sheets for parents and form letters and templates for schools to use. Contact details for OCC and the Wellington Community Law Centre's PLINFO line (Parent Legal Information Line for School Issues) are included on the information sheet provided for parents.

What we know

Students (mostly male) in the 13–15 years age group incur the most stand-downs, suspensions and exclusions. The good news is that stand-down and suspension rates in Aotearoa New Zealand continue to fall (Education Counts, 2014). That said, the Ministry of Education's 2013 statistics (Education Counts, 2014) reveal that while the expulsion rates for Pasifika students were slightly higher than those of Māori students, schools continue to stand down, suspend and exclude more Māori students than any other ethnic group. However, exclusion rates are clearly linked to socioeconomic factors (students attending schools in poorer communities are 5.5 times more likely to be excluded than students attending schools located in affluent areas), and proportionally more Māori and Pasifika students attend schools in lower socioeconomic locations (Education Counts, 2014).

Stand-downs, suspensions, exclusions and expulsions are not measures of student behaviour; they are measures of schools' reactions to student behaviour. What one school may choose to suspend for, another may not (Education Counts, 2014). This is not just an Aotearoa New Zealand issue, nor is it recent. UK authors Munn, Lloyd and Cullen (2000) note that exclusion is not so much about what children do as how schools themselves behave.

While recognising the individual right of each self-managing schools to make informed decisions about their students and to determine their own course of action, this also means that a student in one school might receive different consequences from a student involved in a similar incident at another school. Some schools use stand-downs as a time for reflection and an opportunity to reduce tension and prevent escalation of the action that led to the stand-down (Education Counts, 2014). However, in some instances, students are unlawfully suspended, excluded or expelled from school. These so-called 'kiwi suspensions' occur when students are sent home from school without going through the formal process, as mandated by the Education Act. OCC has advocated for students and their families when students have been sent home for not wearing the school's correct uniform, or non-compliance with school rules around hair length or styles, hair dyeing, or non-regulation jewellery (e.g. nose studs). Kiwi suspensions also occur when parents of children with special needs are told to keep their child at home if, for example, the teacher aide is sick or the school is expecting a visit from the Education Review Office. Sometimes, too, parents of students with challenging behaviours are asked to withdraw their child before they get excluded or expelled. The parents might be told that "the school down the road would be better able to meet your child's needs" or that "getting a fresh start would be in your child's best interests". These 'voluntary' withdrawals are also kiwi suspensions.

Findings from OCC's inquiry into the safety of students at school (Carroll-Lind, 2009) revealed a number of bully-related stand-downs and suspensions involving both the students who bullied and the students who were bullied. While some parents and caregivers (of both primary and secondary school children) requested help to stop their children's bullying behaviours after their children were stood down for violent episodes at school, far more parents complained that their children were unfairly stood down, and in some cases suspended or excluded, when they had responded negatively to students who were bullying them. In one example, after being continually bullied, both girls involved were stood down because the victim had hit her assailant first. The parents of the girl being bullied wanted the school to retract her stand-down. Another case involved a 9-year-old who was suspended for unruly behaviour that his parents considered was due to his continual harassment and bullying by peers.

Competing obligations

A number of parents in the school safety inquiry (Carroll-Lind, 2009) reported dissatisfaction that their children had to face their bullies when they were reinstated at school after stand-down or after a board of trustees' suspension hearing, and that these bullies remained in the same classes as their victims. These parents wanted the students excluded from school so that their children would not have to see their bullies on a daily basis.

In particular, the parents of secondary school boarding students reported feeling afraid that while the students who bullied had been expelled from the boarding hostel, they were allowed to remain in the day school and were therefore likely to re-victimise their victims in subject classes and in break times. In another incident, a student who was stood down for physical bullying, assaulted the same boy again on his first day back at school. The parents of the boy who was assaulted wanted the other student to be expelled.

Schools are required to manage the procedural issues involving paramountcy (students' welfare and best interests must be the first consideration) and natural justice (the obligation to act fairly and reasonably in the circumstances). At times this will mean managing the consequences and impact of decisions made when both the victim and perpetrator continue to attend the same school and the school has obligations to both students. Support is available for schools faced with this situation (e.g. the Ministry of Education's Interim Response Fund and Traumatic Incident Team), but indications from the school safety inquiry are that there are no easy solutions to managing these competing obligations (Carroll-Lind, 2009). *Responsive Schools* (Carroll-Lind, 2010) is a summary of the key messages from OCC's full report on school safety. This resource was developed to support schools in their responses to bullying and violence.

Zero tolerance policies

OCC's school safety report (Carroll-Lind, 2009) noted the number of students who were bullied over a long period of time and then 'lashed out' themselves in desperation. All students have a right to natural justice, which places the obligation on the principal to act fairly and reasonably in the circumstances. As each case is different, they should be treated differently and the responses should vary according to the situation. Parents of students who had suffered ongoing bullying often thought their child's circumstances were not taken into account.

Schools that take a zero tolerance policy to school violence tend to stand down whoever commits a violent act without looking into the circumstances. Zero tolerance does not mean schools should take a harsh and punitive stance by responding to all infringements in the same way. Instead, it should be about encouraging prosocial behaviour that contributes to improving the school climate. The OCC report recommended that schools adopt a zero tolerance *attitude* to violence and bullying (so that they proactively address the bullying behaviours), but not adopt exclusionary zero tolerance *policies* because they do not teach new behaviours and often spell the end of a secondary student's education (Carroll-Lind, 2009). Freed from the obligation to attend school as a direct result of zero tolerance policies, ejected students with challenging behaviours often turn to their out-of-school community of other disenchanted, antisocial peers (Sutherland, 2011).

Missed opportunities

The act of 'severing' a young person from mainstream schooling can result in a range of predictable negative outcomes (Taylor & Fairgray, 2005). According to Principal Youth Court Judge Andrew Becroft (2003), most youth crimes are carried out while the perpetrators are supposed to be in class. The offending happens between 9 am and 4 pm, mostly carried out by teenagers who are truanting or have no contact with school because they have been excluded or are not enrolled. Nearly half of these students disengage from the school system on or before Year 11 (Becroft, 2003). Similarly, Becroft's predecessor, Judge David Carruthers, in his role as chair of the Ministerial Taskforce on Youth Offending (New Zealand Government, 2002), considered the links between lack of education and youth crime to be obvious and overwhelming because most of the young people seen in the youth courts throughout Aotearoa New Zealand have in some way missed out on educational opportunities. Those without school qualifications are more likely to become long-term unemployed or prison inmates (Ludbrook, 2012). Australia shares comparable statistics. The Parliament of Victoria's Drugs and Crime Prevention Committee found that being excluded from school is strongly associated with the offending behaviour of young people (Parliament of Victoria, 2009). Furthermore, a cross-cultural comparison of schools in Victoria and Washington State (USA) reported that even after controlling for demographic, individual and family risk variables, school suspensions increased the risk of antisocial behaviour in both countries (Hemphill, Toumbourou, Herrenkohl, McMorris, & Catalano, 2006; Hemphill et al., 2007).

Principles of natural justice

Schools are required to follow the principles of natural justice in accordance with section 27(1) of the New Zealand Bill of Rights Act 1990, which are incorporated into the Education (Stand-Down, Suspension, Exclusion and Expulsion) Rules 1999. As mentioned earlier, applying natural justice in the school system means that students must be treated fairly, and any decision made that affects their rights (e.g. suspension) should be made using fair procedures. Procedural fairness that ensures the student is guaranteed a fair hearing involves: the right to know of matters alleged; the right to respond; the right to cross-examine; and the right to representation. The decision should be based on relevant evidence, with the standard of proof being the balance of probabilities. A person's defence of the reasons and/or explanation must always be fairly heard, so it is important that the student prepares a verbal or written defence. When there is agreement about the misconduct, it is very important that mitigating factors are provided to place the behaviour in context, including other circumstances (e.g. bereavement or a family separation) that may have contributed to the behaviour. In addition, alternative disciplinary measures should be suggested because the board of trustees must listen with open minds with no preconceived decisions and may take those suggestions into consideration (Darlow, 2011). After all, as stated by White (2002):

> School suspension in particular may be a counterproductive method of dealing with 'recalcitrant' students. It has been argued that it is essential to find creative ways of addressing (and retaining) school 'troublemakers' that do not compound the problem or disrupt the rest of the class or school community other than always through expulsion or suspension. (Cited in Parliament of Victoria, 2009, p. 54)

A person cannot be both judge and prosecutor, so the principal or any teacher, parent or student involved in the incident leading to the suspension cannot take part in the board of trustees' decision making. The principal should leave the board meeting at the same time as the student, parents and other support people, and if the principal is called back for clarification, the student and his or her support group should be present also. If new information is raised at this time, the family can request an adjournment of the meeting. The decision must be reasonable, made in good faith without bias or prejudice, and based only on the facts (Darlow, 2011). In one case the student and his family arrived early for the board of trustees hearing to find the principal chatting with the board of trustees' chairperson and other members of the board who had also arrived early. This perception of bias could easily have been avoided.

Advocating for students during the suspension process

The first duty of an advocate is to ensure that the suspended student and his or her family understand the steps in the suspension process outlined below (as adapted from Darlow, 2011).

Step 1: Principal's decision

Taking the context and relevant information into account, the principal considers whether a suspension is warranted because of gross misconduct, continual disobedience, or behaviour likely to cause serious harm.

Step 2: Informing parents, board of trustees and Ministry of Education

After suspending the student, the principal must immediately inform the parents, board of trustees and Ministry of Education, citing the grounds for suspension. The student remains on the school roll so the principal must take reasonable steps to minimise disruption to the student's education, provide guidance and counselling, and facilitate his or her return to school, if appropriate.

Step 3: Suspension meeting deadline

The student remains suspended until the board of trustees conduct their suspension meeting (which must be within 7 school days or within 10 calendar days, not counting the day on which the student was suspended). The board is legally obliged to hold the suspension meeting and make a final decision within this timeframe.

Step 4: Notification of meeting

The board of trustees must give written notice to the student and his or her family about the time and place of the meeting as soon as possible, but at least 48 hours before the meeting. The letter must contain information about the suspension meeting procedure, a copy of the principal's report to the board outlining the reasons for the suspension, any other material about the suspension to be presented at the meeting, the board's options, and the possible outcomes of the suspension.

Step 5: Suspension meeting

To establish a quorum, at least half the trustees (not counting the principal) must attend a suspension meeting. Students are entitled to bring their parents and support people to the hearing, including representative(s) who help them to put their view across to the board of trustees. The format of the meeting is determined by the board, but the principal's report is usually read out first by the principal. If new information is presented, parents can request an adjournment of the meeting to consider the new information and seek legal advice, if necessary, while still within the legally required 7-day or 10-day timeframe.

Next, the student, parents and support people respond with their version of the facts, including mitigating factors and any written evidence from witnesses or character references and school reports. Reasons why the student should be allowed to remain at school, demonstration of the student's desire to remain at school, and commitment to changing his or her behaviour should be raised at this time, along with alternative ideas for discipline.

Step 6: Board decision process

The board of trustees usually ask the student, family, support people and principal to leave the room while they consider the submissions and reach their decision. Sometimes, in an effort to reach agreement, the board might ask for everyone to stay. The board of trustees can decide on one or other of the following options.

1. *Lift the suspension without conditions:* the student returns to school and the formal disciplinary process ends, with no further involvement from the board of trustees.

2. *Lift the suspension with conditions*: the student can return to school full time but must comply with ongoing reasonable conditions (e.g. drug and alcohol counselling, behaviour management course, counselling). If the student fails to comply with the conditions, the principal may convene a board of trustee reconsideration hearing. The student can remain at school until the board meets and reaches its new decision. However, if another serious incident occurs, instead of calling a reconsideration meeting the principal may impose a new suspension, following the same suspension process as before.

3. *Extend the suspension period, with conditions aimed at facilitating the student's return to school:* the student can only return to school once

the conditions are met or the extended suspension expires. During the out-of-school period the principal must endeavour to provide appropriate schoolwork and guidance and counselling to the student. For extended suspensions of 4 weeks or more, the board of trustees must monitor the student's progress with written reports that must be shared with the parents.

4. *Exclude the student (if under 16 years):* the principal must, within a 10-day period, make an effort to have the student enrolled in an alternative school close by, and inform the Ministry of Education if they are unable to do so.

5. *Expel the student (if 16 years or older):* the principal and Ministry of Education are not obliged to help the expelled student to find a new school.

A suspension can be challenged if the grounds for suspension have not been met or correct procedures have not been followed. The role of the advocate is therefore to ensure that the correct procedures have been followed (e.g. the student and family are clearly informed about the reasons for suspension and have been given sufficient time to prepare their response or defence from their perspective). Arguments used against a disciplinary decision have included:

- there was a conflict of evidence
- the matter had not been corroborated
- there were questionable methods of investigation
- discriminatory treatment of students was proven (e.g. a particular teacher had issues with the student)
- the student's behaviour did not justify the penalty imposed
- the student's general behaviour was not causing problems
- the student had made valuable contributions in other areas and credit was not given for these
- the incident arose from a cultural misunderstanding.

A particularly memorable suspension hearing in which OCC provided advocacy involved an 8-year-old student who, after being locked in the 'withdrawal room' during the lunch hour, smashed a window and then climbed out of it. The board of trustees listened to the advocate's response to the principal's report, considered the circumstances and lifted the suspension. However, the parent chose to move her son to a school that did not detain children in locked rooms.

Procedural issues

Sometimes students might experience 'double jeopardy' (i.e. suspension followed by further punishment on return to school). Frequently reported examples of schools not following procedures involve informal suspension, where the student is told to 'Go home and not come back until …', and partial suspension, where the student is allowed to stay at school but not in class. Another common procedural issue is when a school exerts pressure on parents to withdraw their child. Predetermination works against a student's right to natural justice; for example, when a board of trustees is informed by their chairperson that "We are here because [name of student] has been suspended; however we would like you to know from the outset that we have decided to exclude him." A student perspective on predetermination might be, "They [board of trustees] had already made up their minds before the hearing. They didn't listen. They didn't want to know." As stated by Charles Dickens, "In their little worlds in which children have their existence, there is nothing so finely perceived and so finally felt, as injustice".

Conclusion

This chapter has advocated for students' rights to be upheld within the context of school exclusion. OCC, in its role as an independent advocate for children, has supported students and their families/whānau in all of the exclusion scenarios highlighted at the beginning of this chapter. Schools should consider alternative ways of dealing with misbehaviour because they have a unique opportunity to interrupt the pathway of youth offending through early identification and timely intervention (Sutherland, 2011). Exclusionary practices are not remedies, and Hemphill et al. (2006) suggest adopting proactive approaches (e.g. time-out within the school), as do the authors in Margrain and Macfarlane's (2011) edited book, who provide a wealth of strategies for engaging restoratively with challenging behaviours.

Maintaining students in the school system has long required an interactive perspective on inclusion (see Ainscow, 1999), in recognition that:

- any child may experience difficulties in school at some stage
- help and support must be available to all students where necessary
- educational difficulties result from an interaction between what the child brings to the situation and the programme provided by the school
- teachers should take responsibility for the progress of all the children in their class
- support must be available to teachers as they attempt to meet their responsibilities.

Students have responsibilities, too, which contributes to the complexity of advocacy in school exclusion contexts. Educational advocacy involves advancing the interests, rights and welfare of students, including their participation in decision making that affects them, while at the same time supporting them to follow the Māori whakataukī:

> Whāia te ara mātauranga mōu ake.
> (Seek that educational pathway that realises your destiny.)

References

Ainscow, M. (1999). *Understanding the development of inclusive schools.* London, UK: Falmer Press.

Ainscow, M., Booth, T., & Dyson, A., with Farrell, P., Frankham, J., Gallannaugh, F., Howes, A., & Smith, R. (2006). *Improving schools, developing inclusion: Improving learning series.* London, UK: Routledge.

Alton-Lee, A. (2003). *Quality teaching for diverse students: Best evidence synthesis.* Wellington: Ministry of Education.

Becroft, A. (2003, 29 July). Truants lead crime figures. *New Zealand Herald.* Retrieved from http://www.nzherald.co.nz/nz/new/article.cfm?c_id=1&0bjectid=3515066

Booth, T., & Ainscow, M. (2011). *Index for inclusion: Developing learning and participation in schools* (3rd ed.). Bristol, UK: CSIE Publishing.

Carroll-Lind, J. (2009). *School safety: An inquiry into the safety of students at school.* Wellington: Office of the Children's Commissioner.

Carroll-Lind, J. (2010). *Responsive schools.* Wellington: Office of the Children's Commissioner.

Carroll-Lind, J. (2011). Rights and education. *Children*, *76*, 22–24.

CSIE. (n.d). *Ten reasons for inclusion*. Bristol, UK: Centre for Studies on Inclusive Education. Retrieved from http://www.csie.org.uk/resources/ten-reasons-02.pdf

Darlow, N. (2011). *Schools and the right to discipline: A guide for parents and caregivers* (5th ed.). Wellington: Wellington Community Law Centre.

Education Counts. (2014). *Stand-downs, suspensions, exclusions and expulsions from school*. Wellington: Ministry of Education. Retrieved from http://www.educationcounts.govt.nz/indicators/main/student-engagement-participation/Stand-downs-suspensions-exclusions-expulsions

Education Review Office. (2011). *Alternative education: Schools and providers*. Wellington: Author. Retrieved from http://www.ero.govt.nz/National-Reports/Secondary-Schools-and-Alternative-Education-April-2011

Hemphill, S., McMorris, B., Toumbourou, J., Kerrenkohl, T., Catalano, R., & Mathers, M. (2007). Rates of student-reported antisocial behaviour, school suspensions, and arrests in Victoria, Australia, and Washington State, USA. *Journal of School Health*, *77*(6), 303–335.

Hemphill, S. A., Toumbourou, J. W., Herrenkohl, T. I., McMorris, B. J., & Catalano, R. F. (2006). The effect of school suspensions and arrests on subsequent adolescent antisocial behavior in Australia and the United States. *Journal of Adolescent Health*, *39*(5), 736–744.

Kearney, A. (2013). Barriers to inclusive education: The identification and elimination of exclusion from and within school. *Inclusive education: Perspectives on professional practice* (pp. 40–51). Auckland: Dunmore Publishing.

Ludbrook, M. (2012). *Youth therapeutic programmes: A literature review*. Wellington: Department of Corrections. Retrieved from http://www.corrections.govt.nz/__data/assets/pdf_file/0008/673028/COR_Youth_Therapeutic_Program_WEB.pdf

Margrain, V., & Macfarlane, A. (Eds.). (2011). *Responsive pedagogy: Engaging restoratively with challenging behaviour*. Wellington: NZCER Press.

Ministry of Education (1996). *Special education 2000*. Wellington. Ministry of Education.

Ministry of Education. (2007). *The New Zealand curriculum*. Wellington: Learning Media.

Ministry of Education. (2010). *Review of special education*. Wellington: Author. Retrieved from http://www.minedu.govt.nz/~/media/MinEdu/Files/TheMinistry/EducationInitiatives/PublicResponseSummary.pdf

Ministry of Education (2011). *Success for all: every school, every child.* Wellington. Ministry of Education

Ministry of Education. (2013a). *Pasifika education plan 2013–2017.* Wellington: Author. Retrieved from http://www.minedu.govt.nz/~/media/MinEdu/Files/EducationSectors/PasifikaEducation/PasifikaEdPlan2013To2017V2.pdf

Ministry of Education (2013b). *The Māori education strategy: Ka hikitia—Accelerating success 2013–2017.* Wellington: Author. Retrieved from http://www.minedu.govt.nz/~/media/MinEdu/Files/TheMinistry/KaHikitia/KaHikitiaAcceleratingSuccessEnglish.pdf

Munn, P., Lloyd, G., & Cullen, M. A. (2000). *Alternatives to exclusion from school.* London, UK: Sage.

New Zealand Government. (2002). *Report of the Ministerial Taskforce on Youth Offending.* Wellington: Ministries of Justice and Social Development. Retrieved from http://www.msd.govt.nz/documents/about-msd-and-our-work/publications-resources/archive/2002-youth-ministerial-taskforce.pdf

Parliament of Victoria. (2009). *Inquiry into strategies to prevent high volume offending and recidivism by young people.* Melbourne, VIC: Drugs and Crime Prevention Committee, Parliament of Victorian Government. Retrieved from http://www.parliament.vic.gov.au/papers/govpub/VPARL2006-10No218.pdf

Prochnow, J., & Johansen, A. (2013). Learners with difficult behaviour can be fully included in the classroom. In *Inclusive education: Perspectives on professional practice* (pp. 102–117). Auckland: Dunmore Publishing.

Sutherland, A. (2011). The relationship between school and offending. *Social Policy Journal of New Zealand, 37*, 51–69.

Taylor, L., Fairgray, H. (2005). Natural justice suspended. *Childrenz Issues: Journal of the Children's Issues Centre, 9*(1), 28–31.

United Nations. (1948). *The Universal Declaration of Human Rights 1948.* Retrieved from http://www.un.org/en/documents/udhr/

Young People's Reference Group, Office of the Children's Commissioner. (2011). *Whakarongo mai: Listening in—Stories from the inside.* Auckland: Cognition Institute.

Notes

1 Whānau: Māori word for family, extended family.

Chapter 2 'The kid with ADHD who fished up the land of the kiwi' and other stories from exclusion to inclusion: Human rights, disability and education in the post disability convention world

Paul Gibson, Disability Rights Commissioner, New Zealand Human Rights Commission

Hūtia te rito o te harakeke

Kei hea te kōmako e kō

He aha te mea nui o te ao?

He tāngata, he tāngata, he tāngata.

(If you pluck the heart, te rito, the new growth, from the flax bush,

there will be no place for birds to sing.

What is the most important thing in the world?

It is all people.)

In the above whakataukī the flax bush represents the family and the community, generations past, present and future. Current generations protect the new growth, te rito, and the place for future growth. If we exclude a child, the whole community is affected and there is no place to sing. This chapter seeks to challenge the notion of challenging behaviour, and seeks to exclude exclusion as an option. It weaves together stories of authority and people whose behaviour challenges that authority.

Disabled students—including those who have traditionally been given that label and those included within a modern, social, human rights understanding, such as anyone with a 'disorder'— are over-represented in individual cases of school exclusion. The international human rights framework, which now includes the Convention on the Rights of Persons with Disabilities (the disability convention), has reinforced the right to an inclusive education for all students. Disabled children can and must be included and no longer treated as having 'special needs' in a system catering to the majority and finding ways to formally and informally exclude children who may be different. This chapter explores inclusion and exclusion through the voices and stories of disabled people, children, families, indigenous people, and the stories of nations and nation building. These stories have inspired change and will further change law, practice, values and the attitudes of school leaders, teachers and others in education systems who aspire to build the foundations of diverse, harmonious and prosperous nations.

Robert Martin's story: Becoming a person

My name is Robert Martin and I have an intellectual disability.

"Good on ya Robbie" calls the one who had laughed loudest.

Yes I have an intellectual disability, but that does not mean my voice should not be heard. My story is the story of millions: people all over the world, who are denied humanity because they have an intellectual disability. (McRae, 2014. p. 9)

Each stone, each grain of sand that has found its resting place on the plains of the Horowhenua in Aotearoa New Zealand has descended from the old mountains, the Tararua and Ruahine ranges above. In te reo, the language of Aotearoa New Zealand's indigenous Māori people,

'Horowhenua' means landslide. Each humble stone has its own journey, a story that remains forever untold. Just occasionally the land gives up its secrets, a rare gem is unearthed, whose sparkle catches the eye of a story teller, and a receptive audience listens to the story of an epic journey, to learn, to be inspired, and to take up a call to action. Robert's story, as told in detail in the book *Becoming a Person* by former school teacher and education resource developer John McRae, from which the extracts are taken, is an epic journey from exclusion to global leadership.

During the day, in settled weather, the sea breeze is drawn across the Horowhenua plains to the Ruahine and Tararua ranges, and before dawn a gentle land breeze is exhaled from the ranges, as if they themselves are breathing. 'Ruahine' means wise old woman. The old women mountains watch over the plains below like grandmothers watching over grandchildren, like teachers watching over the school. They once witnessed battles that soaked the land in blood. They have watched over the emergence of some of Aotearoa New Zealand's wisest leaders. Each observes a community freely moving about, at work and at play; farms with fenced-in animals, modern landfills where society discards its waste, and the harakeke—flax bushes used to halt landslides and the advance of the sand dunes. They also see the dilapidated remains of the fences that contain the abandoned institution where people with intellectual disability lived and died. Aotearoa New Zealand created a name for such places, the 'psychopaedic hospital'. It was once Horowhenua's biggest employer and the southern hemisphere's biggest such institution. It was called Kimberley.

'Whenua' means either land or placenta, the critical sustaining umbilical link between mother and baby, the fundamental connection between generations. 'Horowhenua' means the sliding away of the land, the environment, but also the sliding away of the link between generations, the sliding away—the exclusion—of a child from his or her family.

Like the rito being plucked from the heart of the flax bush, an 18-month-old baby named Robert leaves behind a family and is taken to Kimberley, Horowhenua. Despite evidence that children belong and thrive in families, and in particular that intellectually disabled children are more vulnerable and more likely to flourish with the love and stability of their mum and dad, their brothers and sisters, and with the support of their extended family and community, a culture existed where the state and its professionals coerced families into believing that services, not love, should predominate in disabled children's lives. Aotearoa New Zealand institutionalised children at three times the rate of other similar countries. Additional support for families was seldom presented as an option. And worse was to happen inside.

> I've spoken to people all over New Zealand who lived in Kimberley
> and places like it. In fact, all over the world people have told me
> their stories and they are all the same: institutions are places of abuse.
> (McRae, 2014, p. 34)

Services or love? Anyone who stops and thinks, has ever held a baby, tried to quell the tears and tantrums of a toddler, remembers what it was like to be a child, who empathises, or who just has a sense of justice and humanity will intuitively know that what we as a nation did to disabled children and their families was wrong. The abuse each child experienced being taken from their family was frequently compounded by the physical, psychological and sexual abuse of day-to-day life in institutions. While most staff were not abusers, some were, and they preyed on those out of sight, out of mind.

Robert moved from institutions to different abusive foster homes and back to more abusive institutions. He was often IQ tested and, based on the results, discarded. He had very little school experience of any kind, and most of it involved breaking windows, stealing food and general disruption, without what was happening in the rest of his life being noticed and addressed.

> Robert was eight years old and difficult.

"How many of you in the audience have had challenging behaviour?" he asks. In the conference hall a smattering of hands go up, one waving enthusiastically.

"Well good. Keep it up!"

Parts of the hall erupt into enthusiastic laughter. Someone pounds the tray of his wheelchair with a fist and is in danger of toppling headlong onto the floor. Robert joins the laughter. "I had challenging behaviour too. Yes, this paragon of virtue you see before you now was a problem." (McRae, 2014, p. 30)

When he finally left the institution, Robert's advocacy took off. He organised the first-ever recorded strike in a sheltered work environment. He led the establishment of a local self-advocacy group battling patronising and humiliating practices by service providers.

> Don't ever assume that because we have an intellectual disability we
> do not know what you think about us. (McRae, 2014, p. 32)

The self-advocacy group over time evolved into People First, and now has chosen to use 'learning' disability rather than 'intellectual' disability. They were at the forefront of deinstitutionalisation, in reality the fight for freedom for their friends. Robert worked first with IHC, a large Aotearoa New Zealand service provider, and then as a vice president of Inclusion International. He travelled the world speaking about what life is like if you are excluded.

> "I need to be honest with you," he said in a gentle tone. "I always feel
> really uncomfortable when I see people sitting around in pyjamas at
> three in the afternoon. That's not OK". (McRae, 2014, p. 157)

In the mid-1990s he went to Germany.

> When I went there and met people like myself, I soon realised that
> there were none over the age of fifty. None. Older people with
> intellectual disabilities simply did not exist. You see it wasn't only the
> Jews and the Gypsies who went to the gas chambers. It was all those
> who the Nazis said were less than perfect. (McRae, 2014, p. 125)

Gerhardt Kratschmar was a disabled boy from a poor family in Germany. He was the first person killed by the government as part of the t4 programme, killing half a million disabled people before that slippery-sloped into the Holocaust of 6 million Jews. T4 was the post-war designation of the forced euthanasia programme in Nazi Germany. The international framework of human rights conventions began after the Second World War in response to such atrocities.

But still in the 1990s even the most basic of rights of disabled people, such as the right to life, were not being recognised by governments, let alone being realised in the lives of disabled people. Momentum was gathering internationally. What had been disconnected underground movements were coming together to create an unstoppable revolution. Disabled people demanded that their rights be confirmed in international law.

At the United Nations (UN) during the development of the disability convention, against a backdrop of grey-suited diplomats and politicians and many other disabled people, Robert, the one and only person there with an intellectual disability, announced the fact. A hush fell over the audience.

> This convention can't just be about those here today. It has to be meaningful for the people who aren't in the room; to my friends who aren't always seen or heard because they don't communicate in the same way as us here. It has to protect their rights and speak about their lives (McRae, 2014, p. 151)

He spoke often over the period of development, and with humility and authenticity. He was able to build bridges between disabled people's groups and groups representing families. The grey-suited diplomats took a step back and recognised the need for the voices of the lived experience of disabled people to be at the forefront. The Convention on the Rights of Persons with Disabilities (CRPD) was then agreed to in record UN time. Some observers stated that the UN became a different place after Robert spoke. His contribution, describing his life and that of his friends, is reflected in the principles and many articles, including the article on the right to an inclusive education.

The disability convention has reached beyond that UN room and given hope to the most forgotten, abused and rights-deprived people in the darkest corners of our global village. Robert has recently been nominated by the New Zealand Government to stand for the United Nations Committee on the Rights of Persons with Disabilities, the first learning-disabled person to be nominated. The committee oversees the disability convention and examines state signatories' performance against it.

Today, Robert is working alongside people from mental illness institutions, other disabled people and people from child welfare homes towards an apology for abuse in state care, and is working to stop the various forms of abuse that still occur today. Many of the recently reported examples of historical abuse have occurred in special residential schools.

The education article of the disability convention gives disabled students the right to an education that enables them to participate effectively in a free and democratic society. Robert tells of his experience of growing up in Aotearoa New Zealand but knowing nothing of the All Blacks, the Beatles, battles over Springbok tours, or anything of the nation outside. Government officials have been inspired by his idea that as part of a national apology, institutionalised disabled people should have the opportunity for citizenship ceremonies, recognising that part of the healing process is the need for a welcome to be extended to those who have always been excluded.

In the last decade Kimberley has been closed. Robert and his old mates had a minute's silence for those who lived out their lives there, and who may still be there somewhere in unmarked graves. The Ruahine and Tararua, the wise old women mountains, now look down on the Kimberley site and see the prospect of a large aged-care facility. While institutionalisation and exclusion of people with learning disability and mental illness may be reducing, a new kind of institution, the aged-care facility, is rapidly increasing without an understanding of the lessons of the past. If we don't listen to the voices of the affected and learn today, tomorrow we will be haunted by the ghosts of yesterday: each of us may end our days excluded, out of sight, out of mind.

Like te rito of the flax bush giving us all a place to sing, it is a gift to us all when people we can give something to are included alongside us in our families, our communities and our schools:

> Support, care, compassion. They are basic human qualities. They are the things human beings do and if we don't have opportunities to do those things we lose something. We are not human. (McRae, 2014, p. 135)

The troublemaker and the Rainbow Nation

When first researching Robert's journey on the internet, I searched 'Kimberley and human rights' and landed on South Africa's high veldt. The discovery of an abundance of diamonds in the Northern Cape region would change that nation's path. The area known as Kimberley was a particularly troubled spot in a troubled nation. Huge distinctions in wealth between ethnic groups exaggerated tensions and discrimination, and increased distinctions in areas where each lived. This separate living arrangement of the races became institutionalised and compulsory under the Group Areas Act. Kimberley is linked to the birth of the brand of segregated racism given by South Africa the name apartheid. The people in power may have believed they were acting in the best interest of the others, but the others' voice was not seen to matter.

Further south a boy was born and given by his family the name Rolihlahla. It is an isiXhosa name, which means 'pulling the branch of a tree', and informally it means 'troublemaker'. He was to prove too troublesome for the authorities of the time, and spent most of his working adult life excluded from society, labelled a terrorist, in prison. Rolihlahla was given a different name on his first day at school by his teacher. Giving African children English names was a custom among Africans in those days and was influenced by British colonials who could not easily—and often would not—pronounce African names. African teachers succumbed to colonial pressure and overstepped their natural authority. Rolihlahla became known as Nelson.

Nelson Mandela's story is of a troublemaker battling for freedom, inclusion and diversity. He led the creation of the Rainbow Nation. The troublemaker received the highest of all international accolades for his troubles, the Nobel Peace Prize. Under his leadership South Africa went through a truth and reconciliation process, a nation-building exercise, to ensure the voices of the affected and excluded were finally heard: to heal, to say sorry, and to move on.

Dreams of a lucky country

When next searching Kimberley and human rights on the internet, I ended up in the mountains in the north of Western Australia, the lucky country. In the late 19th century Australia's first indigenous uprising against the colonisers occurred in the Kimberley region. Aboriginal communities had relationships with family, land and the dreamtime that were not understood by colonisers, who had declared the land "terra nullius"—previously empty of people. South of Kimberley, rabbit-proof fences line the landscape, erected by settlers in an attempt to control harmful introduced species. All around the nation generations of Aboriginal and mixed-blood children were stolen from their families and excluded from their communities, and sent to live with and learn the good ways of the settlers. Australia proudly celebrates its ancestry of excluded convicts, of those expelled from an overly authoritarian Mother England. Its larrikin rebelliousness is celebrated in its icons such as the punching kangaroo. It refuses to be confined. The national song, Waltzing Matilda, tells of the jolly swagman, who "waltzes Matilda" by wandering the countryside. He was an outsider who illegally filled his tucker bag, and when confronted by the authorities, opts for suicide over the prospect of bowing to authority and being locked up.

The terminal unpalatability of being locked up is not restricted to Australians of European descent. The ghost of the jolly swagman bubbling from the bottom of the billabong reveals itself in the high numbers of Aboriginal people locked up after their challenging behaviour, and in the newest aspiring Australians—asylum seekers taking their own lives behind barbed-wire fences.

Kimberley's uprising can be linked to the stolen generations, the children taken from the "Waltzing Matilda" ways of their ancestors.

The people in power believed they were acting in the best interests of the others, whose voices were not seen to matter. Australia has begun a new nation-building exercise, and has now said sorry to the stolen generations.

The kid with ADHD and the land of the kiwi

Aotearoa New Zealand was founded on a treaty between two peoples. We are reminded of the youth, energy and instability of the land in its constant shaking. Through the Treaty of Waitangi, Kiwis relate to maunga, the mountains of the earth mother, from whom we descend; awa, the refreshed streams filled with the tears of the sky father; waka journeys across vast oceans; and iwi, the shared bones, the nations of people from whom we descend. They give us a place to belong: tūrangawaewae. Each child should have a stable sense of belonging in family, community and school. Many of the children of Christchurch show delays in development after several years of growing up learning to stand on shaky ground.

The land traces its origins to the feats of Māui. When Māui's brothers went fishing, they wanted to exclude their mischievous, defiant, rebellious younger brother. They thought they had left him behind. The conforming brothers had only a little luck fishing. What they did not know was that Māui had stowed away on the canoe. When he emerged, he baited his hook, which was his grandmother's jawbone, with his own blood and fished up the greatest fish of all, the North Island of Aotearoa New Zealand.

Māui was born prematurely, with six toes on each foot. He was discarded, excluded, from his family. But he survived. He was a trickster—cheeky, rebellious, defiant, impulsive and incapable of obedience. In today's education system he would be given a label like ADHD (attention deficit hyperactivity disorder), dosed up with Ritalin and expected to sit quietly in the corner without experimenting and challenging.

Aotearoa does well in educating its children. But when compared internationally we have a tail of underachievement. Māui's tale of defiance and exclusion typifies the tales of children who underachieve. Māui was abandoned at birth. Aotearoa New Zealand is recorded as having the third highest rate of sole-parent families in the world (Torrie, 2011). When Kiwi kids hit high school they learn the double entendre joke of stereotypical abandonment of responsibility: "the Kiwi eats roots shoots and leaves in the dark of the night". The reality of the sightless, flightless bird is a little different: the kiwi does only go out at night, but insects are the main diet, and it is the male who takes responsibility and nurtures the eggs.

In the Māori world the kiwi is the bird of most mana, the tuakana, the oldest and wisest of all the birds. In Pākehā culture the same story of the kiwi's mana has developed in parallel through Alwyn Owen's tale "How the Kiwi Lost His Wings". The kiwi sacrifices its ability to fly, brightly coloured plumage and good eyesight to protect the forest for the benefit of all birds from plagues of insects. The kiwi sees about as much as I do: I'm legally blind. And the kiwi is mobility impaired compared to other birds. Our national icon is disabled.

Māui's grandmother, Muriranga-whenua, was blind and multiply disabled. Today she would likely be excluded, placed in an aged-care facility, and would not get as much opportunity to pass on her wisdom and experience to her grandchildren. Māui's use of her jawbone to fish up the land is a metaphor for teaching and nation building. Aotearoa New Zealand is built on the words of teachers, of wise old women. Settlers to Aotearoa New Zealand have not always honoured their part of the founding Treaty of Waitangi. A nation-building Treaty resolution process has been progressively occurring for a generation, with settlements and government saying sorry to each iwi.

Voices and perspectives of the disability community

A human rights approach to an issue involves using international conventions as standards for accountability, giving voice to the affected, acknowledging everyone's rights in a given situation, balancing competing rights, and prioritising the rights of the most vulnerable. The United Nations Convention on the Rights of Persons with Disabilities (UNCRPD) offers a social/rights-based approach, whereby disablement is a form of social oppression, like racism. People with impairments experience disadvantage in many areas of life not because of inherent difference but because of barriers, attitudes and unfair systems: "Who we are is OK, what happens to us is not".

A new discourse celebrates diversity as opposed to the pervasive striving for an impossible perfection—of body image, of intellect, and of behaviour. Disabled people historically have been excluded at the individual and collective levels when decisions are made about us. The rallying cry used during the development of the disability convention, "Nothing about us without us", was accepted and used by the United Nations.

Disabled people and families from different belief systems all around the world have stories that answer the question 'Where does disability come from?' Some cultures believe disability is random, due to luck, without moral cause, and some the sins of past lives or past generations—a cause of shame. Families of disabled children may particularly carry that shame. Professionals and teachers of a different culture may struggle to elicit the conversations that will make a positive difference to the family. But alongside the stories of shame, when digging a little deeper, stories of disability as a gift can be found: disabled people being given the opportunity to be unique, to do something unique. Strength-based stories of figures like Māui and the kiwi, as well as real-life stories of disabled leaders from different cultures, help build the bridging conversation between shame and support for many families.

Disabled people are experts in their own experience and have solutions to the issues that teachers and schools face. People with lived experience and collective wisdom have expertise that needs to be heard and valued, and drives change in the system. It is no longer acceptable for professionals to claim expertise without listening to, and being actively involved with, those directly affected and their representative voices, such as disabled people's organisations. Part of a rights-based approach includes giving disabled people with similar experiences the opportunity to come together while still being part of inclusive schools and classes. Success in life for a disabled person correlates with integrating the experience of impairment into their own identity, their own positive personal story of who they are.

Disabled people's journeys through life are complex. If I am a disabled person, at a given point in time I need recognition and sympathy for my difference, then encouragement, understanding, and ultimately empowerment. Young disabled people need the experience of 'dignity of risk', the power to make decisions within clear boundaries, and like all other people, need the freedom to make mistakes and learn from them.

Disabled people have rejected the notion of themselves as 'special', and there is no mention of special in the disability convention. People First, representing people with learning disabilities, have workshopped in front of policy makers how the language of special education negatively affects them. Disabled students require access, support, reasonable accommodation and equity in a system co-designed with disabled people.

Families, especially in the earlier years after a child's diagnosis, are less comfortable with the label 'disability' than 'special', because, when you have not been exposed to social/rights-based understandings of disability, or have not personally lived it, special is considered more neutral and less deficit focused. Families are more likely to move from grieving and special to reality and rights if they become connected with other families, disabled role models and strength-based stories.

The right to inclusive education

In Aotearoa New Zealand many—if not most—families of children with disabilities still report having to fight for the right to an inclusive education. A battle is the norm, not the exception. Getting support requires families telling the saddest story, the worst about their child, and the saddest outcome is that the family and the child grow into these expectations: negativity becomes a self-fulfilling prophesy.

The New Zealand Human Rights Commission (HRC) receives more complaints combining the ground of disability and the area of education than any other ground and area. Within this a large proportion relate to a combination of disability behaviour-related issues. The New Zealand Education Act still defaults to the rhetoric of 'special education'. Unlike in tertiary education, where the discourse of rights and reasonable accommodation of disabled students occurs, at primary and secondary level many schools discourage disabled students and families from enrolling, and if enrolled aren't focused on maximising participation and achievement.

Through the monitoring process of the disability convention in New Zealand, the HRC, the Ombudsman, and disabled people's organisations have called for the right to an inclusive education to be made enforceable. This would involve updating the aging legislation to be consistent with the disability convention, as well as detailed policy, programme, and resourcing developments. A lack of resources is often blamed as the cause for non-inclusion. In some cases this is true, but generally, if the leadership of a school commits to making inclusion work, it will work.

The post-convention jurisprudence is slowly developing. The UNCRPD committee released a draft general comment in 2015 to further guide states on how to implement disabled people's right to inclusive education. It states that inclusive education focuses on the attendance, participation and achievement of all students, especially those who, for different reasons, are excluded or at risk of being marginalised. Discrimination includes exclusion through the failure to provide reasonable accomodation.

Other recent international developments include:

- The United Nations Sustainable Development goals. There is a global goal to ensure equal access to all levels of education for persons with disabilities, accompanied by disaggregated data, targets and indicators, by 2030.
- The global impact of the report of the Office of the Children's Commissioner for England, *Nobody made the connection: The prevalence of neurodisability in young people who offend*. It gives the global

evidence that generally the majority of young people locked in the youth justice system have a neurodisability. These include dyslexia, ADHD, Autism Spectrum Disorder, Foetal Alcohol Spectrum Disorder, head injury, communication disabilities as well as learning/intellectual disabilities. It raises the question of the extent to which young people with neuro developmental disabilities are locked out of education as part of their journey into detention.

- The international work of Lumos, founded by Harry Potter author J.K. Rowling, dedicated to reducing by half by 2030 the number of children in orphanages and residential special schools through changing funding models, better support of families, and inclusive education.

Much of the mainstream is not yet inclusive. This failure of regular schools to meet the needs of diverse students understandably drives many families to seek what is perceived to be a safer option, special environments, despite evidence that inclusive regular schools can contribute so much more towards any student having a great life, regardless of the level of their impairment. The variable factor is the supportiveness of the environment. Just as families of past generations were coerced into institutionalisation, some of today's families are coerced into specialism and exclusion. There is no meaningful choice for them.

Several years ago a UK study asked a number of young disabled adults what two things they would most like to change in their lives. Perhaps accessible environments? Accessible format material? Sign language interpreters? Talking therapies for mental illness? Their answer: more sex and more money. Disabled young people have the same needs, dreams, desires, lusts and sense of humour as others. They don't want to be excluded from anything. This does not deny differences, or different means of achieving similar dreams. In my own work with disabled students in primary and secondary schools, their two key issues were: first, bullying, because every single student interviewed or in a focus group had been bullied, and some stated it was then justifiable for them to go on to be a bully; and second, wanting to have friends.

How children perceive teachers and assistants is critical to their success. Inside their mind they are asking, 'Do you know me? Do you understand me? Do you care about me enough to stand up for me?'

Well-intentioned teachers may be devastated to find out how their contact is interpreted. Many students do not believe their teacher cares, and so disconnect from education and from the expected behavioural norms of the class. Conversely, many students are inspired and have their lives transformed by a teacher who listened and proved they cared or stuck up for them. There is a need for more generosity of spirit, creativity and imagination in all levels of the education system, from law and policy through to teaching and support.

In every health setting in Aotearoa New Zealand there is a mandatory code of rights on the wall. This has helped move the culture in the health system. Imagine if every classroom and every principal's office had a code of rights on the wall. Imagine if half of each classroom code was a class treaty negotiated between the students and teacher, consistent with the general code, and expressed in an age-appropriate way, with each student signing up in their own shared words their expectations of each other and of their teacher and classroom supports.

Celebrating and saying sorry

The ultimate form of exclusion is when a whole category of people is structurally excluded. In the state education system we tolerate the existence of schools that discourage and discriminate against certain groups of students, and build separate, segregated schools to embed and institutionalise this exclusion. We then sanitise it with the label 'special'. The structural discrimination born out of Kimberley in South Africa, apartheid, has been dismantled and nationally acknowledged through the truth and reconciliation process. The structural discrimination born out of Kimberley in Australia and culminating in the stolen generations has been acknowledged through a tough, lengthy and contested national conversation, and resulted in the high-profile national apology. The most enduring of judgements is attributed to Ghandi: "The true measure of any society is how it treats its most vulnerable members". At Kimberley, New Zealand, and at other similar institutions, children who were even more vulnerable were New Zealand's stolen generations.

Aotearoa New Zealand is yet to have a national conversation, to confront what was not just a policy error but a large-scale human rights abomination. The disability community—including people with mental illness, as well as people who lived in abusive child welfare homes—are calling for a national conversation about what happened, how to rehabilitate, how to stop current abuse and prevent future abuse, and, ultimately, to hear someone say, 'Sorry'.

Judges and former police commissioners are not only backing this call but also describing the process of acknowledgement and apology of Aotearoa New Zealand's historical abuse in state care as a necessary part of Aotearoa New Zealand's nation building. Kimberley, South Africa, Western Australia and Aotearoa New Zealand, each points to the need to seek out, listen to and act on the forgotten voices. This is a definition of inclusion. This is a lesson for all professionals.

Icons of international rights movements have been celebrated and acknowledged by the Nobel committee. Nelson Mandela, leader of the anti-apartheid movement, received the Nobel Peace Prize. More recently, in a land where girls are often excluded from mainstream education, Malala Yousafzai took a bullet to the head for speaking out and challenging systemic exclusion. She, too, received the Nobel Peace Prize. It is time for the achievements of the leaders of the global disability rights movement to be acknowledged. Internationally, Robert's lifetime achievements culminating in the development of the disability convention have been acknowledged, and he has been nominated for the world's highest accolade, the Nobel Peace Prize.

Let's start a global conversation. Let's celebrate that a kiwi with a learning/intellectual disability has changed the world and been nominated for a Nobel Prize. Maybe then it will be easier to acknowledge the reality of historical abuse, and attract the energy, resources and priority of today's decision makers to address issues of inclusion and exclusion. But first we have to say, 'Sorry'.

References

McRae, J. (2014). *Becoming a person: The biography of Robert Martin*. Christchurch: Potton and Burton.

Owen, A. (2008). *How the Kiwi Lost Its Wings*. Auckland: Penguin.

Torrie, B. (2011). *One child in four in single-parent home*. http://www.stuff.co.nz/national/4945358/

Chapter 3 Is internal suspension associated with better student outcomes than external suspension?

Sheryl Hemphill, Jess Heerde and Barbara McMorris

Research evidence has shown that there is a whole range of unintended, serious consequences of external suspension (temporary removal of a student from school) for students, such as school drop-out, antisocial behaviour, substance use and academic underachievement. Internal suspension (removal from the classroom to sit in another area of the school, such as outside the school principal's office) is seen as a possible alternative to external suspension, perhaps resulting in better outcomes. However, no study has directly compared later student outcomes following external versus internal suspension. This chapter will draw on data from the Victorian arm of the International Youth Development Study to compare young adult outcomes for students internally suspended versus those externally suspended from school in Year 10. The implications of these results for school behaviour management approaches will be discussed.

Key points

- Internal and external suspension rates were high in this community sample of Victorian students.
- External suspension predicted not completing Year 12, not being in paid employment in young adulthood, and young adult antisocial behaviour.
- Internal suspension predicted young adult antisocial behaviour, cannabis use, and other drug use.
- Internal suspension may not be an alternative to external suspension since it was also associated with later problems for students.

Introduction

External school suspension (temporary exclusion from school for a period of time) is a relatively common behaviour management strategy implemented by schools in Australia, New Zealand, the US, and the UK. In Queensland, Australia, 61,791 students at government schools (13 percent) were externally suspended in 2011 (Department of Education, 2012). Official statistics are not reported in Victoria, but in an ongoing study 11 percent of Year 7 and Year 9 male Victorian students and 6 percent of Victorian female students reported being suspended from school. The rates for Victorian males were lower than those reported by male students in Washington State, in the US (16 percent), but identical (6 percent) for female students (Hemphill, Toumbourou, Herrenkohl, McMorris, & Catalano, 2006). In 2006 over 3.3 million students, or 6.9 percent of the total number of US students, were suspended from public elementary and secondary schools (Snyder, Dillow, & Hoffman, 2009), a figure that is increasing. Rates of external suspension peak in Year 9 (ages 14–15 years), when rates of student misbehaviour (e.g. disrupting the classroom, punching another student, antisocial behaviour) are also increasing (Angus et al., 2009; Hemphill, Heerde, Herrenkohl, Toumbourou, & Catalano, 2012).

Concern at the frequent use of external suspension has grown due to research demonstrating that this form of behaviour management is used to address the misbehaviour of disadvantaged students disproportionately more often than other students (e.g. those from minority ethnic groups or of low socioeconomic status) and is associated with negative student outcomes such as dropping out of school, failure to complete school, crime, substance use, and related problems (Arcia, 2006; Butler, Bond, Drew, Krelle, & Seal, 2005; Christle, Jolivette, & Nelson, 2005; Hemphill, Heerde, et al., 2012; Hemphill et al., 2006, 2009; Wu, Pink, Crain, & Moles, 1982). Internal suspension, where a student is removed from the classroom to spend the school day away from peers (often in the office of the leadership team) has been suggested as an alternative to external suspension. However, we know of no existing study that has compared student outcomes following internal versus external suspension.

In this chapter we examine whether or not student outcomes are better following internal versus external suspension. First, the relevant literature on associations between school suspension, student disadvantage and outcomes is reviewed, along with a summary of behaviour management approaches available to schools, including external and internal suspension. Next, the study providing the data to be analysed in the current chapter, the International Youth Development Study, is described. Third, rates of external and internal suspension in Year 10 (ages 15–16 years) for a sample of young Victorians will be presented. Associations between internal versus external suspension and young adult outcomes at ages 18 to 19 years, including health-risk behaviour, employment and education, will be reported, and finally the implications of these findings for behaviour management approaches in schools are discussed.

Associations between suspension, student disadvantage and negative outcomes

External suspension

A prominent concern about the use of external suspension is that it may be a process that reinforces inequalities. As evidence, researchers have found that some students are more likely to experience school suspensions than others. In particular, students who are suspended tend to show the following characteristics: low socioeconomic status, minority ethnicity, and male gender, in Australia, North America and the UK (Hemphill, Heerde, et al., 2012; Hemphill et al., 2006, 2009; Skiba, Michael, Nardo, & Peterson, 2002; Skiba & Rausch, 2006a,

2006b; Vavrus & Cole, 2002). Wu et al. (1982) reported that low socioeconomic status and ethnic minority were more strongly related to suspension than the actual level of student behaviour problems. In other words, there are disparities between student behaviour and resultant external suspensions. A further concern is that those students who could be most advantaged by completing education are being excluded from school due to this behaviour management approach.

In a previous longitudinal study of students in Washington state and Victoria, the use of external suspension was found to *independently* increase the likelihood of student antisocial and related behaviours (such as violence and tobacco use) by 50 to 70 percent 12 months later (Hemphill, Heerde, et al., 2012; Hemphill et al., 2006, 2009). This is the opposite of what might be expected: that student behaviour would improve after suspension. However, findings are remarkably consistent that externally suspended students are more likely to become involved in crime, such that this process is commonly referred to as the "school-to-prison pipeline", (Christle et al., 2005). Factors that may explain links to subsequent antisocial behaviour include the opportunities that being suspended externally from school provide for interaction with antisocial friends, and the impact that external suspension has on academic achievement (Hemphill, Heerde, et al., 2012). Suspended students also tend to drop out of school (Arcia, 2006; Butler et al., 2005). As a result of this exclusionary approach to behaviour management, the societal costs of leaving school early and crime in Australia are large: approximately $38 billion/annum (Black, 2007; Rollings, 2008).

The results reviewed above suggest that, for some students, external suspension leads to further engagement in the very behaviour that was originally targeted to be deterred. That is, external suspension is a reinforcer of antisocial and related behaviours. One potential explanation may be that the students most likely to be externally suspended perceive this officially sanctioned time away from school as a holiday (or at least time away from the difficulties of keeping up at school, which many of these students face) and an opportunity to socialise with others who are not engaged with school (What Works, 2010). This stands in stark contrast to the intended goal of external suspension, which is to reduce or inhibit antisocial and related behaviours by providing consequences for student actions (Skiba & Knesting, 2001).

Internal suspension

Less research has focused on internal suspension in terms of who is suspended and the outcomes for students after suspension. As with the use of external suspension, disadvantaged students are more likely than other students to receive an internal suspension (Hilberth & Slate, 2014; Kerr & Valenti, 2009). In a study of US students receiving internal suspensions, Morrison, Anthony, Storino and Dillon (2001) reported that almost half of these students had previously been referred to the principal's office, one-third had been suspended previously (type of suspension not specified), and they showed low academic achievement.

A few older studies have examined associations between internal suspension and student outcomes. For example, Harvey and Moosha (1977) showed that internal suspension reduced the number of suspensions (not specified as internal or external) in one high school and one junior high school by 29 percent and 42 percent, respectively. In contrast, Mendez and Sanders (1981) found that internal suspension did not improve student attendance at school, resulted in a recidivism rate of 50 percent and yielded a 40 percent difference in rates of graduation for students who completed an internal suspension compared to students who had never received an internal suspension, with internally suspended students far less likely to graduate. In a small, observational study, Stage (1997) found that internal suspension did not reduce disruptive classroom behaviour. One problem with previous studies is that there can be variations in the ways in which internal suspension is implemented. For example, Sullivan (1989) identified the features internal suspension requires to be effective, and these included planning, implementation, and an evaluation of the impact of internal suspension.

Approaches to behaviour management

The use of external suspension fits a zero tolerance approach to behaviour management, which also includes the use of expulsion (through which a student is permanently excluded from the school). Such approaches are particularly common in US schools (American Psychological Association Zero Tolerance Task Force, 2008) and seek to reduce misbehaviour primarily through deterrence by sending a clear message to students that certain behaviours will not be tolerated and will incur serious consequences, regardless of the circumstances (i.e. permanent removal from school). There is an urgent need for more systematic prospective studies on the outcomes of suspended or expelled students (American Psychological Association Zero Tolerance Task Force, 2008). Although Australian (specifically Victorian) schools implement external suspension and expulsion, these schools focus on maintaining student engagement at school (Department of Education and Early Childhood Development, 2009). Indeed, exclusionary approaches are generally only used after the failure of other consequences (e.g. detention, behavioural contracts breached). Similar to Aotearoa New Zealand schools, Victorian schools also implement whole-school restorative practices to both prevent and address incidents of student misbehaviour. These approaches seek to teach students a shared language for misbehaviour and focus on healing relationships and repairing any damage caused (see Chapter 7 in this book for more detailed descriptions of these approaches).

As an alternative to the use of external suspension, some schools use internal suspensions, where the student is removed from the classroom environment but remains on school grounds and spends the day away from peers, often in the office of the principal or assistant principal, or in a separate room with other students on internal suspension. It is possible that from a student's perspective internal suspension is more punishing than an external suspension: the student must still attend school (no holiday) and spend time in close proximity to the leadership team, most likely with school work to do, and at the same time, s/he is separated from his/her classmates (some schools ensure that recess and lunch breaks are held at different times to classmates as well). It also ensures that the student has adult supervision and is not interacting with other students who are not at school (as is the case for external suspension).

Given these features of internal suspension, there are reasons to expect that it may lead to fewer negative outcomes for students than external suspension (Mendez & Sanders, 1981; Sullivan, 1989). First, a key explanatory variable in the relationship between external suspension and negative outcomes seems to be (unsupervised) interaction with antisocial peers (Hemphill, Herrenkohl, et al., 2012). Such unsupervised socialising should be less likely to occur in the case of an internal suspension. However, the reality is that internal suspension may involve excluded students being placed in a common room together, with minimal adult supervision, allowing for interaction between anti-social peers. Second, other important factors that may affect student outcomes after the use of behaviour management approaches, such as diminished connections with school and falling behind in school work, should be less likely to occur because internally suspended students are required to complete school work and remain within the potentially protective environment of the school.

However, a major challenge to the use of internal suspension is schools finding the resources to facilitate its use (i.e. having an appropriate staff member supervise internally suspended students).

Being able to demonstrate whether internal suspension, compared with external suspension, is associated with fewer negative outcomes for students could provide clear policy guidance for educational authorities to better resource the use of internal suspensions. Hence, in this chapter we report results which, for the first time, compare the outcomes of Victorian students who have received internal versus external suspension. The data for this comparison are drawn from the International Youth Development Study, which will be briefly described in the next section, followed by a presentation of findings from the comparison of student outcomes after receiving an internal versus external suspension, and a discussion of the implications of these results for schools and policy makers.

The International Youth Development Study

The International Youth Development Study (IYDS) began in 2002 with the recruitment of almost 6,000 students from Victoria, Australia, and Washington State, in the US. The IYDS has focused on the development of substance use and related behaviours such as antisocial behaviour for over a decade in Victoria. In addition, students were asked about their experience of internal and external school suspension and a range of influential factors that may positively and negatively affect their development into early adulthood.

Participants

The IYDS used a two-stage cluster sampling approach:

- random selection of public and private schools, stratified according to geographical location, using a probability proportionate to grade-level-size sample procedure
- one class at each grade level (Year 5, 7 and 9) within each school, selected at random.

The findings presented here report on the Victorian sample, comprising 927 (481 female, 446 male) students who were first surveyed in 2002 when they were 10–11 years old. These students have been reassessed annually from 2002 to 2010/2011, with the exception of 2005. Other IYDS cohorts have not been surveyed as frequently due to funding constraints and are therefore excluded from these analyses. Data analysed here are from 2007, when participants were aged 15–16 years, and from 2010/11 when participants were aged 18–19 years.

Measures

The self-reported measures of Year 10 suspension (internal, external), influential factors, and young adult behavioural and social outcomes are contained within a modified version of the Communities that Care survey, used in the IYDS. The survey has acceptable psychometric properties in the US (Glaser, Van Horn, Arthur, Hawkins, & Catalano, 2005) and has been used in Victoria (Hemphill et al., 2011). The influential factors known to influence young adult outcomes that were assessed in Year 10 spanned intrapersonal, peer group, family and community factors (see Table 3.1 for information about all the measures used in this chapter). These measures are included here because it is important to show that internal and external suspension each independently predicts young adult outcomes after taking into account other potential factors in these students' lives.

Table 3.1: Description of measures used for analyses

	No. of items in scale	Response options	Cronbach's alpha
Year 10 suspension			
Past-year internal suspension (e.g. "When you attended school, did you ever receive an internal or in-school suspension (i.e. removed from regular classes but still required to attend school)?")	1	Yes/No	N/A
Past-year external suspension (e.g. "When you attended school, did you ever receive an external or out-of-school suspension?")	1	Yes/No	N/A
Year 10 influential factors			
Individual-level risk factors			
Academic failure (e.g. "What were your grades/marks like last year, putting all of your grades together?")	2	4-point scale (*very good* to *very poor* for item 1 and *definitely yes* to *definitely no* for item 2	Pearson's correlation = .63
Low commitment to school (e.g. "How often do you feel that the schoolwork you are assigned is meaningful and important?")	7	*Never* (1) to *almost always* (5)	.79
Rebelliousness (e.g. "I do the opposite of what people tell me, just to get them mad.")	4	*Definitely no* (1) to *definitely yes* (4)	.82
Peer group risk factor			
Interaction with antisocial friends (e.g. "How many of your best friends in the past year have: been suspended; carried a weapon; sold illegal drugs?")	9	*None of my friends* (0) to *4 of my friends* (4)	.88
Family-level risk factors			
Poor family management (e.g. "Would your parents know if you did not come home on time?")	9	*Definitely no* (4) to *definitely yes* (1)	.84
Family conflict (e.g. "My family argues about the same things over and over.")	3	*Definitely no* (1) to *definitely yes* (4)	.82
Parent attachment (e.g. "Do you share your thoughts and feelings with your mother?")	4	*Definitely no* (1) to *definitely yes* (4)	.80

	No. of items in scale	Response options	Cronbach's alpha
Community-level risk factors			
Community disorganisation (e.g. "How much do each of the following statements describe your neighbourhood: lots of empty or abandoned buildings?")	5	Definitely no (4) to definitely yes (1)	.61
Young adult (age 18–19) outcomes			
Non-completion of Year 12 (i.e. whether students completed secondary school)	1	Yes/No	N/A
Study since secondary school (e.g. "Have you done any further study since secondary school?")	1	Yes/No	N/A
Not currently employed (e.g. "Are you currently employed?")	1	Yes/No	N/A
Source of income is not paid employment	1	Yes/No	N/A
Antisocial behaviour (e.g. "Have you ever attacked someone with the idea of seriously hurting them?")	10	No (1) to Yes, > once in past 12 months (4)	.74
Tobacco use (e.g. "Have you smoked cigarettes in the past year?")	1	Never (0) to 40+ times (8)	N/A
Alcohol problems (e.g. "Has your drinking or being hung-over ever led you to neglect some of your usual responsibilities at work, education, home, or caring for children?")	9	No (1) to Yes, only in past 12 months (4)	
Alcohol use (e.g. "In the past year (12 months), on how many occasions (if any) have you had alcoholic beverages (like beer, wine or liquor/spirits) to drink—more than just a few sips?")	1	Never (0) to 40+ times (8)	N/A
Heavy alcohol use (e.g. "In the past 30 days on how many occasions (if any) have you had five or more alcoholic drinks in a row?")	1	Never (0) to 40+ times (8)	N/A
Cannabis use (e.g. "In the past year (12 months), on how many occasions (if any) have you used marijuana (pot, weed, grass)?")	1	Never (0) to 40+ times (8)	N/A
Other drug use (e.g. "In the past year (12 months), on how many occasions (if any) have you used LSD (acid/trips, tabs) or other psychedelics?")	7	Never (0) to 40+ times (8)	.77

Procedure

Ethics approval was obtained from the University of Melbourne Human Ethics in Research Committee. In Year 10 (age 15–16 years) approval was also sought from relevant educational authorities, and permission to administer the 2006 survey was obtained from each school principal. The Year 10 survey was group administered within the students' classrooms and required approximately 50–60 minutes to complete. Students no longer attending school in Year 10, or who were absent on the day of the survey, were surveyed individually by trained personnel. Both parental written informed consent and written student assent were obtained for each participant. In 2010/11 participants provided informed consent before individually completing the survey online, on the telephone or by posting a paper-and-pencil version of the survey. Participants received a gift voucher after completing each survey.

Findings from the International Youth Development Study

In this section rates of Year 10 internal and external suspension are presented, in addition to rates of young adult outcomes at age 18–19. This is followed by the results of the analyses examining associations between external suspension and young adult outcomes, and associations between internal suspension and young adult outcomes.

Rates of internal and external suspension in Year 10

Rates of internal suspension were more than double those for external suspension (see Figure 3.1). More boys than girls were externally suspended from school ($p = .006$), but for rates of internal suspension there were no statistically significant differences between boys and girls. Thirty-five students (4 percent of the total sample) reported both internal and external suspensions in Year 10.

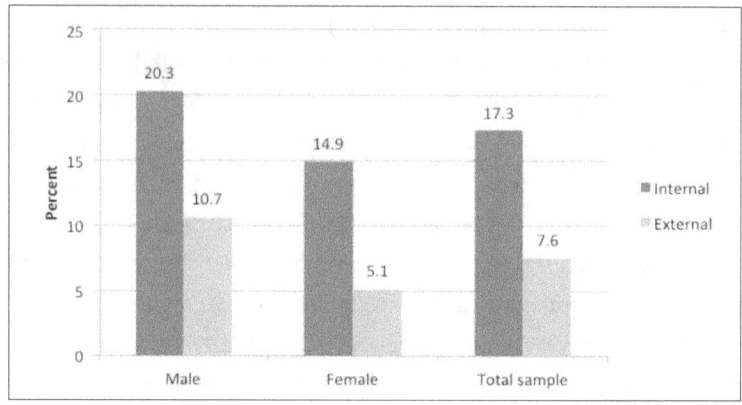

Figure 3.1: Rates of internal and external suspension in Year 10 Victorian students, 2007

Rates of behavioural and social outcomes in young adulthood

Three years later, in young adulthood, around three-quarters of all participants were in paid employment, currently employed and had completed further study since finishing secondary school (see Figure 3.2). These young people reported very high rates of alcohol use, in excess of 80 percent. Over half of the participants had used tobacco in the past year, and almost one-third had used cannabis. Twenty percent of these young adults had left school early (prior to the completion of Year 12) and a similar proportion reported engaging in antisocial behaviour (e.g. carrying a weapon, stealing).

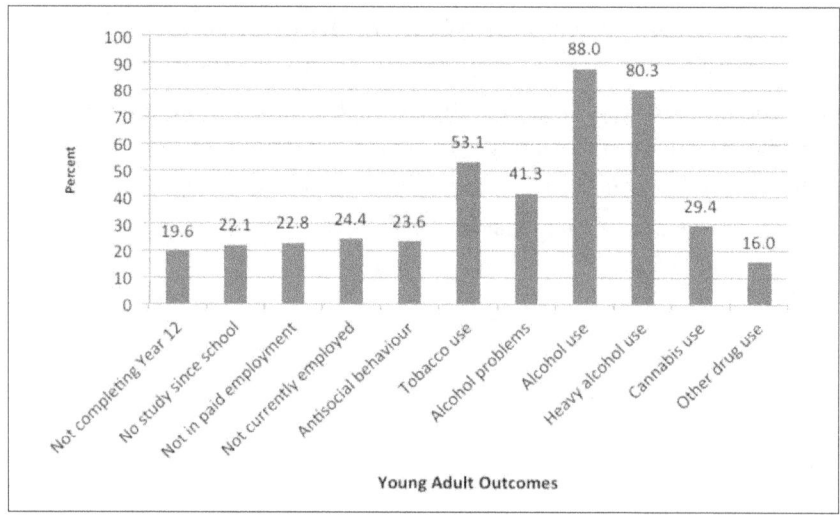

Figure 3.2: Rates of young adult outcomes in 2010/11

Associations between internal versus external suspension and young adult outcomes

Direct associations between internal versus external suspension and young adult outcomes

In general there were similarities in associations between internal and external suspension and young adult outcomes; that is, internal suspension was also linked to negative outcomes in young adulthood (see Figure 3.3). The bars in Figure 3.3 represent odds ratios, a measure of the strength of the association, whereby the longer the bar, the stronger the association. Internal suspension predicted (in order of the size of the association) cannabis use in the past year, use of other drugs in the past year, antisocial behaviour, heavy alcohol use in past year, tobacco use in past year, alcohol problems, and not completing Year 12. The likelihood of reporting these outcomes was at least doubled and sometimes tripled after being internally suspended from school compared with not being internally suspended.

External suspension (versus not being externally suspended) was linked to young adult reports of source of income is not through paid employment, not studying since secondary school, not completing Year 12, antisocial behaviour, alcohol problems, tobacco use, cannabis use, and the use of other drugs in the past year. The likelihood of not completing Year 12 was six times higher and antisocial behaviour was four times greater after external suspension.

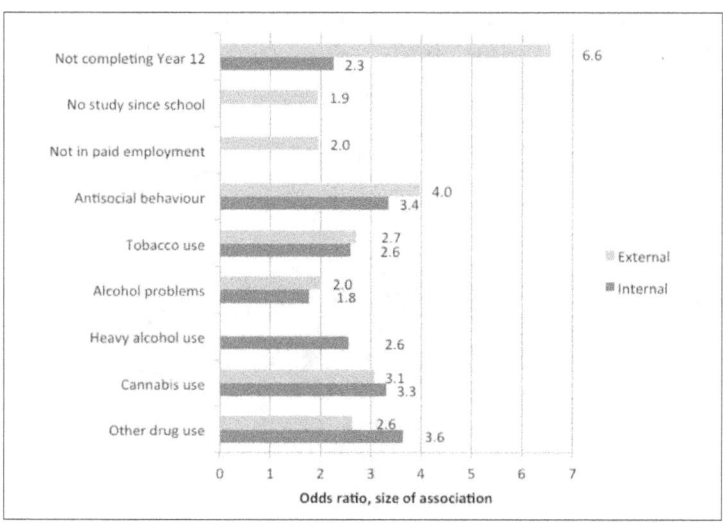

Figure 3.3: Direct associations between Year 10 internal and external suspension and young adult outcomes in 2010/11

Associations between internal versus external suspension and young adult outcomes in analyses controlling for other influences

In attempting to understand the links between internal and external suspension and young adult outcomes, it is important to explore whether associations remain relative to other factors we know influence young adult outcomes. In 'adjusted' analyses we included other factors such as prior behaviour, rebelliousness, family conflict, poor family management, interaction with antisocial peers, and disorganisation in the local community. Even after these Year 10 factors were included, having experienced internal and external suspension (versus not having experienced internal and external suspension) independently predicted specific young adult outcomes, but these outcomes were often different depending upon the type of suspension. Internal suspension predicted engagement in antisocial behaviour, cannabis use and use of other drugs in the past year, with the likelihood of each of these outcomes in young adulthood approximately doubled compared with classmates who did not experience an internal suspension. For students who reported external suspension in Year 10 their likelihood of not completing Year 12 was three times higher compared with classmates who did not experience external suspension. Similarly, odds of the source of income not being paid employment 3 years later were almost double for participants who were externally suspended in Year 10. These two outcomes can have serious social implications. Finally, having reported an external suspension at age 15–16 also resulted in a slightly higher likelihood of reporting antisocial behaviour by age 18–19 ($p = 0.054$).

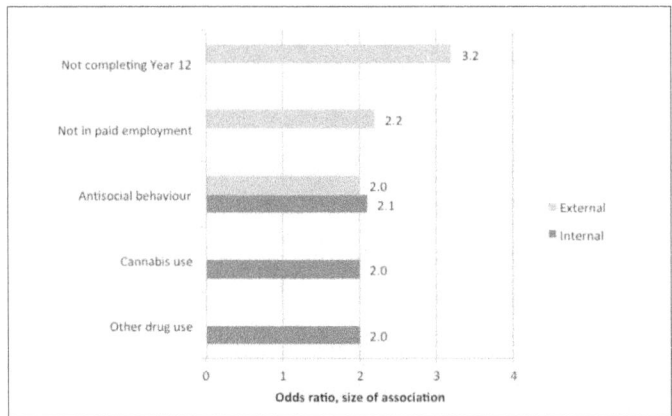

Figure 3.4: Adjusted associations between Year 10 internal and external suspension and young adult outcomes in 2010/11

Summary of findings

Several major points are worth noting in the findings described above. First, reports of both forms of suspension in Year 10 (2007) were associated with a range of negative young adult outcomes in 2010/11, such as antisocial behaviour, and alcohol and drug use. Even in analyses that took into account other factors we know to be related to negative behaviour, both internal and external suspensions continued to predict increased odds of negative outcomes. For internal suspension, links remained with young adult antisocial behaviour, cannabis use and use of other drugs. External suspension continued to be related to adult outcomes, such as not completing Year 12, having a source of income that is not through paid employment, and engaging in antisocial behaviour. In sum, both forms of suspension independently predict negative outcomes after students have left school. These findings have key implications for schools and policy makers.

Possible explanations of the findings

There are several potential reasons why both forms of suspension have a negative impact on behaviour reported by young people more than 3 years later. Both internal and external suspension remove the student from the learning environment, whether the immediate classroom setting or the wider school context. Already disrupted learning (as is often the case with students who are suspended) is further interrupted by these forms of removal, creating an even larger gulf for students to keep up with their classmates. It is well established that low achievement at school is related to a range of negative outcomes such as early school leaving, school dropout, unemployment and dependence on welfare (Battin-Pearson et al., 2000; Bond et al., 2007; Henry, Knight, & Thornberry, 2012; McMillan & Marks, 2003). By removing vulnerable students from the classroom through the use of suspension, schools may be further directing these students down a pathway that will have an impact on their life opportunities even after they have left school.

Another possible reason for these associations between suspension (internal or external) and negative young adult outcomes could be the environments (or more specifically the peers) to which young people are exposed while suspended. Irrespective of whether the suspension is internal or external, it is still highly likely that suspended young people are interacting with others who are also suspended, since many schools place internally suspended students in a common room. Similarly, it is likely that externally suspended students are afforded increased opportunity to interact with other peers within their school environment who are suspended, as well as antisocial peers from outside their school environment who may have been externally suspended, are truant from school, or who have dropped out of school.

Differential association theory postulates that a young person commits antisocial behaviour when in the company of others who endorse and reinforce the behaviour (Shoemaker, 2004; Sutherland, 1947). Similar to this is a phenomenon called 'peer deviancy training'. According to this account of behaviour, students who engage in problem behaviours and are placed in a group together can train each other to be more deviant through their interactions, and this can develop a culture that reinforces antisocial behaviour by group members (Dishion & Piehler, 2007; Dodge, Dishion, & Lansford, 2006). Through this positive reinforcement, students increase their levels of misbehaviour. Suspended (internal or external) students have time to interact with antisocial peers who are not in class. Peer involvement is of particular importance when there is minimal adult supervision of students, particularly that relating to monitoring students' whereabouts and social interactions during the suspension period.

Implications of the findings for behaviour management in schools

Findings from the International Youth Development Study have important implications for behaviour management approaches used in schools. First, both forms of suspension (internal and external) in Year 10 (when students are aged 15–16 years) were associated with a range of negative young adult outcomes at ages 18–19, such as antisocial behaviour, and alcohol and drug use. Even in analyses that took into account other factors we know to be related to negative outcomes, both internal and external suspensions continued to predict negative outcomes. These findings suggest that even when students are suspended and remain at school (internal suspension), they are at increased risk of engaging in antisocial behaviour, and cannabis and other drug use after they leave secondary school. Hence, the hypothesised benefits of keeping students at school while suspended are not supported. This is valuable to know since it is highly resource intensive for schools to ensure staff availability for internal suspension. Given that internal suspension does not seem to offer any benefits in terms of student outcomes, it is difficult to justify the added expense of implementing this approach.

One option available to schools is to adopt a proactive rather than a reactive approach to student misbehaviour through the use of prevention and early intervention. Preventive approaches seek to minimise the likelihood that student misbehaviour will occur, thereby reducing the need to respond to it. There is a range of prevention approaches available, so it is important that schools identify evidence-based approaches (i.e. those that have been demonstrated to work). These programmes can help students to learn self-regulation, and social, problem-solving, interactional, and conflict resolution skills that can reduce engagement in misbehaviour.

An emerging example of a comprehensive and preventive approach is whole-school restorative practices. Restorative practices refer to a continuum of intervention and prevention processes that view misbehaviour as a fundamental violation of people and interpersonal relationships in schools and the community (Morrison, 2002) and seek to repair relationships and ensure perpetrators are held accountable (Shaw, 2007). Misconduct is not treated simply as rule breaking or a violation of the institution. Hence, restorative practices focus on restoring relationships through acknowledging the losses experienced by victims and holding the offending student accountable for the harm s/he has caused, and may involve the exploration of a number of possible options.

In New Zealand and Australia restorative practices have further developed to focus not only on incidents once they occur, but to seek to prevent such incidents arising in the first place. These approaches seek to teach students a shared language around misbehaviour and focus on healing relationships and repairing any damage caused (see Chapter 7 in this book for more detailed descriptions of these approaches). There is an urgent need to conduct rigorous research on the impact of school-based restorative practices on student behaviour, school suspension rates, and other factors such as school climate (McMorris, Beckman,

Shea, Baumgartner, & Eggert, 2013). Encouraging schools to adopt proactive rather than reactive approaches to classroom management (e.g. whole-school adoption of restorative practices) may reduce the use of suspension.

In addition, school policies that are inclusive of all students and their families are needed. There has been an attempt to reflect this in federal policy in Australia. For example, the Melbourne Declaration of Educational Goals identifies two main goals: the promotion of equity and excellence, and all young Australians becoming successful learners, confident and creative individuals, and active and informed citizens. This includes providing

> all students with access to high-quality schooling that is free from discrimination based on gender, language, sexual orientation, pregnancy, culture, ethnicity, religion, health or disability, socioeconomic background or geographic location. (Curriculum Corporation as the legal entity for the Ministerial Council on Education, 2008, p. 7)

There is also an express aim to ensure that socioeconomic disadvantage and other forms of disadvantage (e.g. homelessness, disability, remote location and refugee status) often experienced by suspended students are not major determinants of educational outcomes. It is explicitly stated that this is not just focused on equality of opportunities, but on equitable outcomes as well.

Hence, schools need to find ways to ensure students from disadvantaged backgrounds achieve equitable outcomes. Findings from the current study indicate that suspensions are not congruent with these federal goals. Identifying the reasons for student misbehaviour and addressing them may be a more effective way of handling misbehaviour. Such reasons may be located within the student, his/her family, the classroom environment, and/or the school environment.

Schools need to consider the broad range of explanations, including those within the classroom and school environments. Areas worthy of consideration within the school itself are the quality of teacher–student relationships, the use of classroom management approaches, and enhancement of the curriculum. In some instances, schools may not be equipped to address the reasons for student misbehaviour themselves. However, it remains important that school staff be able to direct students and their families to appropriate sources of help and support. First and foremost in these considerations there needs to be a focus on finding ways for the student to remain connected and engaged with learning and the school community.

In order to best assist students and their families when needed, schools need to actively engage with parents and the community. Ensuring that parents are comfortable visiting the school and that they have opportunities to raise issues of concern is essential. Through having links with the local community, schools will be better informed about appropriate services for students and their families and will have the necessary networks to refer them on when necessary.

Conclusions

Both internal and external suspension in Year 10 (ages 15–16 years) predicted negative young adult (ages 18–19 years) outcomes such as antisocial behaviour and drug use in a sample from Victoria, Australia. The negative outcomes differed for internal and external suspension. These findings suggest that the use of internal suspensions is not to be recommended, even though it has been identified as a possible alternative to external suspension because it retains students at school. However, schools find it difficult to allocate resources for internal suspensions. It has been demonstrated here that internal suspension is itself related to negative young adult outcomes.

Schools and education systems need to find alternative ways of managing student misbehaviour in order to create safe, orderly and high-quality contexts for learning, and these approaches should be evidence-based. Identifying underlying explanations for student misbehaviour, which may be located within the student, his/her family, the classroom environment and/or the school environment, and addressing these reasons with resources may be a more effective way of handling misbehaviour.

First and foremost there needs to be a renewed focus on discovering ways for the student to remain connected and engaged with learning and the school community. Preventive approaches that seek to minimise student misbehaviour from occurring in the first place are also important ways to reduce reliance on school suspension. Schools are primarily environments for learning, and learners do make mistakes. Creative solutions and alternatives to exclusionary sanctions are needed to assist students who engage in misbehaviour to learn new ways of behaving and reduce the need to implement internal and/or external suspension.

Acknowledgements

The authors are grateful for the financial support of the National Institute on Drug Abuse (R01-DA012140) for the International Youth Development Study's initial data collection. The content is solely the responsibility of the authors and does not necessarily represent the official views of the National Institute on Drug Abuse or the National Institute of Health. Continued data collection in Victoria, Australia, has been supported by three Australian Research Council Discovery Projects (DPO663371, DPO877359 and DP1095744) and a National Health and Medical Research Council grant (project number, 594793). The authors wish to express their appreciation and thanks to project staff and participants for their valuable contribution to the project.

References

American Psychological Association Zero Tolerance Task Force. (2008). Are zero tolerance policies effective in schools?: An evidentiary review and recommendations. *American Psychologist, 63*(9), 852–862.

Angus, M., McDonald, T., Ormond, C., Rybarczyk, R., Taylor, A., & Winterton, A. (2009). *Trajectories of classroom behaviour and academic progress: A study of student engagement with learning.* Mount Lawley, WA: Edith Cowan University.

Arcia, E. (2006). Achievement and enrollment status of suspended students: Outcomes in a large, multicultural school district. *Education and Urban Society, 38*(3), 359–369.

Battin-Pearson, S., Newcomb, M. D., Abbott, R. D., Hill, K. G., Catalano, R. F., & Hawkins, J. D. (2000). Predictors of early high school dropout: A test of five theories. *Journal of Educational Psychology, 92*(3), 568.

Black, R. (2007). *Engaging students in school: An Education Foundation Australia fact sheet.* Australia Melbourne, VIC: Education Foundation Australia.

Bond, L., Butler, H., Thomas, L., Carlin, J., Glover, S., Bowes, G., et al. (2007). Social and school connectedness in early secondary school as predictors of late teenage substance use, mental health, and academic outcomes. *Journal of Adolescent Health, 40*(4), e9–e18.

Butler, H., Bond, L., Drew, S., Krelle, A., & Seal, I. (2005). *Doing it differently: Improving young people's engagement with school.* Melbourne, VIC: Brotherhood of St Laurence.

Christle, C. A., Jolivette, K., & Nelson, C. M. (2005). Breaking the school to prison pipeline: Identifying school risk and protective factors for youth delinquency. *Exceptionality: A Special Education Journal, 13*(2), 69–88.

Curriculum Corporation as the legal entity for the Ministerial Council on Education, Employment, Training and Youth Affairs (MCEETYA). (2008). *Melbourne declaration on educational goals for young Australians.* Melbourne, VIC: Ministerial Council on Education, Employment, Training and Youth Affairs.

Department of Education and Early Childhood Development. (2009). *Effective schools are engaging schools: Student engagement policy guidelines.* Melbourne, VIC: Author.

Department of Education, Employment and Workplace Relations (2010). *What works. The work program booklet: Core issues: 2: Reducing suspensions.* Canberra, ACT: Author

Department of Education, Training and Employment. (2012). *Reports and statistics Queensland state schools: School disciplinary absences by region.* Version 4, 5/7/2012. Retrieved http://education.qld.gov.au/schools/statistics/pdf/sda-by-region.pdf

Dishion, T. J., & Piehler, T. F. (2007). Dynamics in the development and change of child and adolescent problem behavior. In A. S. Masten (Ed.), *Multilevel dynamics in developmental psychopathology: Pathways to the future* (pp. 151–180). New York, NY: Taylor & Francis Group / Lawrence Erlbaum Associates.

Dodge, K. A., Dishion, T. J., & Lansford, J. E. (2006). Deviant peer influences in intervention and public policy for youth. *Social Policy Report, 20*(1), 1–20.

Glaser, R. R., Van Horn, M. L., Arthur, M. W., Hawkins, J. D., & Catalano, R. F. (2005). Measurement properties of the Communities That Care Youth Survey across demographic groups. *Journal of Quantitative Criminology, 21*(1), 73–102.

Harvey, D. L., & Moosha, W. G. (1977). In school suspension: Does it work? *National Association of Secondary School Principals (NASSP) Bulletin, 61*(405), 14–17.

Hemphill, S. A., Heerde, J. A., Herrenkohl, T. I., Patton, G. C., Toumbourou, J. W., & Catalano, R. F. (2011). Risk and protective factors for adolescent substance use in Washington State, United States, and Victoria, Australia: A longitudinal study. *Journal of Adolescent Health, 49*(3), 312–320.

Hemphill, S. A., Heerde, J. A., Herrenkohl, T. I., Toumbourou, J. W., & Catalano, R. F. (2012). The impact of school suspension on student tobacco use: A longitudinal study in Victoria, Australia, and Washington State, United States. *Health Education & Behavior, 39*(1), 45–56.

Hemphill, S. A., Herrenkohl, T. I., Plenty, S. M., Toumbourou, J. W., Catalano, R. F., & McMorris, B. J. (2012). Pathways from school suspension to adolescent nonviolent antisocial behavior in students in Victoria, Australia, and Washington State, United States. *Journal of Community Psychology, 40*(3), 301–318.

Hemphill, S. A., Smith, R., Toumbourou, J. W., Herrenkohl, T. I., Catalano, R. F., & McMorris, B. J. (2009). Modifiable determinants of youth violence in Australia and the United States: A longitudinal study. *Australian and New Zealand Journal of Criminology, 42*(3), 289–309.

Hemphill, S. A., Toumbourou, J. W., Herrenkohl, T. I., McMorris, B. J., & Catalano, R. F. (2006). The effect of school suspensions and arrests on subsequent adolescent antisocial behavior in Australia and the United States. *Journal of Adolescent Health, 39*(5), 736–744.

Henry, K. L., Knight, K. E., & Thornberry, T. P. (2012). School disengagement as a predictor of dropout, delinquency, and problem substance use during adolescence and early adulthood. *Journal of Youth and Adolescence, 41*(2), 1–11.

Hilberth, M., & Slate, J. R. (2014). Middle school black and white student assignment to disciplinary consequences: A clear lack of equity. *Education and Urban Society, 46*(3), 312–328.

Kerr, M. M., & Valenti, M. W. (2009). Controls from within the classroom: Crises or conversations. *Reclaiming Children and Youth, 17*(4), 30–34.

McMillan, J., & Marks, G. (2003). *School leavers in Australia: Profiles and pathways*. Camberwell, VIC: Australian Council for Educational Research.

McMorris, B. J., Beckman, K. J., Shea, G., Baumgartner, J., & Eggert, R. C. (2013). *Applying restorative justice practices to Minneapolis public schools students recommended for possible expulsion: A pilot program evaluation of the Family and Youth Restorative Conference Program*. Minneapolis, MN: School of Nursing and the Healthy Youth Development, Prevention Research Center, Department of Pediatrics, University of Minnesota.

Mendez, R., & Sanders, S. G. (1981). An examination of in-school suspension: Panacea or Pandora's Box? *National Association of Secondary School Principals (NASSP) Bulletin, 65 (January)*, 65–69.

Morrison, B. E. (2002). Bullying and victimisation in schools: A restorative justice approach. *Trends and Issues in Crime and Criminal Justuce, 219*. Canberra, ACT: Australian Institute of Criminology.

Morrison, G. M., Anthony, S., Storino, M., & Dillon, C. (2001). An examination of the disciplinary histories and the individual and educational characteristics of students who participate in an in-school suspension program. *Education and Treatment of Children, 24*(3), 276–293.

Rollings, K. (2008). Counting the costs of crime in Australia: A 2005 update. *Research and Public Policy Series, 91*. Canberra, ACT: Australian Institute of Criminology.

Shaw, G. (2007). Restorative practices in Australian schools: Changing relationships, changing culture. *Conflict Resolution Quarterly, 25*(1), 127–135.

Shoemaker, D. J. (2004). *Theories of deliquency: An examination of explanations of deliquent behavior*. New York, NY: Oxford University Press.

Skiba, R. J., & Knesting, K. (2001). Zero tolerance, zero evidence: An analysis of school disciplinary practice, *New Directions in Youth Development, 92* (Winter), 17-43.

Skiba, R. J., Michael, R. S., Nardo, A. C., & Peterson, R. (2002). The color of discipline: Sources of racial and gender disproportionality in school punishment. *Urban Review, 34*(4), 317–342.

Skiba, R. J., & Rausch, M. K. (2006a). School disciplinary systems: Alternatives to suspension and expulsion. In G. G. Bear & K. M. Minke (Eds.), *Children's needs III: Development, prevention, and intervention* (pp. 87–102). Bethesda, MD: National Association of School Psychologists.

Skiba, R. J., & Rausch, M. K. (2006b). Zero tolerance, suspension, and expulsion: Questions of equity and effectiveness. In C. M. Evertson & C. S. Weinstein (Eds.), *Handbook of classroom management: Research, practice, and contemporary issues* (pp. 1063–1089). Mahwah, NJ: Lawrence Erlbaum Associates.

Snyder, T. D., Dillow, S. A., & Hoffman, C. M. (2009). *Digest of education statistics 2008 (NCES 2009-020)*. Washington, DC: National Centre for Education Statistics, Institute of Education Sciences, US Department of Education.

Stage, S. A. (1997). A preliminary investigation of the relationship between in-school suspension and the disruptive classroom behavior of students with behavioral disorders. *Behavioral Disorders, 23*(1), 57–76.

Sullivan, J. S. (1989). Elements of a successful in-school suspension program. *National Association of Secondary School Principals (NASSP) Bulletin, 73*, 32–38.

Sutherland, E. H. (1947). *Principles of criminology.* Philadelphia, PA: Lippincott.

Vavrus, F., & Cole, K. (2002). "I didn't do nothin": The discursive construction of school suspension. *The Urban Review, 34*(2), 87–111.

Wu, S. C., Pink, W. T., Crain, R. L., & Moles, O. (1982). Student suspension: A critical reappraisal. *The Urban Review, 14*(4), 245–303.

Chapter 4 What results from psychological questionnaires?

Tim Corcoran

> Most participants in conversations about their own lives would expect to have the opportunity to engage from the perspective of their own meanings, in a conversation that will be constitutive of what happens next. However, the effect of interactions that work to exclude this possibility is to position the persons whose lives are being spoken about as non-participants in the production of the conditions of their own lives. (Drewery, 2005, p. 312)

Key points
1. How we talk about the people society exclude.
2. Language helps us to understand the world (i.e. know).
3. Language helps us to perform in the world (i.e. do, act).
4. Inspect the value of psychological discourse and practice.

Introduction
Before joining the academic rank and file I spent 10 years in the Queensland public service working as a psychologist in two government departments. It was early on during this time that I felt compelled

to undertake research in the area of exclusion. It doesn't take too much explanation to see why. I started out, straight from qualifying with an undergraduate degree, to working at the adult prison on the outskirts of town. It was during my 2 years inside that I became more and more interested in how it is that we talk about the people we want to exclude. When I say 'we', my immediate consideration is the communities we live in and potentially belong to. For example, my research has examined how language is used in state-based legislation to provide the means to lawfully exclude people from society (Corcoran, 2003, 2005). I also wanted to turn attention to my own profession (and similar social, education and health services) to question how what they were doing was enabling or disabling inclusive communities (Corcoran, 2007, 2012).

From prison I went on to work as the district psychologist for state-run schools (P-12)[1] in the region. Once there I was stunned by the fact that, again, my case load was populated by those the community was looking to reject. This time it was schools petitioning for the permanent exclusion of care-worn students. This chapter reports on research conducted during my time as a school psychologist.

The discussion presented here critically questions the contributions made by professional activities to social practices such as school exclusion. I start with a brief review of Achenbach's (1991) Youth Self-Report (YSR). The YSR is a formal psychological questionnaire, utilised around the world for over 25 years, to screen young people aged between 11 and 18 years for potential psychopathology. In the second section I introduce five young males, participants in a research project I conducted on formal school exclusion. The results obtained from these five young people are considered from two points of view: first, to see how a student excluded from their school might perform on this kind of measure, and second, to examine critically how the YSR allows those under assessment to respond to its questions. The analysis centres on the discursive resources (i.e. language) used and made available in the YSR.

The final section extends Drewery's position (see above) cautioning practitioners and community members about the use of professional tools such as questionnaires and how these must be carefully checked

---

[1] Preschool to Year 12.

for how they limit the possible range of meanings that can be in play, simply because they are and always will be closed 'conversations'. Practitioners should consider their professional activities—assessment practices included—as opportunities not simply for proclamation but also for elaboration. For ultimately, in our social engagements—even with those we intend to exclude—if we are committed to the prospect of change, we have to show a commitment to keeping open possibilities for new meanings to develop.

Introducing the YSR

Achenbach's YSR—or any professional questionnaire or assessment tool for that matter—should be situated and recognised as existing within a network of socio-political practices that help to maintain its relevance and credibility as a professional instrument. If and when support regarding the usefulness of a particular tool or practice wanes, the old knowledge gets discarded and replaced by new ways of knowing. For instance, it was not that long ago that measuring the shape of a person's head was thought to be able to reveal knowledge of their psychological attributes (known as phrenology and popular in the early 19th century). Social or community support of the 'psy' disciplines (i.e. psychiatry, psychology) enables specific knowledge to be valued. Institutional and disciplinary practices combine in intricate relationships to provide ways of understanding people, suggesting to people who they are at any moment in time and who they may become some time in their future.

Incorporated in the language we employ and sustained by social practice, knowledge of this kind helps construct human nature and our understanding of relationships and community. The availability of psy-related discursive resources is central to understanding another person. The ongoing interplay between people, the language they use and institutional practices such as education, health, and law and order affect all aspects of contemporary life. Although of primary concern here are the resources made available to both students and adults involved in state-sanctioned exclusion, it is important for any community member to acknowledge the role their use of language plays in legitimising preferred ways of being human. The fact is, we have choices regarding the language we choose and, as such, all involved must in good faith be aware of the enduring consequences their words play in discriminating for exclusion.

The YSR is part of a family of assessment procedures known as the Achenbach System of Empirically Based Assessments (ASEBA). ASEBA materials are researched, developed and produced primarily at the Research Centre for Children, Youth, and Families, a non-profit scientific and educational corporation situated at the University of Vermont. Achenbach's initial work dates back to the 1960s, but it was with the publication of his book *Developmental Psychopathology* (Achenbach, 1974) that work developing the range of what would become ASEBA materials began in earnest. Achenbach's first manual was published in 1983 (in collaboration with Craig Edelbrock) and was entitled the *Manual for the Child Behaviour Checklist and Revised Child Behaviour Profile* (Achenbach & Edelbrock, 1983). The YSR was first published in 1987 (Achenbach & Edelbrock, 1987) and the Young Adult Self Report (YASR) followed 10 years later (Achenbach, 1997).

The YSR (Youth Self-Report) is designed to be self-administered by young people aged between 11 and 18 years. It begins by seeking demographic information (e.g. gender, age, ethnicity, year level in school and whether the respondent is currently working). It then moves on to questions on what is called the competence scale, designed to assess adaptive strengths and divided into activities and social categories (see Figure 3.1). Competence scale questions require short answers; for example, list your favourite sports or hobbies, or describe any concerns you may have about school. The activities and social competence scales together with an academic item (Question VII, addressed below) combine to produce a total score. This total competence score is then converted into a statistic, a T score, using gender as its main variable. The T score is plotted along a normal, borderline-clinical and clinical range. The normal range is supposed to represent the general population, and the clinical range people in the community more likely to be affected by psychopathology.

The second part of the YSR involves 112 questions producing the syndrome scales. The student answers these questions using a common three-point rating scale ranging from 0 = not true, to 1 = somewhat or sometimes true, and 2 = very true or often true. Like the competence scale, the syndrome scales are split into several subscales: an internalising syndrome scale, an externalising syndrome scale and other syndrome scales These scales are further split into subscales (see Figure 3.1). This second part of the YSR is scored similarly to the competence scale. Total scores for the internalising and externalising components are first converted to T scores and plotted against a normal–borderline–clinical range. The total score involving all three components is then also converted to a T score and plotted against a standardised-to-population range. I will return later in the chapter to say more about how the YSR was standardised.

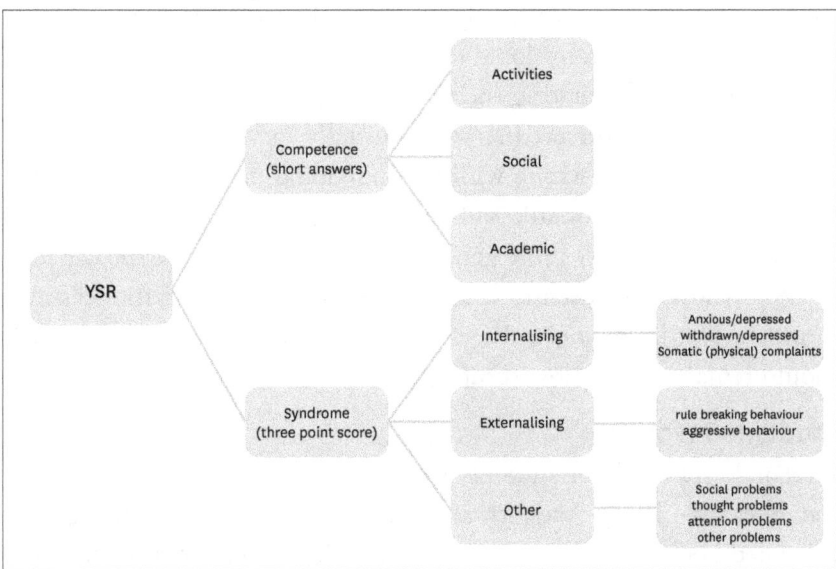

Figure 3.1 Diagram of the YSR components and subscales

The most common reason given for using the YSR as a research tool has been to provide grounds for explaining developmental psychopathology (Ebesutani, Bernstein, Martinez, Chorpita, & Weisz, 2011; Ferdinand, Blüm, & Verhulst, 2001; Hofstra, Van der Ende, & Verhulst, 2002; Rosina, Crisp, & Steinbeck, 2003). In layman's terms this means studying the development of psychological or psychiatric disorders like depression or anxiety. A note of warning though: Achenbach himself said the questionnaires "should not be automatically equated with any particular diagnoses or inferred disorders" (1997, p. iii). Rather, he suggests they may be "used as a take-off point for clinical interviewing" (1991, p. iii). In light of the psychopathological focus of previous studies, it seems practical to utilise student scores sourced from my own research into school exclusion via Achenbach's standardised normal–borderline–clinical range.

The research study

As revealed in the Introduction, the study discussed here developed from my tenure as a practising psychologist. Its main aim was to examine how language is used in a variety of social practices (e.g. legislation, psychological tools, research interviews) to facilitate or resist acts of exclusion (school exclusion and adult incarceration). Subsequently, the student's YSR results were analysed to consider the kind of discursive resources a typical professional tool makes available to its respondents, the practitioners facilitating their use, and, potentially, the wider community. Clinically oriented language usually focuses on pathology, or what is to seen to be wrong with the individual (i.e. some form of disorder), and this kind of talk is ubiquitous in psychological research and practice and in society more generally. Such discourse has the capacity to be privileged in discussion about the individual practitioner's aim to measure or know more about—in this case, students—and as such should remain under close scrutiny.

Students involved

Five male state school students gave their consent to be involved in the research. These students and their parents/carers were initially informed about the study via an information sheet provided to them by a staff member, usually the guidance officer based at the school. The reported reasons for exclusion extended from misconduct (e.g. tobacco possession at school) and disobedience (e.g. swearing at school staff) to physical assault. The age of respondents ranged from 12 to 17 years. Each student was known to have recently experienced his first formal exclusion from school. This meant the student could not return to the school that had formally made the application for exclusion but could enrol at another state school. It should also be noted that through my role as district psychologist, a prior therapeutic relationship existed with three of the five students (Bill, Mick and Keith).

Below I have listed the student's pseudonym used for the study, their age, and the reason they reported for being excluded from school.

- Mick was 12 years old at the time he completed the questionnaire. He reported swearing at teachers to be the main issue leading to his school exclusion.
- Bill was 13 years old at the time he completed the questionnaire. He reported truancy and swearing to be the main precursors to his school exclusion.
- Keith was 13 years old at the time he completed the questionnaire. Keith reported that swearing played a significant role in his exclusion from his school.
- Charlie was 13 years old at the time he completed the questionnaire. He reported a history of suspensions for fighting with peers prior to his exclusion from school. Charlie stated that he was excluded after an altercation with one of his teachers that reportedly involved Charlie striking the staff member.
- Ron's situation was somewhat different from that of the other respondents. Ron completed the questionnaire as a 17-year-old and, according to the legislation guiding school exclusion, his age placed him in the category of non-compulsory student. Ron's enrolment was 'cancelled' after he was found with alcohol and tobacco in his possession during school hours within school grounds. Ron also reported a history of "destructive" relationships with teachers.

YSR responses—competence scales

To some it might seem strange—perhaps even wrong—to question the results of clinical interventions. But second opinions or reconsiderations are just that: opportunities for those interacting with professional practices to raise concerns about their potential ramifications. With its capacity to construct and impart certain knowledges about adolescents, the YSR invites careful revision. For example, its competence scales are constructed from three subscales: activities, social and academic. From the questionnaire responses, two of the five students, Mick and Ron, are noteworthy because they both received total competence T scores in the clinical range. Both students scored within the normal range on the social category, but it was the activities subscale that presented as most concerning. Mick's score placed him on the ceiling of the borderline-clinical range, whereas Ron's was situated well within the clinical range. The activities subscale is constructed from questions relating to the number of sports the student is involved in, other activities such as hobbies or music, and jobs (e.g. part-time work) or chores they might be required to do around the home. Ron's scores on this subscale differed from Mick's and placed him in the clinical range, largely due to his reported limited involvement in sports and chores.

The issue of chore involvement around the home is a questionable variable on which to construct an understanding of the person, for a couple of reasons. First, response to this question is completely dependent on the practices established within the family home, and these are set by the adults in the household. It could be the case that the family is relatively wealthy and employs individuals from outside the household to do the washing and cleaning. Alternatively, in an extended family, a grandparent or other relative might opt to take care of the household chores. In another scenario, the adults might take it upon themselves to do all of the housework and not ask for help from the children. In any event, there are several plausible reasons why a person might not be involved in household chores, or in part-time work for that matter. Second, Ron reported that he lived independently (i.e. not with either of his parents). In his situation he did not see that he was involved in the general upkeep of his living environment, nor did he report being engaged in part-time work.

There is another issue that needs to be raised regarding the YSR's competence scales. Specifically this involves the academic subscale and how this score is constructed. According to the manual, when tabulating the respondent's score, direction is made not to include school subjects such as "physical education, art, music, home economics, driver education, industrial arts, typing, or the like" (Achenbach, 1991, p. 212). A strange and somewhat perplexing situation arises in that the YSR favours subjects such as "English or language arts", "history or social studies", "arithmetic or math" and "science", as well "computer courses, foreign language and business". No doubt there is a bias established in the way the YSR views academic endeavour. This point is given away by the questionnaire's use of the term 'academic' and fuels contemporary debates regarding what is to be considered fundamental as far as learning activities in schools are concerned. In Australia presently this debate is being vigorously contested in academia and in mainstream media. Positioned to one side are those who see education systems as having been infiltrated by liberal ideologues hell bent on deconstructing traditional educational practice and authority (see, e.g. Donnelly, 2013). Opposed to this view is the belief that education is about more than the three Rs and must equip young people with the skills and capacity to live productively in contemporary society (see, e.g. Biesta, 2014). Questions about the YSR and its competence scales remain valid due to its bias in this regard.

YSR responses—Syndrome Scales

Table 4.1 (see below) lists the internalising, externalising and total T scores from the YSR's syndrome scales for each of the students. Of particular importance is how these scores plot against the Achenbach normal–borderline–clinical range. For the YSR, the normal range involves a T score up to 64, the borderline-clinical range score is set between 65 and 69, and the clinical range begins with a T score of 70. Immediately evident from the results provided in the table is that no student is placed within the clinical range. While this may seem remarkable for a group of individuals excluded from their community, there are still some interesting scores to note for discussion. First, the fact that this group of male students did not score above the normal range on internalising conditions would seem to support the view that males are 50 percent less likely to present with anxiety or depression than females during adolescence (Ryan, 2005). Remember that the internalising scale involves three subscales: anxious/depressed, withdrawn/depressed and somatic complaints. In a recent systematic review of international research, an Australian-based team examined the possibility that child and adolescent mental health problems are increasing in the 21st century (Bor, Dean, Najman, & Hayatbaksh, 2014). In their summation, the review also pointed to a greater and increasing experience of internalising problems for adolescent females when compared to males of similar age.

Table 4.1: *T* scores from YSR syndrome scales

Student	Internalising	Externalising	Total *T* score
Mick	63	66	63
Bill	48	52	51
Keith	63	66	68
Ron	54	52	50
Charlie	58	67	59

Three of the five students did score in the borderline-clinical (B-C) range on the externalising score. This result comes as no surprise given this component is constructed using the rule-breaking behaviour and aggressive behaviour subscales.

Taking one example, further review of the scores indicates that Mick scored within the B-C range on the aggressive behaviour subscale but scored within the normal range on the rule-breaking behaviour subscale. Mick reported in the interview undertaken for this study that he had been excluded from his school because of general disobedience (e.g. continued swearing at school staff), which he stated did not involve any form of physical aggression. A closer look at Mick's responses to several questions on the aggressive behaviour subscale supports his contention. He answered 'not true' to questions such as 'I get in many fights' and 'I physically attack people'. He did, however, answer 'very true' to questions such as 'I argue a lot' and 'I disobey at school'.

One student, Charlie, reported a physical element to his exclusion. The incident allegedly escalated when his teacher refused to return a note that was being passed around the classroom. As Charlie tells the story, he and the teacher stepped outside the classroom to discuss the issue further. At interview he reported that he pushed his class teacher after the teacher had intentionally 'walked into me' on their way out of the class. Once outside the class Charlie said that he struck the teacher with an open hand on the shoulder. The teacher then returned the item to Charlie but informed him that he would not be allowed to return to class. In a similar outcome to Mick's, Charlie scored in the B-C range on the aggressive behaviour subscale and in the normal range on the rule-breaking subscale. Charlie reported 'sometimes true' to the question 'I get in many fights' but 'not true' to the question 'I physically attack people'.

Keith was the only student in the study who ended up with a total *T* score on the syndrome scales in the B-C range. As with Mick's and Charlie's responses, Keith's score on the aggressive behaviour subscale provided the dominant influence on his total score. While Keith responded with a score in the normal range on the rule-breaking subscale, his score on the aggressive subscale put him in the clinical range. But even with this score Keith's responses to the questions 'I get in many fights' and 'I physically attack people' were the same as Charlie's. The recurrent issue evident across Mick's, Charlie's and Keith's responses, according to the YSR, was that aggressive behaviour was of greatest concern. But the results from the YSR risk being taken out of context if then applied to each of these students as a reified personal quality, e.g. 'he is an aggressive person'. To say this of any of these boys would be to totalise an outcome which is itself, ambiguous as presented. Were the Aggressive subscale further devolved to verbal and physical acts such revisioning might draw closer to the understandings made by the student. In their current form, as discursive resources, these items would seem to hold little authenticity for the three excluded students.

How value is mobilised through language

> The scientific discourse of individual psychology did not form in a pure space of knowledge, but neither was it called into existence through the force of social exigencies. It was made possible by other ways of thinking of the nature, origin and treatment of mental pathology, and by certain conceptions of the role and objectives of good government and the laws of economic and social life. (Rose, 1985, p. 7)

Clinical and scientific practices

The YSR belongs first and foremost to the discipline of psychology, and within this field the self-reporting questionnaire has an established tradition. The use of questionnaires can be examined discursively and appraised from several vantage points. Danziger, for example, has criticised the tenuous relationship constructed between respondents and questionnaires in psychological studies generally, and in particular the reliance placed on an acceptance of the language used as being transparent and unambiguous. As he puts it,

> epistemic access to the world is collective—it is always mediated by the social conditions under which groups of investigators work. Moreover, in psychology these conditions are relevant not just for the investigators but also for those who function as the objects of investigation. (1990, p. 195)

A young person completing the YSR is asked for their response to a question such as 'I act too young for my age'. There is no doubt that any meaningful understanding and response is ultimately reliant upon an interplay between environment, history and culture. When Roger Daltrey (lead singer of the British rock group the Who) screamed the classic lyric "I hope I die before I get old", how old is old exactly? For that matter, how young is too young?

Achenbach's (1997) previously cited direction that the results obtained via use of the YSR should not be automatically equated with diagnostic categories (e.g. those delivered in the *Diagnostic and Statistical Manual of Mental Disorders*, better known by its acronym, the DSM) does not, in my opinion, do enough to mitigate the potential for inappropriate application. In some ways it is like placing a warning label or graphic image on a packet of cigarettes: such action does not stop all people from smoking and provides the barest amount of caution. In its appropriation of clinical language the YSR functions, to continue the analogy, like low-tar cigarettes. That is, its influence is no less harmful, but it attempts to cast an image of not being as definitive as other pencil-and-paper assessments such as intelligence or personality tests.

The scientist-practitioner model dominates current-day professional psychological training and practice (Johnson & Kaslow, 2014). This model aims to produce generalised accounts of human behaviour attained via the application of scientific rules (e.g. the use of statistics for predictive purposes). As noted already, in the Achenbach questionnaires the scales are converted to T scores, thereby providing what is often referred to as standardised results or results that have wide-ranging social application. In the sampling procedures used to develop and validate the YSR, two distinct groups—a normative sample (said to be representative of the general population) and a clinically referred sample (representing people in the community affected by psychopathology)—were sought. In constructing the YSR, respondents were reportedly segregated on the basis that their parents did not report the young person having received either mental health support services and/or remedial school classes in the preceding 12 months (Achenbach, 1991). Yet, the normal/clinical dichotomy on which the questionnaire is founded should be examined further, particularly in light of the YSR syndrome scale responses received here.

How did the group in the present study respond so underwhelmingly in relation to their placement on the normal–borderline clinical–clinical range? The students would be considered likely candidates to belong in the clinical range of the questionnaire given their prevailing circumstance (i.e. having been forcibly excluded from their communities due to engaging in rule- or law-breaking acts). Yet not one student could be. Given these results, the clinical ranges used in the YSR deserve closer scrutiny and must surely be questioned for their applicability to the students involved in this study. In a broader sense, the example serves as a reminder for us to question diligently the grounds on which our knowledge claims are made, for these often influence practitioners in forming and delivering potentially life-changing decisions—decisions like excluding someone from school.

Value & meaning

In Australia, as in other countries, the actions of government very much contribute to the immediate and medium-term sociopolitical context affecting schools and their wider communities. The practice of school exclusion is a pertinent example. At a time when the rhetorical upper hand is usually sought by politicians via their claims to being 'hard' on rule breakers, it is questionable how our governments uphold and support certain values. Consider the following present-day sociopolitical issues:

- the values of social justice and respect, and the treatment of Aboriginal and Torres Strait Islander peoples
- the values of inclusion and trust, and the treatment of asylum seekers
- the values of tolerance and understanding, and the denial of same-sex marriage rights
- the value of freedom, and the availability to detain, without charge, individuals suspected to be national security risks
- the value of care, and the state of mental health services in Australia.

People use these values to position themselves in relation to life's challenges. Such values are repeatedly negotiated between a government and its citizens and play an important role in the kinds of relationship constructed. As practitioners working with young people or parents with children at school, we must remain aware of an ongoing predicament constructed and maintained by, on the one hand, the context of rule or law breaking supporting exclusionary practice, and, on the other hand, an inevitable frustration with governments swayed by the consistency of universal approaches. We know, don't we, what counts as appropriate behaviour, and we can agree on this in ways that make sense to all involved.

With its focus on psychopathology, the YSR would seem to be well placed to assess the kinds of legislatively targeted behaviours implicated in school exclusion (e.g. disobedience and misconduct; see Corcoran, 2003). In fact, closer attention to the rule-breaking behaviour subscale provides the discussion with an indication of contemporary values and standards according to the YSR. There are 15 questions that contribute to the rule-breaking behaviour subscale, and while it is not necessary to list all of these here, there is one worth further consideration. The question I draw attention to is one that immediately raises the relational context of everyday life. Question 26 of the YSR states: "I don't feel guilty after doing something I shouldn't". A respondent's answer could be considered indicative of the culture and historical period in which s/he lives and demands reflection beyond the partitioned response of the individual. For instance, understanding emotions like shame or guilt can be explained via the use of different discourses (Corcoran, 2014a). Organism and molecular grammars work to provide reductionist accounts of human action examining emotion as physiological phenomena (e.g. acute anger or great sadness treated as biochemical imbalance in the brain; see Breggin, 2014). In contrast, our person-oriented grammars potentially offer richer understanding of the kind of practical-moral knowledge necessary to make meaning of emotion in contemporary life (Harré, 1998). Stearns (1995, p. 52) put it succinctly saying the relational context of emotional performance can be envisioned at the broadest societal level in that '[e]motions and emotional standards ... affect public institutions. Laws change in the light of emotional values'. How else would we be able to account for what is understood to be disobedience or misconduct?

The enactment of guilt and other emotions is performed with an understanding of socially and culturally constructed knowledges and, according to Vygotsky (1978), we learn and practise such life skills within a zone of proximal development. Consequently, the familial home or role model influences could play a significant part in how a person understands and experiences guilt. Question 26 directs the respondent's answer to their knowledge of *doing something I shouldn't*. If a 15-year-old is permitted to smoke cigarettes at home, it is highly improbable that they are going to feel guilty after being caught smoking at school. This particular example again brings to the fore the relational context existing between the student, their home and the school. The value the student places on his/her school-based relationships, particularly with adults in positions of authority, could have a determining influence on how the student experiences their own transgression of the school's rules (Corcoran, 2014b). Will the experience of guilt affect the respect s/he has for staff at the school? Will s/he feel that s/he has let them down? Or is the meaning surrounding their experience tied to the student's knowledge that the teacher who found him/her smoking is a smoker too, and that privately both see the practice of prohibiting smoking at school as draconian?

Conclusion

The YSR is an example of professional practice using particular language to construct knowledge about people. While it may be argued that the students could have registered clinically skewed scores because all were recipients of state-sanctioned exclusion, generally they did not. The reason for this? It is neither practical nor responsible to suggest a definitive answer to such a question. Possibly the students wished to answer in such a way as to have their responses considered favourably. If so, were they in fact trying to keep open a conversation that for them often seems already closed? Also possible is that the students had been selected to participate in the study because the situation they had found themselves in was novel to them (i.e. it was their first formal school exclusion). Given this circumstance, the search for causal psychopathology may be a misguided and redundant move. Perhaps rather than belonging to a supposedly predictable and static clinical population—because of their participation in rule-breaking behaviour—their involvement may otherwise and more legitimately be understood *in situ* as relational action. As we try to make sense and put into words what people do in joint action, we are always presented with choices. Interrogating both the aims and the objectives of professional practice and the language used to achieve these ends is pivotal to keeping open future possibilities when working with those society wants to exclude.

The use of standardised questionnaires has not played a significant role in my professional engagement with people. This is largely due to the relationship I maintain with these tools of the trade. As a discursive practice I remain wary of the potential of questionnaires for two principal reasons. First, questionnaires are fundamentally 'closed conversations': a person's responses and consequent positioning are made to fit within the strict parameters of a preordained normativity. Second, as potential resources for getting to know people, they often promote a world view informed by clinical knowledge. While I generally support the inclusion of these discourses in conversations regarding psychosocial wellbeing, I cannot but remain concerned with their focus on deficit-based explanation reducing dynamic social activity to individual behaviour. Clinical discourse plays a purposeful role in psychological practice, and while its aims can be debated, the central issue for me is a pragmatic one questioning how such language may best be understood and the relative importance it should receive. In recognising the limitations and potential of our way with words, we can be satisfied with evidence conveyed in a closed language of standardised questionnaires; or, as Achenbach himself inferred (though not quite in these terms), we can commit to keeping conversations open, making space for future-oriented opportunities. Even when exclusion seems the only option available, the potential for change is sustained in the presence of dialogue and the language we use.

References

Achenbach, T. M. (1974). *Developmental psychopathology*. New York, NY: Wiley.

Achenbach, T. M. (1991). *Manual for the youth self-report and 1991 profile*. Burlington, VT: University of Vermont Department of Psychiatry.

Achenbach, T. M. (1997). *Manual for the young adult self-report and young adult behaviour checklist*. Burlington, VT: University of Vermont Department of Psychiatry.

Achenbach, T. M., & Edelbrock, C. (1983). *Manual for the child behaviour checklist and revised child behaviour profile*. Burlington, VT: Queen City Printers.

Achenbach, T. M., & Edelbrock, C. (1987). *Manual for the youth self-report and profile*. Burlington, VT: University of Vermont Department of Psychiatry.

Biesta, G. J. J. (2014). *The beautiful risk of education*. London, UK: Paradigm.

Bor, W., Dean, A. J., Najman, J., & Hayatbakhsh, R. (2014). Are child and adolescent mental health problems increasing in the 21st century?: A systematic review. *Australian and New Zealand Journal of Psychiatry*. doi: 10.1177/0004867414533834

Breggin, P. (2014). *Guilt, shame and anxiety: Understanding and overcoming negative emotions*. New York: Prometheus.

Corcoran, T. (2003). Constructing dialogic relationships: School legislation and the principal's gamble. *Australia and New Zealand Journal of Law and Education, 8*(2), 97–109.

Corcoran, T. (2005). Legislative practice as discursive action: A performance in three parts. *International Journal for the Semiotics of Law, 18*(3/4), 263–283.

Corcoran, T. (2007). Counselling in a discursive world. *International Journal for the Advancement of Counselling, 29*(2), 111–122.

Corcoran, T. (2012). Health inclusive education. *International Journal of Inclusive Education, 16*(10), 1033–1046.

Corcoran, T. (2014a). *Are* the kids alright?: Relating to representations of youth. *International Journal of Adolescence and Youth*. http://dx.doi.org/10.1080/02673843.2014.881296

Corcoran, T. (2014b). Doing restorative practices justice: Questioning the psychology of Affect Theory. In G. Goodman (Ed.), *Educational psychology reader* (rev. ed., pp. 598–610). New York, NY: Peter Lang.

Danziger, K. (1990). *Constructing the subject: Historical origins of psychological research*. Cambridge, UK: Cambridge University Press.

Donnelly, K. (2013, 9 October). The lost art of discipline. *The Australian*. http://www.theaustralian.com.au/news/the-lost-art-of-discipline/story-e6frg6n6-1226735038124#sthash.CV83wHKr.dpuf.

Drewery, W. (2005). Why we should watch what we say: Position calls, everyday speech and the production of relational subjectivity. *Theory and Psychology, 15*(3), 305–324.

Ebesutani, C., Bernstein, A., Martinez, J. I., Chorpita, B. F., & Weisz, J. R. (2011). The Youth Self Report: Applicability and validity across younger and older adults. *Journal of Clinical Child and Adolescent Psychology, 40*(2), 338–346.

Ferdinand, R. F., Blüm, M., & Verhulst, F. C. (2001). Psychopathology in adolescence predicts substance use in young adulthood. *Addiction, 96*, 861–870.

Harré, R. (1998). *The singular self: An introduction to the psychology of personhood*. London, UK: Sage.

Hofstra, M. B., Van der Ende, J., & Verhulst, F. C. (2002). Pathways of self-reported problem behaviours from adolescence into adulthood. *American Journal of Psychiatry, 159*(3), 401–407.

Johnson, W. B., & Kaslow, N. J. (Eds.). (2014). *The Oxford handbook of education and training in professional psychology*. Oxford, UK: Oxford University Press.

Rose, N. (1985). *The psychological complex: Psychology, politics and society in England 1869–1939*. London, UK: Routledge.

Rosina, R., Crisp, J., & Steinbeck, K. (2003). Treatment adherence of youth and young adults with and without a chronic illness. *Nursing and Health Sciences, 5*, 139–147.

Ryan, N. D. (2005). Treatment of depression in children and adolescents. *Lancet, 366*, 933–940.

Stearns, P. (1995). Emotion. In R. Harré & P. Stearns (Eds.), *Discursive psychology in practice* (pp. 37–54). London, UK: Sage.

Vygotsky, L.S. (1978). *Mind in Society: The development of higher psychological processes*. Cambridge, MA: Harvard University Press.

PART TWO: RESOLVING SCHOOL EXCLUSION CONTEXTS

Chapter 5 A way forward? Finding room for flexible behaviour management approaches in inflexible school structures

Sheryl Hemphill, Sarah Drew, David Broderick, Lynn Gillam and Lyndal Bond

Key points

- Student and staff perspectives revealed that there is an urgent need for creative, adaptive and flexible approaches to behaviour management.
- While research evidence shows that preventive practices are desirable, current school behaviour management practices are often set in a punitive mode.
- Both students and staff seemed open to the potential benefits of restorative practices.
- The way forward involves actions to bridge the gap between punitive and preventive approaches.

Introduction

Behaviour management in schools is a widely debated and well-researched topic. Much of the current discussion is about how to ensure order is maintained within school while using approaches that are inclusive of all students. To develop approaches that meet the needs of both students and staff it is important that the voices of both be heard. However, rarely in the research literature are the perspectives of both students and staff collected and compared.

How Does School Discipline Affect Student Behaviour, Wellbeing, and Educational Progress? was an Australian Research Council-funded project (2008–2010). Qualitative interviews with 50 students and nine principals, and eight focus groups with 56 school staff, revealed the impacts of suspension for students in different social circumstances, and the efforts of staff to explore innovative alternatives to suspension. This chapter will draw on interview data from students and principals, and data from staff focus groups, to examine connections and disconnections in student and school staff views.

First, the relevant literature in this field will be reviewed. Next, the study in which interviews and focus groups were conducted will be described. In describing the data this chapter juxtaposes two issues: (a) students' need for flexible approaches to behaviour management that avoid exclusion, coupled with the school's capacity to embrace more individually tailored approaches; and (b) the challenges encountered by staff when trying to enact less punitive behaviour management approaches. Finally, the implications for school behaviour management policies and practices are discussed.

Overview of approaches to behaviour management

Schools have a range of behaviour management approaches available to them, on a continuum from punitive to supportive to preventive. *Punitive or punishing approaches* include detentions, excluding students from school activities (e.g. camps, excursions), internal suspensions, external suspensions, and expulsions. Punitive approaches fit with a zero tolerance approach to behaviour management. Such approaches are particularly common in schools in the US (American Psychological Association Zero Tolerance Task Force, 2008), as well as Australia (New South Wales Department of Education and Training, 2008) and the UK (Department for Children Schools and Families, 2008). Such approaches seek to reduce misbehaviour through deterrence, by sending a clear message to students that certain behaviours will not be tolerated and will incur serious consequences *regardless of the circumstances*.

Concern about the use of punitive approaches has grown following research demonstrating that disadvantaged students are more likely to experience punitive approaches irrespective of their behaviour (Hemphill et al., 2009; Hemphill, Heerde, Herrenkohl, Toumbourou, & Catalano, 2012; Hemphill, Toumbourou, Herrenkohl, McMorris, & Catalano, 2006; Skiba, Michael, Nardo, & Peterson, 2002; Skiba & Rausch, 2006a, 2006b; Vavrus & Cole, 2002; Wu, Pink, Crain, & Moles, 1982). Research also shows that punitive approaches are associated with negative student outcomes, such as dropping out of school, failure to complete school, crime, substance use, and related problems (Arcia, 2006; Butler, Bond, Drew, Krelle, & Seal, 2005; Hemphill et al., 2006, 2009, 2012).

Supportive approaches include restorative justice approaches (students make amends for the harm they do), providing remediation and/or counselling, and recognising positive behaviours. Restorative justice approaches view misbehaviour as a fundamental violation of people and interpersonal relationships in the school and the wider school community (Morrison, 2002) and seek to heal and make amends for the violations within the community affected by the incident (not just the misbehaving student) (Thorsborne & Vinegrad, 2004). Misconduct is not seen primarily as school rule-breaking or a violation of the institution. The use of restorative justice approaches within schools is growing and is now undergoing more research.

Preventive approaches focus on addressing influential factors that may affect student behaviour to stop misbehaviour occurring in the first place. Whole-school restorative practices is an example of a preventive approach that aims to help both students and staff to develop a shared language they can use for behavioural issues (see Chapter 7). This approach requires further research to demonstrate its effectiveness. Examples of other approaches are evidence-based prevention programmes designed to develop positive interactional skills in students, such as social skills, problem-solving skills, communication skills, and conflict resolution skills.

Although the theoretical and empirical understanding of the

impact of different behaviour management approaches is extensive, implementing this knowledge within a complex school environment remains challenging for many schools. Discrepancies have been found, for example, between teachers' perceptions of what is good classroom management in theory and their perceptions of "realistic" best practice (Lewis, 1999). In addition, promoting an inclusive school environment that meets the needs of all students to keep young people engaged in schooling is a key challenge facing all schools.

A critical element in promoting inclusive school environments is identifying those factors that increase student disengagement and disconnection from school. Developing a clearer understanding of how young people experience aspects of schooling and behaviour management can greatly assist school administrators to better meet the needs of the most vulnerable students and ensure that behaviour management strategies do not result in further disengagement from school.

Overarching study: International Youth Development Study

The International Youth Development Study (IYDS) began in 2002 with the recruitment of almost 6,000 students from Victoria in Australia, and Washington State in the US to complete a quantitative survey. The IYDS has focused on the development of substance use and related behaviours such as antisocial behaviour for over a decade. Briefly, the IYDS used a two-stage cluster sampling approach to recruit students: random selection of public and private schools using procedures to ensure a state-representative sample was recruited, and the selection at random of one class at each grade level (Year 5, 7 and 9) within each school.

Sub-study focused on behaviour management in schools

In 2007, funding was received from the Australian Research Council to undertake the project entitled How Does School Discipline Affect Student Behaviour, Wellbeing, and Educational Progress? The aim was to continue to collect quantitative survey data from students, but to add interviews with students and principals, as well as focus groups with school staff, to examine issues related to behaviour management in schools in more depth. Specifically, the study sought to investigate the impacts of suspension for students in different social circumstances and the efforts of staff to explore innovative alternatives to behaviour management.

The student-focused component of the study examined the ways in which young people understand and experience behaviour management, and external school suspension in particular. While external school suspension is utilised in many schools, relatively little is known about the *students'* experiences of this practice. The staff component of the study identified the behaviour management approaches schools are currently using and the challenges faced by schools in using these approaches, as well as the impact on staff of dealing with negative behavioural incidents.

Data gathering

Accessing student perspectives

Relying on one-to-one interviews with 50 young Victorians (26 females, 24 males), including 30 in Year 11 or 12 and 20 who were 1 to 2 years post-secondary school, the study reported on the perspectives of students from a range of socioeconomic backgrounds with equally diverse experiences of behaviour management. Participants were selected to ensure that a wide range of students were interviewed. The participant sample included students who had experienced external suspension, students who had engaged in antisocial behaviour but had not experienced external suspension, and students who had neither engaged in antisocial behaviour nor experienced external suspension.

Accessing staff perspectives

Nine secondary schools agreed to participate in principal interviews and staff focus groups that were designed to complement the content covered in the student interviews. These schools were selected to include all sectors (government, Catholic and independent). They included both metropolitan and non-metropolitan schools in Victoria, and ranged from low to high school suspension rates according to quantitative survey data from the IYDS. In total, qualitative data were collected from 71 school staff, including nine school principal interviews and eight focus groups with 56 staff, covering classroom teachers, student welfare co-ordinators, school psychologists, and staff in senior leadership roles.

The topics of the semi-structured interviews and focus groups included staff opinions about how they felt school discipline and behaviour management approaches worked in their school; whether staff felt behaviour management approaches contribute to student disengagement; how students know about the rules and consequences at the school; which students mostly seemed to get into trouble; and staff feelings or emotions in relation to behaviour management issues, including teacher stress.

Outcomes of the study

Student perspectives on behaviour management

The results of the student component of this study demonstrated that many factors influence the outcomes of a suspension event. Specifically, the study showed that there is no single pathway into suspension and no single pathway out of suspension. The stories shared by the young people involved in this research revealed that students from any social background may experience external suspension. The consequences of suspension, however, are likely to be more detrimental for those who are already emotionally vulnerable and/or socially disadvantaged. The experiences of suspension of disengaged female participants, for example, differed substantially from those of male participants, who had clearer post-secondary career ambitions. The results from this study also illustrated the ways in which experiences of external suspension depend on factors both internal and external to school. Examples include student perceptions of procedural fairness, their sense of connection to the school community, and their experience of concurrent stressful life events, as well as parental response to suspension.

Family factors affecting suspension and school completion

Parent attitudes to suspension

When describing their experience of suspension, many participants discussed the role played by their parents in this experience. For almost all participants who had experienced external suspension, parental reactions and responses to this event appeared to be branded vividly in their memories. Parental reactions also appeared to mediate participants' emotional responses to the suspension and also seemed to affect their appraisals of the event. Pomeroy (2000) presents similar results, indicating that experiences of suspension are often strongly shaped by parental reactions.

Many participants described their parents' reaction to their suspension as the most worrying or unpleasant element of the suspension experience.

> The only thing that bothered me was the home part of it because of mum and dad's anger towards it rather than the teacher's. It sort of made me try to be a better student rather than muck up again … just to avoid mum and dad again. (Harley: Year 11 student, male, government school)

> My parents were furious at me and I got grounded. (Sebastian: post-secondary student, male, government school)

> She [mum] wasn't very happy. Mum actually took time off work to do it because she knew that if she left me there by myself I probably wouldn't do it [school work]. (Jacqui: Year 11 student, female, government school)

In contrast, some suspended participants reported that their parents "didn't care" or disagreed with the school's decision to suspend their child. It is particularly noteworthy that each of the participants described below denied the presence of any negative effects stemming from their respective suspensions and appeared somewhat dismissive of the events surrounding the suspension:

> But like mum and dad didn't care that I got suspended or whatever. It [suspension] was just at school, like they didn't care that I wagged so it didn't bother me [laughing]. (Isla: Year 11 student, female, government school)

> Mum was a bit like 'Oh well … you shouldn't even be disciplined for that'… so I kind of got a bludge off that. (Liam: Year 11 student, male, government school [early departure])

> Mum kind of knew that the teacher was giving me a hard time to

start with so she never really took anything she said seriously. Because even mum was getting annoyed because she would be trying to sleep during the day and she'd just be getting phone calls flat-out from this teacher about stupid things that could just wait. (Fiona: post-secondary student, female, government school [early departure])

These findings appear to indicate that the manner in which parents respond to their child's suspension plays a very important role in shaping the experience of this event. The American Academy of Pediatrics Committee on School Health (2003) state that young people who experience suspension are often those least likely to receive parental supervision while absent from school. A similar suggestion is made by Kirk (2009), who argues that "results reveal that suspension and parental supervision have a highly significant negative association" (p. 501), a factor that may increase the likelihood of antisocial behaviours or arrest.

When describing parental responses to suspension, participants reported that anger and disappointment were common reactions. Importantly, many suspended participants described their parents' reaction as the *worst* aspect of this event, and these responses in turn shaped participants' experiences of suspension. Notably, the small proportion of participants who described their parents as being dismissive of their suspension were themselves dismissive of this event. This finding emphasises the important role played by factors external to school, such as families, as an element shaping suspension experiences.

Socioeconomic factors and school completion

Socioeconomic factors, including parental levels of education, have consistently been presented as strong predictors of school achievement and school completion (Marks, 2007; McMillan & Marks, 2003; Rothstein, 2004). However, in this study parental attitudes to schooling appeared more closely linked to school completion than socioeconomic status or reported parental levels of education. Notably, in this study student-reported parental levels of education were substantially lower than might be expected based on school completion and tertiary education statistics from this particular generation of parents.

Despite this demographic information, when asked to describe their parents' attitudes to schooling, an overwhelming majority of participants described parental attitudes as strongly favourable to school completion. This pattern existed regardless of socioeconomic status, as measured by the Socio-Economic Indexes for Areas (SEIFA) scores or reported parental levels of education. In particular, many students spoke of their parents' insistence that they complete secondary schooling. This trend was particularly strong for those whose parents had very limited education themselves, such as those whose educational opportunities were disrupted by political turmoil in their country of origin or economic hardships.

These findings highlight the important role played by parents in shaping school experiences. Adopting school-based intervention programmes that focus on strengthening relationships between school and parents may serve to reduce the negative long-term effects of external suspension (e.g. school drop-out), particularly for disadvantaged or vulnerable young people (Skiba & Peterson, 2000; Sheldon, 2002). In this situation, schools and families can work collaboratively to support the student by identifying areas for intra- and interpersonal development, and ensuring the student's individual learning needs are met.

Student perspectives on components of the suspension process

Internal versus external suspension

Some participants regarded internal suspension as "worse" than external suspension. This is particularly noteworthy given that internal suspension is typically classified by schools as a less severe behaviour management measure than external suspension. For these students the term 'worse' referred to internal suspension being a less desirable option than external suspension.

> It [suspension] was in-school and in-school is worse because it's really boring [laughing]. (Trucanh: Year 11 student, female, Catholic school)

> I just wish I did something worse so that I could have an at-home suspension—like a three-day ban from school, that'd be fine. Ah when you did that it's not really to the kid, I just see that as really, 'Okay sweet, I'll just sit at home and play Playstation' or whatnot. But yeah, the in-school suspension was just boring. I couldn't get

anywhere or do anything so it worked effectively. (Brian: post-secondary student, male, independent school)

From the perspective of these young people, this undesirability centred on the lack of freedom afforded by internal suspension in comparison to external suspension. From a behaviour management perspective these findings appear to indicate that internal suspension may indeed be a more effective deterrent for students against unproductive behaviour. Hemphill, Heerde and McMorris (Chapter 3, this volume), however, suggest that, while internal suspension appears to be more effective, the eventual outcomes of internal suspension may be just as negative as external suspension in terms of antisocial behaviour, substance abuse and course completion.

Internal suspension may have advantages in terms of school connectedness because, while students may perceive internal suspension as "boring", this approach ensures that students continue to receive support and tuition. Internal suspension, therefore, potentially encompasses the benefits of external suspension—removal from the classroom and isolation from peers—without the diminished connection to schooling and unsupervised time away from school. Internal suspension is, however, still inconsistent with adopting an inclusive approach for all students.

Finally, Leonie had extensive experience of both internal and external suspension from school. She found internal suspension to be more effective than external suspension:

> Instead of [external] suspension they should be sat in a separate room and do their work without their friends there but still be let out at lunch time and recess and whatever but not have the interaction that they did in their school time. Then they actually might realise because the worse punishment would be being ripped away from your friends in your class and it was. (Leonie: Year 11 student, female, government school [early departure])

Her early departure from school, however, questions the efficacy of internal suspension as a strategy to re-engage young people with education.

Restorative practices

Interviews also examined young people's understanding of justice.

Notably, participants described justice in terms of rectifying harm or *righting wrongs*. The two responses below focus on the repair of harm as opposed to the punishment of those responsible, a notion commonly attributed to restorative practices (Bazemore, 2001; Morrison & Ahmed, 2006; Wearmouth, McKinney, & Glynn, 2007).

> I think it's just the ability to have something that was wrong be rectified. Like, for instance, if something bad happened, for that bad thing to be fixed. That is doing justice. So pretty much fixing— putting everything back to the way it should be is justice for me. (Donald: Year 11 student, male, Catholic school)

> I don't know. It's kind of something that if something has gone wrong it's kind of owed or you want it to be restored back to how things were. That's kind of how I see justice. (Rachel: Year 11 student, female, government school)

These and other students from the study indicated that student participants possessed sophisticated moral reasoning abilities allowing for a nuanced interpretation of justice and injustice. In particular, young people in this study emphasised the importance of equitable treatment, the maintenance of public and personal safety, and the acceptance of repercussions for wrongdoings provided that key elements of procedural justice are upheld. The findings indicate that young people possess a nuanced rather than concrete conceptualisation of fairness that is dependent upon contextual factors.

Student perceptions: summary

The interviews with students revealed a number of important considerations in relation to their perceptions and experiences of schools' behaviour management approaches. These considerations affected not only students but also their parents. Students were keenly aware of how their actions at school affected their parents, and the students themselves were affected by parents' reactions to their external suspension. The interviews also revealed the contrasts drawn between experiences of both internal and external suspension. Notably, several participants classified internal suspension as a less desirable option than external suspension, despite perceptions of this form of suspension as being less punitive. The next section of this chapter reports the results of the focus groups and interviews with school staff, and identifies themes that are both similar to and different from those raised by students.

Staff perspectives on behaviour management

Overview of findings from school staff

Staff from all schools expressed dedication to dealing effectively with behaviour management to achieve positive student outcomes, though staff at some schools reported having more success than others with their chosen behaviour management approaches. There was a predominance of punitive strategies described, with some preventive and supportive approaches also discussed. Staff from all schools described issues up to the level of suspension, whereas few staff talked overtly about expulsion. When expulsion was discussed, it was described using language such as a student withdrawal or transfer to another school. The reason so few talked of expulsion seemed to be that the process to expel a student was relatively slow, whereas a suspension could be implemented quickly. School staff made the distinction in the kinds of misbehaviour engaged in according to the age of students, with general "acting up" or "misdemeanours" more prevalent in younger age groups, and more specific and serious behavioural challenges in older age groups.

Specific areas identified by school staff

There were four specific content areas raised by school staff during qualitative data collection:

- the predominance of references to punitive approaches, and language consistent with such approaches
- the frustrations and benefits of using alternatives to punitive practices, including restorative practices
- the importance of student–teacher relationships
- concerns about behaviour management.

Each of these areas will be described in the sections that follow.

Predominance of punitive approaches

School staff used a range of terms during interviews and focus groups that reflected a punitive approach to behaviour management. These terms included: repeat offender, re-offending, misdemeanour, serious misdemeanour, the mistake, the behaviour, the incident, punishment, consequences, investigative process, disciplinary hearing and imposing sentences. They used phrases such as "kids who are not parented well", "there's no excuse for kids not knowing what our standards are", "the severity of the intention of the punishment", "punch hard and then sort of embrace", and "we mean business".

The predominance of punitive approaches reflected in the language used by school staff may, in part, explain the continued use of these approaches in schools. If student misbehaviour is still categorised in terms consistent with a punitive approach, then it seems unlikely that alternative methods of behaviour management will be adopted. Placing an emphasis on having a common language for students and staff in whole-school restorative practices may be one way of countering this tendency to use language focused on punitive approaches. Research on how the language used in restorative practices may shift schools' practices to being more supportive and preventive is an important direction for future research.

When talking in the context of punitive approaches, school staff commented that young people's behaviour is worse than it was in the past. They referred to lack of discipline at home and in society:

> Like, kids aren't scared of teachers any more, they're not scared of police any more, they're not scared of their parents any more, you know, and that's—that's a societal change and that's certainly changed over my time in teaching. So the traditional ways of disciplining you had—we had to change otherwise you won't survive as a teacher ... There's been a hell of a shift in the way kids react to discipline. (Year 11 male teacher, focus group participant)

This participant continued:

> It's also true that the number of students who need severe discipline has increased over the years. The number of kids that are—are not happy at school, the number of kids with severe social problems and those problems are reflected in what happens at school, their behaviour at school, the number of kids involved there has increased exponentially I reckon in the last five, 10 years.

School staff recognised that despite the emphasis on punitive practices, there may be a number of reasons for student misbehaviour:

the students' backgrounds, age and individuality were also factors in behaviour management. One staff member commented, "Some kids use that as an excuse sometimes … their background is their excuse for not doing the right thing", and observed "Certainly Year 11 and 12 because they are really at a different level or stage in their lives and you can deal with them one to one, one on one, you know, as an almost human being" (Year 11 male teacher, focus group participant). One principal commented:

> As angry as we might get at these children who we perceive to be trying to needle us, we've got to realise that they're children and they're doing that for some reason. They might be bored, bored with the curriculum, angry, had a bad day, didn't have enough to eat. They might be teenagers so they might be on an emotional rollercoaster. Their amygdala might be enlarged and they can't control themselves … whatever it is we have to rise above that.

She went on to say,

> But times have changed and kids are no longer to be seen and not heard … kids are people and they just happen to be younger. (Female principal secondary school, interview participant)

Some participants took the next step: from identifying a range of possible influences on student behaviour to noting that responses to students therefore need to vary:

> You know, there's sometimes you need to get a student out of the classroom. Or you need to solve an issue that could only get bigger, you've got to use a range of techniques and it's not all yelling or restorative, it's—it's, you know, picky really, thinking what's going to be best for that class, that student, that situation. (Year 11 male teacher, focus group participant)

Continuing with this line of thinking, other participants said:

> And that's the key, isn't it? It's an individual thing for each situation as it arises. You can't have a blanket thing and this is what we do. Just, doesn't work. (Year 11 female co-ordinator, focus group participant)

> They'll try and distance the child from the actions and then work out why it's happening. (Year 11 male teacher, focus group participant)

> It's trying those different approaches that work, and you can sort of see, you can gauge from the student in the way they respond to it what works with them. (Year 11 male teacher, focus group participant)

> Or there's the misbehaviour in the classroom, the students—and then [you] say to the student what is going on? And they say, 'Oh well, Dad walked out last night, we haven't had any food for the last three weeks,' or whatever it might be. And then you say, 'Okay, right, now we talk to the teacher and say this is the reason why I'm not taking this any further'. (Year 11 male teacher, focus group participant)

Alternatives to punitive approaches

There was genuine interest expressed by staff in possible alternatives to punitive approaches for student misbehaviour. Many commented, however, on the lack of alternatives to punitive approaches available. There was some evidence that school staff working in the busy environments of schools may find they end up using the punitive strategies with they are familiar with and for which they have the resources, even though they have the best intentions to use supportive approaches.

> I think one of the frustrating things for us … is that there are not a lot of options for serious offences. I don't have a great big bag of tricks that I can do, so, you know, you don't have much else other than suspension, and even that's been tempered somewhat slightly … So it's a lot about working with them and trying to set strategies in place and alternative things for them or things that might hold them here for a bit longer to try and get them back on track. A lot of work's put into that. (Year 11 female teacher, focus group participant)

And from another teacher,

> I think it would be fantastic if we could be more creative with our consequences for severe behaviour, but it's really just a matter of time and resources that we often don't have the time to be so creative. (Year 11 female teacher, focus group participant)

This limited range of options can be a cause of frustration for staff:

> It is frustrating, isn't it though, that we can't—our most serious punishment before an expulsion is an out-of-school suspension

and a lot of parents view that as another day off and not a worthy
punishment. So our most serious punishment is not valued by the
parents. That—I've found that very frustrating. (Year 11 male teacher,
focus group participant)

The comment above also reveals a disconnect between the staff perception that parents do not regard suspension as an appropriate punishment and reports by students that their parents did take suspension seriously.

Similar to the students' comments in the last section, some teachers talked about the effectiveness of internal in comparison to external suspension. It is worth noting, however, that while internal suspension is presented as an alternative, it is still a punitive approach.

So we've sort of got this in-school suspension going, so same thing,
but instead of the kids staying home, they're put in a room ... It does
mean more work for us, though, cos you've got to chase the teacher
up to organise work, find a spot to put them generally—keep an eye
on them for the day, and it does take a bit of work. End of the day
it's probably more effective than out-of-school. (Year 11 male teacher,
focus group participant)

Restorative practices approaches

At the time the current study was conducted, schools in Victoria were increasingly adopting restorative practices in their schools. As a result, several staff talked about this approach in the focus groups and interviews.

Instead of, you know, just focusing on educating the student
intellectually, we try to educate the whole person and, you know, give
them a sense of social justice, respect, responsibility, all those sorts of
things and by employing the restorative practices sort of questioning
and all those sort of practices, it ... has instilled that in the kids,
you know, seeing how it impacts on the class as a whole and the
individual who they just—who their behaviour [affected]. (Year 11
male teacher, focus group participant)

Even though staff perceived that restorative practices require time, the outcomes they achieved were perceived to be worth their investment of time.

> It's very time consuming. Takes a lot of time, you know. When you have issues that need to be dealt with, sometimes you could be spending two periods on one issue. But it's worth it because the—you can see the body language of the kids change as they are allowed to speak about what's been happening and then discuss it with whoever's been upsetting them, you know, with the anger or bullying or whatever. And there's been really positive things happening. (Year 11 male teacher, focus group participant)

School staff recognised that in order to manage student misbehaviour effectively, the teacher needs to have a working relationship with the student. In addition, teachers emphasised the importance of consistency in approach, and how the efforts of one teacher may be very rapidly undone by another with a different approach.

> The only disappointing things that I've had happen is where you have really worked at building a relationship with a student and it only takes one other teacher to walk past them, and you might have just spoken to them about something, whether they're out of uniform or whatever, you've had a chat, you know where they're at, and another teacher walks past and can't get that relationship with them from the start, then you've got no hope in hell of disciplining them when [another teacher] bails them up and follows a totally different path ... five more teachers go 'No, you're out of uniform' and that kid's turned off completely. (Year 11 female teacher, focus group participant)

School staff also commented on their relationship with and responsibilities to "good" students, and in particular the time that may be required to manage student misbehaviour. This may also explain why some teachers do not go down the path of exploring why the student engaged in misbehaviour: because it distracts from the teachers' responsibility to the other well-behaved students in the class who are ready to learn. Considerations about the *needs of the one* versus the *needs of the many* present a serious dilemma for teachers.

> [For one student] we've recently done, spent hours upon hours of doing work, chasing up notes, chasing up every little bit we've done, documenting every stage that we've done this. Now that takes for one student—you know, it doesn't happen very often, but that's hours of work, and then we're thinking well, what about the 700 other good—

> really good kids? If I could put my time into those good kids who are on the brink that perhaps have got some issues, I'd love to put some time in ... I'd love to be able to put some time into those kids that I know that—are saveable, that—that really need that one-on-one support. (Year 11 male teacher, focus group participant)

Similarly, another teacher said:

> Finding out why the kid misbehaved ... that's really good ... that's what you want to do, you want to find out. But often the really difficult part is you've got three or four students misbehaving in a class—so your—the opportunity to actually have that conversation with that student and find out why they're misbehaving or what's going wrong is impractical in that circumstance. Or you can't go outside and spend 15 minutes with the student—why are they misbehaving—cos you've got a responsibility or duty of care for the other 25 in the classroom ... Sometimes you need to be really authoritarian and say no, this is the way it is. (Year 11 male teacher, focus group participant)

More research is needed to understand how teachers and school staff balance the needs of the student engaging in misbehaviour with the needs of the others students in the class.

Concerns raised by school staff about safety

Reflecting the difficulties of finding effective ways of managing student misbehaviour, staff also raised concerns about their own safety and the stress they experience following an incident they have dealt with.

> And when you've got a couple that are bigger than me, I can understand smaller teachers, female teachers, without being sexist, feeling intimidated by this group. (Year 11 male teacher, focus group participant)

Another staff member reported:

> Some of the staff take days and weeks to get over an incident, especially when it's been quite a volatile one ... But this is a top-end really stressful thing, you just can't get it out of your head for ages and they stay with you forever. (Year 11 male teacher, focus group participant)

School staff perspectives: summary

Punitive practices for managing student behaviour continued to be used in Victorian schools at the time of this study for a variety of reasons. School staff referred to lack of time and resources and the need to take a firm approach with young people. Staff also recognised that there are number of factors that influence the behaviour of students and described how they adjusted their responses to address these factors. While some schools are already trying out different approaches, in the busy school environment schools may find themselves falling back into old patterns of behaviour management. There was evidence that staff believed they had to hold the line in a society where traditional support for good behaviour, the home and the community was deteriorating.

When staff talked about managing behaviour, the predominant vocabulary was that of punitive practices. While language associated with punitive practices persists it is unlikely that supportive and preventive approaches will take hold. School staff were able to identify the benefits of restorative practices in their schools even though it can require more time to implement, and this presents enormous challenges in an already crowded curriculum. The increasing use of restorative practices in schools in Victoria, however, does show a change in language use associated with behaviour management, and this may provide a way forward.

Implications of student and staff perspectives for behaviour management in schools

Continuing to explore creative behaviour management approaches is likely to benefit all concerned—students and their families, teachers, principals, and the broader community. The challenge for schools, policy makers and the research community is to address the barriers and progress the opportunities to move forward identified by this study. The chief barrier appears to be that schools are set in a punitive mode to address challenging behaviour in students. The language of discipline is punitive, and a suggested alternative to external suspension, internal suspension, is also punitive. However, the opportunities are promising. Firstly, the participants in this project agreed that there is an urgent need for creative and flexible alternatives to punitive discipline.

Essentially, there is a commitment to change. Secondly, the early indications from growing restorative practices in schools reveal both a change in the language of discipline and a commitment to the value of restorative approaches.

Currently school staff are able to present many reasons why the status quo should continue while still expressing a need for change. The challenge is to make an *authentic* commitment to addressing the barriers to change. This requires assigning responsibility to those with the power to act. The crowded curriculum and lack of time to try out and evaluate new approaches is largely outside the jurisdiction of schools. It is the responsibility of politicians and policy makers who assign the budget and thus the time available to schools. School staff identified a lack of alternative options for behaviour management. It is incumbent upon researchers and policy makers to help schools to access evidence-based prevention approaches. Researchers need to convey their findings in ways and venues that are readily available to schools and ensure that evidence-based programmes can be accessed by schools. Education systems and policy makers need to ensure that schools have access to resources to support the use of preventive approaches. Ensuring funding is tied to proactive, preventive approaches rather than reactive, incident-focused approaches may facilitate a shift in schools' focus. One action schools can take responsibility for is to be aware of the range of influences on student behaviour and use this awareness to guide decisions about the consequences for that behaviour.

School staff in this project expressed awareness of, and talked about, approaches to modifying courses of action depending on the factors influencing students' behaviours. However, again, schools require assistance to find ways within busy schedules and competing demands to take time to reflect on the courses of action taken and the likely impact of these on the student in the short and long term. Schools also have it within their mandate to enhance the involvement of parents in school suspension processes. Parents who feel genuinely included may not dismiss suspension so readily.

Finally, there needs to be an authentic conversation about the safety of school staff as they go about their business of educating and managing young people. Currently making schools safe is associated with removal of the child, a punitive approach. Yet does this actually make the school safer? Experiencing, witnessing and handling challenging and violent behaviour damages not only the immediate victim but also other children who observe it and the teacher charged with confronting it. This study proposes restorative approaches as one way forward from punitive to more desirable preventive behaviour management, and thus potentially safer schools. There is an urgent need for further rigorous research on restorative practices in schools to investigate the efficacy of this approach in terms of both reducing misbehaviour and enhancing the move towards preventive practices in responsive schools.

Acknowledgements

The authors are grateful for the financial support of the National Institute on Drug Abuse (R01-DA012140) for the International Youth Development Study initial data collection. The content is solely the responsibility of the authors and does not necessarily represent the official views of the National Institute on Drug Abuse or the National Institute of Health. Continued data collection in Victoria, Australia, has been supported by two Australian Research Council Discovery Projects (DPO663371, DPO877359). The authors wish to express their appreciation and thanks to project staff and participants for their valuable contribution to the project. We particularly acknowledge the contributions of Ruby Walter in the collection of qualitative data from school staff.

References

American Academy of Pediatrics Committee on School Health. (2003). Out-of-school suspension and expulsion. *Pediatrics, 112,* 1206-1209.

American Psychological Association Zero Tolerance Taskforce. (2008). Are zero tolerance policies effective in schools?: An evidentiary review and recommendations. *American Psychologist, 63*(9), 852–862.

Arcia, E. (2006). Achievement and enrollment status of suspended students: Outcomes in a large, multicultural school district. *Education and Urban Society, 38,* 359–369.

Bazemore, G. (2001). Young people, trouble and crime: Restorative justice as a normative theory of informal social control and social support. *Youth and Society, 33*(2), 199–226.

Butler, H., Bond, L., Drew, S., Krelle, A., & Seal, I. (2005). *Doing it differently: Improving young people's engagement with school*. Melbourne, VIC: Brotherhood of St Laurence.

Department for Children, Schools and Families. (2008). *Permanent and fixed period exclusions from schools and exclusion appeals in England, 2006/07*. London, UK: Department for Children, Schools and Families.

Hemphill, S. A., Heerde, J. A., Herrenkohl, T. I., Toumbourou, J. W., & Catalano, R. F. (2012). The impact of school suspension on student tobacco use: A longitudinal study in Victoria, Australia, and Washington State, United States. *Health Education and Behavior*. doi: 10.1177/1090198111406724

Hemphill, S. A., Smith, R., Toumbourou, J. W., Herrenkohl, T. I., Catalano, R. F., McMorris, B. J., et al. (2009). Modifiable determinants of youth violence in Australia and the United States: A longitudinal study. *Australian and New Zealand Journal of Criminology, 42*(3), 289–309.

Hemphill, S. A., Toumbourou, J. W., Herrenkohl, T. I., McMorris, B. J., & Catalano, R. F. (2006). The effect of school suspensions and arrests on subsequent adolescent antisocial behavior in Australia and the United States. *Journal of Adolescent Health, 39*, 736–744.

Kirk, D. S. (2009). Unravelling the contextual effects on student suspension and juvenile arrest: The independent and interdependent influences of school, neighbourhood, and family social controls. *Criminology, 47*(2), 479–520.

Lewis, R. (1999). Teachers' support for inclusive forms of classroom management. *International Journal of Inclusive Education, 3*, 269–285.

Marks, G. N. (2007). Do schools matter for early school leaving?: Individual and school influences in Australia. *School Effectiveness and School Improvement, 18*(4), 429–450.

McMillan, J., & Marks, G. N. (2003). Declining inequality?: The changing impact of socio-economic background and ability on education in Australia. *The British Journal of Sociology, 54*(4), 453–471.

Morrison, B. (2002). Bullying and victimisation in schools: A restorative justice approach. *Trends & Issues in Crime and Criminal Justice, 219*, 6 pages.

Morrison, B., & Ahmed, E. (2006). Restorative justice and civil society: Emerging practice, theory, and evidence. *Journal of Social Issues, 62*(2), 209–215.

New South Wales Department of Education and Training. (2008). *Long suspension and expulsion summary 2008*. Sydney, NSW: New South Wales Department of Education and Training.

Pomeroy, E. (2000). *Experiencing exclusion*. Staffordshire, UK: Trentham Books.

Rothstein, R. (2004). *Class and schools: Using social, economic, and educational reform to close the Black-White achievement gap*. New York, NY: Teachers College Press.

Sheldon, S. B. (2002). Parents' social networks and beliefs as predictors of parent involvement. *The elementary school journal*, 301–316.

Skiba, R. J., Michael, R. S., Nardo, A. C., & Peterson, R. (2002). The color of discipline: Sources of racial and gender disproportionality in school punishment. *Urban Review, 34*(4), 317–342.

Skiba, R. J., & Peterson, R. L. (2000). School discipline at a crossroads: From zero tolerance to early response. *Exceptional Children, 66*(3), 335–347.

Skiba, R. J., & Rausch, M. K. (2006a). School disciplinary systems: Alternatives to suspension and expulsion. In G. G. Bear & K. M. Minke (Eds.), *Children's needs III: Development, prevention, and intervention* (pp. 87–102). Bethesda, MD: National Association of School Psychologists.

Skiba, R. J., & Rausch, M. K. (2006b). Zero tolerance, suspension, and expulsion: Questions of equity and effectiveness. In C. M. Evertson & C. S. Weinstein (Eds.), *Handbook of classroom management: Research, practice, and contemporary issues* (pp. 1063–1089). Mahwah, NJ: Lawrence Erlbaum Associates.

Thorsborne, M., & Vinegrad, D. (2004). *Restorative practices in schools: Rethinking behaviour management*. Buderim, QLD: Margaret Thorsborne & Associates.

Vavrus, F., & Cole, K. (2002). "I didn't do nothing": The discursive construction of school suspension. *The Urban Review, 34*(2), 87–111.

Wearmouth, J., McKinney, R., & Glynn, T. (2007). Restorative practice in schools: A New Zealand example. *Educational Research, 49*(1), 37–49.

Wu, S. C., Pink, W. T., Crain, R. L., & Moles, O. (1982). Student suspension: A critical reappraisal. *The Urban Review, 14*(4), 245–303.

Chapter 6 The relationship between the compulsory school experience and youth offending

Alison Sutherland

Key points

1. There is a relationship between school experience and the child and youth offending.
2. School experience can aggravate pre-existing family and/or community risk factors to propel a vulnerable student along the pathway towards chronic criminal offending.
3. A healthy school climate can make a positive difference to young people at risk of future offending.
4. Schools have a unique opportunity to identify students most at risk of future offending by applying both appropriate screening tools and preventive interventions.

Introduction

Based on my PhD research, and drawing on my experience as a practitioner supporting schools with students exhibiting severe behavioural problems, this chapter explores the relationship between the school experience and child and youth offending. While acknowledging that family, child-centred and/or community risk factors generally underpin criminal behaviour, I focus on the schools' role in propelling a vulnerable young person along the pathway towards offending. I argue that while school attendance does not necessarily cause a young person to commit crimes, the cumulative effect of negative school experiences can result in a student's alienation from the education system. It is this estrangement that aggravates pre-existing risk factors and propels a vulnerable student along the pathway towards chronic criminal offending. I emphasise the unique opportunity schools have to identify students most at risk of future offending, suggest appropriate screening tools, and conclude with preventive interventions that could be implemented through the education system.

Young offenders in Aotearoa New Zealand

While most young New Zealanders make significant, positive contributions to their whānau/families, peer groups, schools and communities, a number offend at some stage while they are growing up. The majority do so in a limited way, committing minor offences that do not come to the attention of the police. In 2013, 5,990 offences were committed by children in Aotearoa New Zealand aged 10 to 13 years; 19,166 were committed by youth aged 14 to 16 (Statistics New Zealand, 2014). What is particularly concerning is that the majority of youth and child offences are committed during school hours (Becroft, 2004). The focus of this chapter is on the link between young people's offending and their non-engagement with the school system. Why were these students out of school? What is the role that schools play in a young person's pathway towards a criminal career?

The role of schools in youth offending

School attachment and educational success are key protective factors in preventing criminal behaviour by young people (Gottfredson, 2001). However, school attendance has also been implicated in propelling a vulnerable student at risk of offending further along the criminal pathway (Rutter, Maughan, Mortimore, Ouston, & Smith, 1979). This is because susceptible students may have been exposed to one or more of the following school risk factors.

Inadequate school transition

Students experience a number of school transitions, including entry into primary school, from class to class, primary to intermediate, intermediate to secondary, and school to school. Some children are exposed to more school-to-school transitions than others due to the mobility of their family, thus increasing their exposure to this particular risk. Each transition brings its own unique risk factors and challenges that rely on the previous acquisition of essential social skills (Kellam, Ling, Merisca, Brown, & Ialongo, 1998). The child is required to adapt to an unfamiliar classroom or whole school environment and create new teacher and peer relationships. They are expected to respond appropriately to a range of new demands and rules while negotiating new roles for themselves (Reinke & Herman, 2002).

The transition from primary to secondary school is particularly challenging because it involves the movement from one teacher to multiple teachers, a few subjects taught in one classroom by one teacher to multiple subjects taught by a number of teachers in different classrooms, differing teacher styles, greater and more complex academic demands, and greater demands for self-monitoring and self-reliance as the students move around several classrooms (Wasserman & Miller, 1998). This transition period is especially risky for girls, who are more likely than boys to experience pubertal maturity at the same time as they encounter the transition from primary to secondary school (Pepler & Craig, 2005).

Anti-social peer relationships formed at school create a toxic contagion effect

Both inside and outside the classroom, students develop social hierarchies and groups that have a significant influence on their performance and that play a large role in shaping both their appropriate and inappropriate behaviours (Reinke & Herman, 2002). When discontented, embittered and alienated youth are punished by being grouped together in detention, this provides a breeding ground for the development of criminal ideology (Cohen & Felson, 1979). Particularly at risk are students who exhibit verbally and physically aggressive behaviours and become isolated from 'normal' peers. The process of peer rejection, spiralling to severe disruptive behaviours and youth offending, begins in the primary school years and accelerates during the intermediate and high school years, becoming more serious, more frequent and more covert as the young people mature (Church, 2003; Gardner, Lane, & Hutchings, 2004).

An unhealthy school climate

An unhealthy school climate is linked with a poorly organised, malfunctioning school that has a prevalent sense of despondency among students and staff, accompanied by high rates of teacher and student absenteeism (McEvoy & Welker, 2001). Such schools are characterised by teachers who are routinely late to class, leaving students unsupervised and vulnerable to bullying. They have cramped classrooms and overcrowding, buildings in poor physical condition and high student: teacher ratios. Many of the teachers have had insufficient training on effective behaviour management (Leone et al., 2003). An unhealthy school climate not only contributes to a young person's academic failure, lack of school attachment, school drop-out and criminal offending, but may also escalate aggressive students' violent behaviour towards property and others (Edwards, 2001).

Ineffective teaching and assessment methods

These methods that lead to academic failure can also drive a student towards offending. Children who are struggling academically are more likely to turn to crime than those who are performing adequately or well (Flannery, 2000). This is verified by young offenders having significant deficits in reading, maths, and written and oral language compared to their non-offending peers (Leone et al., 2003). While low achievement can be symptomatic of a student's behavioural and/or learning difficulties rather than low ability, it has also been attributed to teachers' low expectations for students from lower socioeconomic disadvantaged families and/or minority groups (Macfarlane, 2004).

A negative teacher–student relationship

Negative teacher–student relationships create a vicious cycle that begins with an escalation of the student's antisocial behaviour in response to the teacher's requests, a punitive reaction to this response from the teacher, leading to an intensification of negative behaviour from the student (Kennedy & Kennedy, 2004). Instead of allowing that the child's behaviours are escalating as a response to their own treatment of the child, teachers are more likely to blame the student's challenging behaviours on his or her unwillingness to be co-operative, a mental health disorder, or some other external factor such as the child's dysfunctional upbringing. When teachers cannot cope with the stress and frustration associated with working with these difficult students, they react to minor problems with irritability, fear, counter-aggression and disciplinary responses, which further escalates the frequency and severity of the child's aggressive behaviours (Reinke & Herman, 2002).

Traumatisation of students

Traumatisation of students may occur through deliberate or unintentional mistreatment by school personnel. Both have been identified as school-based risk factors (Halkias et al., 2003; Piekarska, 2000), the difference between the two being determined by the adult's intent to cause harm to the student while seeking compliance. Deliberate mistreatment involves punitive disciplinary strategies and control techniques that are based on fear and intimidation; for example, verbal assaults, sarcasm and ridicule, isolating a student from his or her peers, allowing or ignoring peer humiliation, sexual harassment, publically humiliating a student by drawing attention to their perceived deficits (including learning difficulties), calling them liars and criminals, and personal attacks regarding their appearance, family and choice of friends. Unintentional mistreatment includes involuntary provision of a low quantity and quality of human interaction, and providing limited opportunities for individual students to develop self-worth.

At the extreme end of teacher abuse is the use of corporal punishment, the purposeful infliction of pain or confinement as a penalty for an offence, and racism or other forms of prejudice directed at students who are already marginalised within the school setting (Cunningham, 2003; Puketapu-Andrews, 1997). Traumatisation of students also occurs in schools that are guilty of omission and neglect. Minority groups with special requirements are overlooked and ignored, their needs considered too difficult to address because of inefficient targeting of insufficient resources. A student who perceives that his or her culture has no place within the school is likely to feel unwelcome, unsupported and defensive.

School policy abuse

School policy abuse occurs when a school's senior management team, supported by their board of trustees, victimise students by using legitimised, inappropriate punitive disciplinary practices to deter students' behaviours (Morrison & Skiba, 2001). Intolerant, zero-tolerance policies such as extended school stand-downs, suspension, exclusion and early school exemptions provide opportunities for at-risk, alienated youth to associate, unsupervised, with deviant peers (Leone et al., 2003). The effect of these zero-tolerance practices is to transfer undesirable behaviour from the school setting, where it was contained, out into the community (Becroft, 2004).

Young offenders' perceptions of school

Believing that it is by listening to young people detained for serious criminal offences that we are better able to understand the role school plays in the pathway to criminal offending, I invited young offenders to share their stories about their primary and secondary school experiences (Sutherland, 2006, 2007). The main themes that came from the young people's stories were "I couldn't do it", "I didn't fit", "I couldn't sit and be quiet the way the other kids did", "I couldn't survive at school unless I self-medicated", and "In school, it wasn't safe to be me; it was not me to sit and be quiet and do my work".

For many of the youth there was a strong sense of unfairness, of perceived victimisation that led to frustration and a search for ways to get out of attending school. It was their viewpoint that having to attend school was imposed on them: it was never their choice. They described feeling alienated from the school system and from their pro-social peers. Many found learning difficult, especially towards the end of primary school. The majority were bored with classroom routine and behavioural expectations and used this to justify their antisocial, impulsive and aggressive behaviours. They had little desire to comply with teachers' instructions, and while there was an expectation that other students should follow the school rules, they did not accept that the rules applied to them. Truancy was routine, as were discipline, detentions and stand-downs. Suspension and/or exclusion were common. The most dominant complaint was they were treated unfairly by their teachers and deputy principals. No-one listened to their explanation of an incident before determining that they were at fault, nor were others involved in the incident punished. While the principal was generally someone they wanted to take an interest in them and their achievements in school, they disliked coming to the attention of the deputy principal for any reason. These feelings intensified when the young person sharing the story was Māori and the deputy principal was not. Despite their own misconduct, it was the Māori participants' perception that the deputy principal was motivated by racism.

Their preferred teachers, according to the female students, listened to their personal issues and concerns, offered mutual respect, were kind, sensitive and flexible, and looked beyond their disruptive behaviours to see what was troubling them. Secondary to the girls' need for a nurturing teacher was a teacher with skills and techniques that enabled them to learn. The boys preferred teachers who would support them in the classroom and provide them with a sense of ability and accomplishment in an environment that lacked conflict. Once learning was happening, they wanted someone who related to them as individuals, showed them respect, kindness and understanding, and was flexible in his or her classroom behaviour management skills. While a positive bond with a teacher can be a protective factor for at-risk children (Sprott, Jenkins, & Doob, 2000), attachment to a teacher did not stop the criminal developmental pathway of these young offenders. The primary benefits of teacher attachment for the young person were a higher level of academic achievement than might otherwise have been mastered, and positive stories of the school experience to share with their children.

Their worst teachers were those who hurt, harassed, shamed or humiliated them in front of their peers. They also disliked teachers who punished them for minor misdemeanours and who were ineffective in their teaching practice. The girls complained about moody teachers, those favouring other girls or who isolated them from their friends, those who focused on their negative rather than their positive qualities, and teachers who delivered boring lessons. The boys disliked teachers who focused too much attention on them: this was interpreted as being "picked on". They also complained about teachers who were unhelpful, difficult to understand, overly strict or yelled. Several boys reported receiving excessive physical force to gain compliance, including being manhandled, smacked by hand or with an item, being "wedgied" and choked. Long periods spent in time out, and being suspended and/or excluded, were also described as being traumatic for them.

Friendships played a major role in their school-life world. However, rather than being rejected by pro-social peers and left with little alternative but to mix with, and be negatively influenced by, their antisocial peers, they reported shunning their pro-social peers, seeking out friends who shared similar rebellious interests such as smoking, truanting, petty theft, drinking alcohol and using drugs in and out of school. These relationships with antisocial peers were particularly toxic for the female offenders, who attached themselves to older or same-age boys at school, accepting the role of 'girlfriend' while seeing them as role models—people they wanted to be like. To be accepted into the boys' group, the girls allowed themselves to be used sexually. Labelled as promiscuous by onlookers, what they sought was a sense of belonging and acceptance. Once part of the boys' group, the girls honed their aggression skills and participated in criminal activities.

Both sporting and academic achievement at school have been identified as protective factors from youth offending, primarily because success within the educational arena is considered to strengthen attachment to school. Several of the young offenders achieved success in school sports. However, like attachment to positive teachers and friendships with pro-social friends, participating in sports was not sufficient to stop the vulnerable young person from offending. This may be because participation and success in school sports is only a protective factor when connected with some other component, such as a supportive home environment and a parent or parents who actively encourage pro-social activities. It is possible that academic rather than sporting achievement is a stronger protective factor against future criminal offending, as none of the participants reported gaining success in any external or significant school examinations. Several connected underachieving academically with their behavioural problems at school, although there was some confusion as to whether their behaviour caused them to underachieve or their lack of ability led to their antisocial behaviour. Some participants reported having learning difficulties such as dyslexia, but most of them attributed their lack of academic success on a "disability", such as oppositional defiant disorder (ODD) and/or attention deficit hyperactivity disorder (ADHD).

Distorted moral reasoning and the blaming of others pervaded the young offenders' stories. It was their perception that they were victims of an unfair system and therefore were morally justified in breaking the school rules and disrupting the learning of others. All antisocial behaviours could be rationalised. For example, fighting and physical aggression towards others was just being playful, in self-defence or to gain or maintain a place in the social hierarchy. Bullying was retaliation for perceived insults, because they had been bullied in the past, or their victims deserved it because of their diversity or positive relationship with teachers. Unprovoked assaults on others was blamed on their uncontrollable anger. Vandalism of school property was a way of venting their anger. Tagging was a form of social currency that provided them with an identity and status among their peers. Smoking, swearing, drinking alcohol and using drugs should be acceptable in school because they did it at home. Despite contrary evidence that taking drugs contributes to academic and behavioural problems, they perceived that it relaxed them, made them more compliant and therefore better students in the classroom.

From school to criminal offending

The majority of the young offenders' memories of their school experience involved negative incidents with teachers and deputy principals. Recalling frequently applied consequences for what they regarded as their normal behaviour, the young people felt victimised. They complained about the double standard between what was allowed in the home environment and what was considered a punishable offence at school. Where the young person habitually smoked cigarettes, the effects of withdrawal and the need to smoke during the day increased their anxiety and aggravated any existing conflict between themselves and teachers. The drive to have an illicit cigarette had them reaching out to peers who were similarly involved in rebellious, antisocial behaviour. Repeatedly apprehended, their sense of unfairness and alienation from school grew. Forced to be educated against their will, they were offered what to them were meaningless subjects that had no relevance to their reality. Aggravated by a lack of academic success, they found their resentment towards adults with unwarranted authority over them grew. Feeling oppressed and discriminated against, they believed they were justified in retaliating with increased acts of antisocial behaviour. The school system—under-resourced and ill-equipped to tolerate severe, often aggressive, behaviours that disrupted the learning process and endangered teachers and other students—applied zero-tolerance policies. Finally freed from the imposed obligation to attend school, the ejected students turned to the out-of-school community, joining other disenchanted, antisocial youth. With no legitimate means to satisfy their physical and emotional needs, these unsupervised children and adolescents, many of whom were previously involved in petty criminal activity, became exposed to the more serious criminal elements that exist on the streets.

The majority of the young offenders who shared their stories come from lower socioeconomic neighbourhoods and were of Māori and/or second-generation Pacific Island descent. Both these groups carry the negative consequences of what Ogbu (1991) describes as "involuntary minority ethnic status". He defines involuntary minorities as people who are raised or brought into a society against their will, unlike voluntary immigrants, who willingly enter a country with the option of being able to return to their homeland and origins if they so desire. When these children with multiple, complex problems enter the unfamiliar school system, they are exposed to school-based risk factors which they are often ill equipped to cope with. Starting from the first punitive incident, feelings of confusion, resentment, frustration and anger begin to grow. They believe their culture, interests, abilities and voices have no weight in the school system—they do not belong. Repeated throughout the young offenders' stories were long periods of boredom, humiliation and discrimination. They described excessive use of physical force, being yelled at, targeted, misunderstood and insulted. With each negative school experience the damage accumulated and feelings of victimisation intensified until the student was completely alienated from the school system. Gradually the frequency and severity of the behaviours intensified, finally resulting in a volatile altercation that ensured the student was ejected from school. If the explosive outburst did not result in removal from school, the student escalated the behaviour until it had the desired outcome.

The transition from school attendance to a criminal career develops through this 'tsunami effect'. The first and most crucial layer of the tsunami effect is the foundation of critical risk factors the child brings into the school setting. These include familial risk factors, low socioeconomic status, involuntary minority ethnic status, and association with criminally minded peers and associates. The second wave is the accumulation of negative school experiences that fester and build up resentment, frustration and anger in the vulnerable child. Initially an adverse school experience may appear to have little effect, but for a minority of students each perceived affront is added to their store of negative school experiences until the pressure forces the student to search for a way to exit the compulsory school system.

Identifying potential young offenders at school

The tsunami effect is a visible process within the school setting. Symptoms of the young person's alienation from the school system become apparent through their behaviours. These include persistent expressions of boredom, overt defiance, hostility directed at teachers, stealing, damaging school property, running away from school, substance abuse and truanting. The degree of a student's negative reaction to a teacher's request and to minor disciplinary consequences is an indicator of the scale of their alienation from school, as are the lengths they will go to avoid being apprehended when truanting. The less they care about being caught, the greater the young person's alienation from school.

Because all children are obliged by law to attend school, the school setting provides a unique opportunity to identify the children most at risk of future criminal offending. However, it is imperative that early identification of potential criminal offenders is approached carefully. Teachers are considered to be the most accurate informants for identifying socially maladjusted children, but some teachers, when asked to nominate highly non-compliant or antisocial children, name more pupils than are identified by a uniformly administered checklist procedure (Church, 2003). This has raised concerns about the use of such informal checklists being used in schools to identify children considered to be at risk for violence, predominantly because they result in false positives. Children who are wrongfully identified as being at risk of future criminal offending can become labelled and targeted for inappropriate, preventive discipline, which is likely to increase the young person's anger, hostility and aggressive behaviours (Burns, Dean, &

Jacob-Timm, 2001). Students have a right to be free from uninformed stigmatisation by the school, and schools and teachers have no right to assign a potentially stigmatising label to any child without some sort of fair decision-making procedure that includes parental participation. Teachers and other educational personnel also have an ethical and moral obligation to ensure that early identification of children considered to be at risk of future criminal offending is used in ways that benefit the child rather than the school (Gresham, Lane, & Lambros, 2000).

Screening tools

To assist schools in the identification of children most at risk of future violent, serious and/or chronic offending, a number of screening strategies have been developed. These include informal checklists and profiling, and the Systematic Screening for Behaviour Disorders (Walker & Severson, 1992). However, perhaps the most promising multi-gate screening instrument that assesses young people considered to be at high risk of becoming serious and/or violent juvenile offenders is Augimeri, Koegl, Levene and Webster's (2004) Early Assessment Risk List (EARL). Supervised by the Canadian developers, I further developed the EARL for the diversity of Aotearoa New Zealand's population. Closely resembling the original EARL-20B (for boys) and EARL-21G (for girls), the EARL-NZ covers a wide range of variables related to the child, his or her family and neighbourhood, the child and family's responsiveness to intervention, as well as other social factors such as poverty, negative peer influence and ethnic minority status. Both the EARL-NZB and the EARL-NZG are designed for evaluating children under the age of 12 years who are exhibiting disruptive behavioural problems that could be indicative of future antisocial, aggressive or violent conduct, providing a platform to assist in the creation of effective, culturally sensitive, clinical risk management plans for high-risk children and youth. A similar multi-gate assessment instrument to the EARL, designed specifically for the adolescent, is the Structured Assessment of Violence Risk in Youth (SAVRY) (Borum, Vossequil, & Berglund, 1999). Like the EARL, the SAVRY provides valuable information for intervention planning and monitoring of ongoing progress.

Recommendations for school-based interventions

There is no single easy solution to the problem of youth offending, but there are some school-based interventions that might reduce the potential to offend among some at-risk children and adolescents. The following recommendations, based on my research and practitioner experience, are grounded in the paradigm that young people who later become serious criminal offenders exhibit severe behavioural problems at school.

Start by addressing the transition into school

Working collaboratively with early education centres, iwi and child-welfare agencies, ensure that all children, especially those identified as coming from an 'at-risk' family background, are transitioned sensitively into their new school environment. Create effective transition programmes for students moving from one class to another, or from one school to another. Particular focus should be on vulnerable students transitioning into secondary school.

Provide opportunities for aggrieved young people to feel heard

This could be achieved by creating an independent grievance process in all schools, which can be accessed by students and their parents/caregivers. When they feel they have been treated unfairly, they go to the school office and fill in a grievance form, which is numbered so that one can't be overlooked or discreetly ignored. A committee of three, made up of one school representative and two independent community representatives (with at least one being the same ethnicity and socioeconomic background as the aggrieved student), meet regularly to discuss grievances. All parties (the child, family and school personnel) are informed of the outcome.

Introduce a token economy into school

Pay targeted 'at-risk' youth to be at school (e.g. Year 9 and 10 get a $2 token per day; Years 11–13 get a $3 token per day). Have a well-stocked shop on campus with appropriate products (including lunches) where token dollars can be spent. Spending of tokens can be deferred as a consequence (i.e. they can't spend their points for one day) but cannot be taken away unless the student leaves school. School tokens would be non-transferable to other students, but could be traded in for vouchers to local specialist shops. To reduce stealing in school and the wider community, create contracts with large trading stores (e.g. The Warehouse) for a credit system to be used targeting students who are identified as being at high risk of criminal offending. They earn credits for good behaviour, a good work ethic and school achievement, which can be spent on appropriate items at the contracted trading store.

Make school attendance more desirable

Offer a nutritious breakfast, morning tea and lunch at minimum cost. Create opportunities for students from low socioeconomic neighbourhoods, or a member of their family, to earn rather than pay for the food.

Acknowledge that many students smoke cigarettes

Many students have at least one, probably more, cigarettes before they begin their school day. Recognise that some are suffering from nicotine withdrawal. Address this by offering giving-up-smoking courses and provide alternatives to smoking, such as nicotine patches. If they believe the school is trying to help rather than judge them, students may feel less inclined to truant or slip away to have that illicit cigarette, thus putting them on the school's disciplinary cycle.

Address academic failure

It is my opinion that the majority of Aotearoa New Zealand primary schools have got it right, and that the newly introduced National Certificate of Educational Achievement and unit standards at secondary school level provide opportunities for our at-risk young people to achieve. However, it is Years 5 to 9 that are the most critical times for vulnerable students. In high-risk neighbourhoods, create 'cadet schools' that offer youth-interest options requiring minimum academic prerequisites and few compulsory subjects (e.g. sports, culture and languages, music, drama, photography, dance, business enterprise, and agriculture/horticulture). Allow young people and their families to choose which school they will attend, and facilitate their choice by providing transportation. Reduce disciplinary hazards by replacing school uniforms with a dress standard. Allow blazers and other prestigious items of clothing to be earned through achievement. Reduce the focus on literacy and numeracy by presenting it in a more palatable way for low-achieving students, centring the learning around the theme rather than the subject (e.g. teach numeracy in darts; literacy in research on sports heroes, vehicles, music idols, or other high-interest topics).

Make the safety of other students a priority

Widely publicise that physical aggression towards others, students and school personnel is physical assault and is unacceptable. Make it mandatory for schools to report severe incidents of physical assault to the community's Police Youth Aid.

Address toxic student–teacher relationships

Some teachers are unable to gain their students' respect or compliance and so they resort to behaviour that students interpret as bullying. Teacher bullying is an issue that needs to be dealt with through compulsory professional development on how to get alongside an alienated student and how to manage one's own reactive response to unacceptable behaviour. Consider creating a system where individuals have some choice in the selection of their teachers. Girls identified as being most at risk of criminal offending should be strategically placed with nurturing and caring female teachers. Where personality conflict between a teacher and student is apparent, or the at-risk student believes there is conflict, provide non-punitive mediation between the two in a situation where the power is perceived to be equal. Where there is an obsessional dislike for one particular teacher, a process should be put in place whereby the student is discreetly moved out of his or her class.

Introduce a cultural advocacy role into the educational system

Ideally, the person responsible for a student's school discipline will be from the same culture as the student. However, this is clearly not practical in a multicultural society. While most schools have student advocates such as a guidance counsellor, social worker and/or student leaders, the majority of children and adolescents on the pathway to offending are either not represented culturally or socioeconomically by student advocates, or do not trust the people the school nominates.

Do not punish by sending students home
Have a purpose-built venue where students can be sent to calm down and reflect. Have a protected television monitor tuned into their classroom so that they can observe the lesson and class activity. As soon as they are ready (minutes, not allocated hours as a punishment), return them to their classroom. Put in consequences for the behaviour that does not disrupt the child's learning.

Reduce school policy abuse
Create a procedure where, before any student can be excluded, expelled or indefinitely suspended, s/he must first be referred to a specialised group of practitioners for a critical risk assessment. This should be followed by a family and multi-agency meeting so that an evidence-based support plan can be put in place.

Follow up unexplained leavers
Like the 'hidden curriculum', there is a 'hidden exclusion' process where disagreeable students are unofficially pushed out of school, supposedly in his or her best interests but predominantly because it benefits the school that is rejecting the child. Ministry of Education representatives could follow up with phone interviews to parents/caregivers of under-aged students who 'left school of their own accord' during the school year to ascertain their reason for leaving. This is especially important for those students from an isolated community who leave school when there is no other school in the area to take them. For their education to continue, they are forced to move away from the protection of their immediate family and community.

Address ineffective and harmful punitive systems
Young people perceive systems, like detention, as meaningless, mindless and boring. Schools might argue that detentions should be boring and undesirable because this will discourage the students from repeating undesirable behaviours, but the young offenders say it doesn't work. Rather than being deprived of their friends' company, many of their friends are in detention with them. Confined together in the detention room away from pro-social peers, they became empowered against the one teacher supervising them, reinforcing their belief that they are the 'cool bad guys'. Detention contributes to the alienation of young people

in schools. As the number of detentions accumulates, students fight back by refusing to attend. This show of non-compliance results in further punitive action from the school; if a student misses one detention, the consequence is another detention and then another one, until the student is no longer able to comply and the school has no other option than to stand down or exclude.

Instead of this 'double-up' system, keep the original detention and offer an alternative consequence. Never punish by insisting on writing output, as this is not an equitable process and is particularly traumatising for students who have difficulty reading and/or writing. Think laterally; for example, invite the parents into the school to accompany the student on detention. Alternative suggestions for school discipline could include special weekend or holiday camps provided by the community agencies where the young people can work off their detentions—the camps could incorporate a variety of programmes, including physical challenges, anger management, marae-based/cultural interventions, and sessions with successful, culturally appropriate role-models. Literacy and numeracy extension using computer learning could also be offered. Never take away the school-based activity the student most enjoys and/or succeeds in, as this may be the only attachment the individual has with the school.

Start each year and new term with a clean slate
Create a policy where penalties cannot be carried over.

Support alienated students
Offer separate taster apprenticeships, cadetships and internships to at-risk youth who are entering secondary school and who are deemed to be alienated from school. The training would be paid at a very minimal rate, lead to hours towards a trade, and be dependent on the young person attending and passing block courses in a nominated secondary school. The block courses should be relevant to the training and to the students' life experiences, and would include practical maths, applied English (incorporating reading and writing), and their legal rights and responsibilities. Successful students could be encouraged to achieve credits towards unit standards and the National Certificate of Educational Achievement.

Persistent reoffenders

Schools can never be a case of 'one size fits all' because children come into the school setting with differing backgrounds, abilities, attitudes and life experiences. Because of this, there will always be some young people who cannot be helped through school and community interventions. They are not interested in learning, have given school up as being too hard, and only attend to be with their friends or because it is somewhere to go. As negative role models for susceptible young people they provide a 'contagion effect', where their behaviours are copied and contaminate their peers. A small number of students, especially those who exhibit the most challenging and non-conforming behaviours, are unable to behave appropriately: they are not emotionally, physically, cognitively or psychologically equipped to fully participate in the mainstream classroom.

Because of these factors, a full inclusion education policy cannot work for them because it is not equitable and inevitably leads to alienation and exclusion. Full inclusion not only sets antisocial children up to fail, but also jeopardises the learning of other children who have no other option but to co-exist with their behaviours in the classroom. Their severe behaviours provide a contagion effect for those who are bordering on criminal activity, while adding stress and burning out teachers who are trying to make a difference. Fundamental to the success of a blanket inclusion model is the motivation of the student to be in a mainstream classroom. Children on the pathway to offending do not want to be in any classroom, nor do they want to follow the school rules—but they do want to learn. They especially want to learn about ways to make money. It is this desire for money that is the key to intervening in the trajectory to youth offending.

Because schools provide a unique window of opportunity to observe all children together in a compulsory setting, they have a social and moral responsibility to identify and report to the appropriate agencies children at risk of harm, including those who present as being on a pathway towards criminal offending. However, once the most at-risk children have been identified within the school setting, it is the responsibility of appropriate social agencies to provide the resources, including the professional expertise, to intervene or intercept in the pathway to youth offending. While school may be the ideal venue for interventions to be implemented, it is the community who must take responsibility for the welfare of its youth.

> "Better to build schoolrooms for the boy,
> Than cells and gibbets for the man."
> (Eliza Cook, "A Song for the Ragged Schools")

References

Augimeri, L., Koegl, C. J., Levene, K. S., & Webster, C. D. (2004). *Early Assessment Risk Lists for Boys and Girls: EARL-20B and EARL-21G.* Toronto, ON: Earlscourt Child and Family Centre.

Becroft, A. (2004, 17 May). *Never Too Early, Never Too Late.* Paper presented at the New Zealand Youth Justice Conference, Wellington.

Borum, R., Vossequil, B., & Berglund, J. (1999). Threat assessment: Defining an approach for evaluating risk of targeted violence. *Behavioral Sciences and the Law, 17,* 323–327.

Burns, M. K., Dean, V. J., & Jacob-Timm, S. (2001). Assessment of violence potential among school children: Beyond profiling. *Psychology in the Schools, 38*(3), 239–246.

Church, J. (2003). *The definition, diagnosis and treatment of children and youth with severe behaviour difficulties: A review of research.* Wellington: Ministry of Education.

Cohen, L. E. & Felson, M. (1979). Social change and crime rate trends: A routine activity approach. *American Sociological Review, 44,* 588–608.

Cunningham, J. (2003). A 'cool pose': Cultural perspectives on conflict management. *Reclaiming Children and Youth, 12*(2), 88–92.

Edwards, C. H. (2001). Student violence and the moral dimensions of education. *Psychology in the Schools, 38*(3), 249–257.

Flannery Jr., R. B. (2000). *Preventing youth violence.* New York, NY: Continuum.

Gardner, F., Lane, E., & Hutchings, J. (2004). Chapter 3: Three to eight years. In C. Sutton, D. Utting, & D. Farrington (Eds.), *Support from the start* (pp. 43–56). London, UK: Department for Education and Skills.

Gottfredson, D. C. (2001). *Schools and delinquency.* New York, NY: Cambridge University Press.

Gresham, F. M., Lane, K. L., & Lambros, K. M. (2000). Comorbidity of conduct problems and ADHD: Identification of "fledgling psychopaths". *Journal of Emotional and Behavioural Disorders, 8*(2), 83–93.

Halkias, D. F., Fakinos, I., Hyman, I., Cohen, D., Akrivos, D., & Mahon, M. (2003, 21 May). *Victimization of children in Greek schools: Stress and trauma symptoms related to school bullying.* Paper presented at the 9th Panhellenic Conference in Psychological Research, Rhodes, Greece.

Kellam, S., Ling, X., Merisca, R., Brown, C., & Ialongo, N. (1998). The effect of the level of aggression in the first grade classroom on the course and malleability of aggressive behavior into middle school. *Development and Psychopathology, 10*, 165–185.

Kennedy, J. H., & Kennedy, C. F. (2004). Attachment theory: Implications for school psychology. *Psychology in the Schools, 41*(2), 247–259.

Leone, P., Christle, C., Nelson, M., Skiba, R., Frey, A., & Jolivette, K. (2003). *School failure, race, and disability: Promoting positive outcomes, decreasing vulnerability for involvement with the juvenile delinquency system*. National Center on Education, Disability, and Juvenile Justice, University of Maryland, MD.

MacFarlane, A. (2004). *Getting them early*. Hamilton: University of Waikato.

McEvoy, A., & Welker, R. (2001). Antisocial behavior, academic failure, and school climate: A critical review. In H. M. Walker & M. H. Epstein (Eds.), *Making schools safer and violence free: Critical issues, solutions, and recommended practices* (pp. 28–38). Austin, TX: PRO-ED Inc.

Morrison, G. M., & Skiba, R. (2001). Predicting violence from school misbehaviour: Promises and perils. *Psychology in the Schools, 38*(2), 173–182.

Ogbu, J. U. (1991). *Minority status and schooling*. New York, NY: Garland Publishing Co.

Pepler, D. J., & Craig, W. M. (2005). Aggressive girls on troubled trajectories: A developmental perspective. In D. Pepler, K. Madsen, C. Webster, & K. Levene (Eds.), *The development and treatment of girlhood aggression* (pp. 3–28). Hillsdale, NJ: Lawrence Erlbaum Associates.

Piekarska, A. (2000). School stress, teachers' abusive behaviours, and children's coping strategies. *Child Abuse and Neglect, 24*(11), 1443–1449.

Puketapu-Andrews, G. (1997). Korero awhina: Counselling: Part II. In P. Te Whaiti, M. McCarthy, & A. Durie (Eds.), *Mai i rangiatea: Maori wellbeing and development* (pp. 60–74). Auckland: Auckland University Press.

Reinke, W. M., & K. C. Herman. (2002). Creating school environments that deter antisocial behaviors in youth. *Psychology in the Schools, 39*(5), 549–559.

Rutter, M., Maughan, B., Mortimore, P., Ouston, J., Smith, A. (1979). *Fifteen thousand hours: Secondary schools and their effects on children*. Cambridge, MA: Harvard University Press.

Sprott, J., Jenkins, J., & Doob, A. (2000) Human resources development Canada. In *Early offending: Understanding the risk and protective factors of delinquency*. Ottawa, ON: HRDC Publications Centre.

Sutherland, A. (2006). *From classroom to prison cell: Young offenders' perception of their school experience*. Unpublished doctoral thesis, Victoria University of Wellington.

Sutherland, A. (2007). *Classroom to prison cell*. Wanganui, NZ: Stead & Daughters.

Walker, H. M., & Severson, H. H. (1992). *Systematic screening for behaviour disorders*. Oregon. Silvereye Educational Publications.

Wasserman, G. A., & Miller, L. S. (1998). The prevention of serious and violent juvenile offending. In R. Loeber & D. Farrington (Eds.), *Serious and violent juvenile offenders: Risk factors and successful interventions* (pp. 197–247). London, UK: Sage Publications.

Chapter 7 Writing the wrong: Using restorative practices to address student behaviour

Michelle Kehoe, Sheryl Hemphill and David Broderick

Key points

- Students' perspectives are vital to understanding their opinions on matters that affect them.
- According to students, restorative practices increased their reflective thinking and pro-social behaviour.
- Students perceived that communication throughout the school community was more effective because of restorative practices.
- Sustaining restorative practices in schools requires a whole-school approach.

Introduction

This chapter discusses the use of restorative practices (RP) as an effective means to address student misbehaviour. It draws on the findings of a Victorian research study that examined teachers and students' perspectives on the use of RP. The findings suggested that RP increases effective communication in the school and increases students' pro-social skills.

This chapter further presents the need for teachers, school leadership and practitioners to acknowledge and promote the value of ongoing training and professional development. Despite positive findings in this study, the chapter concludes that we need to continue to challenge current thinking and practices to create sustainable change.

School-based RP

School-based RP are holistic methods used to build healthy relationships in the school environment. The RP approach seeks to address student behaviour as it occurs, as well as building pro-social skills in students (Blood & Thorsborne, 2005; McCluskey, Lloyd, Kane, et al., 2008). The RP approach has an underlying philosophy that suggests that when a wrongdoing has occurred, the relationship between those parties involved is damaged. School-based RP developed from restorative justice. Restorative justice is a philosophy and collection of practices used at different stages of the justice system, such as meetings with victims, not just as an alternative to retributive or punitive actions but something done in tandem with traditional processes (Daly, 2002; McCluskey, Lloyd, Kane, et al., 2008). The history and origins of restorative justice practices has been widely discussed and can be reviewed in various academic papers and books (Daly, 2002; Daly & Immarigeon, 1998; Morrison & Ahmed, 2006; Wachtel, 2012). The aim of RP emphasises a relational approach that seeks to repair the damage caused to the relationship by supporting both the victim and the perpetrator to allow all those involved to heal and move forward (Morrison, Blood, & Thorsborne, 2005; Zehr & Mika, 1998). In schools, RP require a student to reflect on their behaviour and acknowledge any wrongdoing, and offer them the opportunity to agree on an outcome (Morrison et al., 2005). In addition, the RP approach promotes personal accountability and allows the students an opportunity to have a voice in issues that affect them (Shaw, 2007).

The current study

The current research, on which this chapter is based, sought to explore the use and perceived impact of RP from the perspectives of students and teachers. Six schools, in Melbourne, Victoria, participated in the research study during October and November 2012. There were three primary and three secondary schools, including state, Catholic and independent schools. The participants were teachers (one-on-one interviews) and Year 6 and Year 9 students (focus groups). The main purpose of the research was to establish the current use of RP in schools and the perceived impact of using the technique on the school environment, teachers' attitudes and student behaviour. Both teachers and students involved in the research project reported the use of many practices associated with RP, such as restorative circles, affective questions, written reflections, a consistent school policy, and conferencing to manage incidents as they occurred. The various ways of using RP can be considered as being on a continuum (see Figure 7.1).

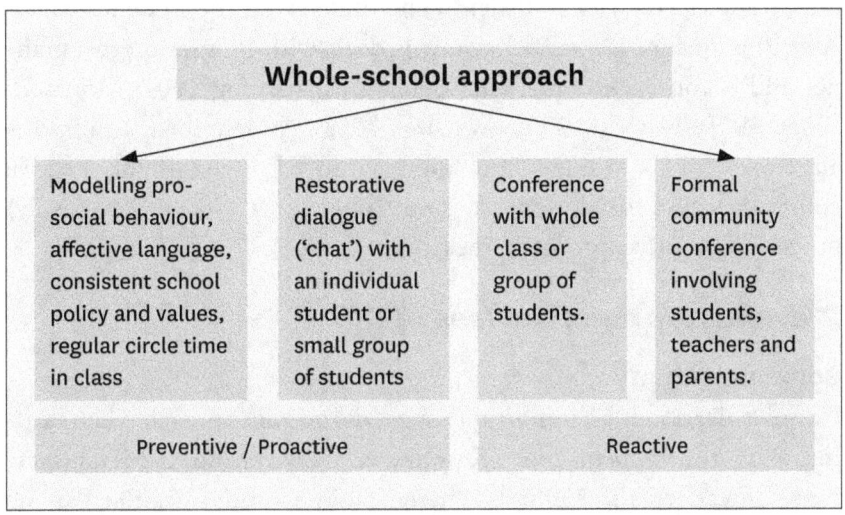

Figure 7.1: The RP Continuum

Source: adapted from Armstrong, 2007; Morrison, Blood, & Thorsborne, 2005; and Wachtel , 2012.

The continuum shows both preventive/proactive and reactive approaches to managing student behaviour. In schools that use the various approaches outlined, the approach is described as a "whole-school" approach to RP (Morrison, Blood, & Thorsborne, 2005). The whole-school RP approach engages students in formal and informal ways to promote pro-social skills and embraces RP as a philosophy throughout the school environment. The main purpose of the whole-school approach is to prevent future misbehaviour and potential exclusion from the school community.

The preventive/proactive approach to RP (as shown in Figure 7.1) entails the direct teaching of prosocial skills, modelling those skills to students, the use of affective language, and regular communication, in particular through the use of regular classroom circle time to enhance students' social skills. For the school administration it involves ensuring consistent school policy and procedure that reflect the RP philosophy and values (Armstrong 2007; Morrison, Blood, & Thorsborne, 2005; Wachtel , 2012).

The reactive approach involves addressing issues as they occur, whether this involves an individual student, a small group of students or a whole class. Similar to the proactive/preventive approach, when reacting to a situation the use of communication and language is an important aspect, used to listen to and understand the student's issues. Any consequence for misbehaviour is dealt with in a restorative manner and is consistent with school policy (Armstrong 2007; Morrison, Blood, & Thorsborne, 2005; Wachtel, 2012). As described, an important feature of the whole-school approach to RP is the use of effective communication to address issues. not only as they occur (reactively) but as a preventive, proactive measure.

Preventive/proactive uses of RP

Communication

Communication is an important aspect of the RP approach when dealing with student behaviour (Kaveney & Drewery, 2011; McCluskey, Lloyd, Stead et al., 2008; Wachtel, 2012). Communication can be used in a reactive manner, such as the use of a verbal conversation or a written letter by the student to reflect on their behaviour; or in a proactive manner, such as through demonstrating or modelling appropriate behaviour or language (Blood & Thorsborne, 2005). Schools in the current research study emphasised the importance of communication to establish expectations, engage students, and build positive relationships. One form of communication in achieving these expectations was verbal communication.

Verbal communication and restorative dialogue in an RP school are achieved through the use of affective language. Affective language involves the teacher and student addressing each other with statements such as, "When you disrupt the classroom I feel disappointed"

(Wachtel, 2012). The consistent use of such language is designed to empower the individual student into reflecting on their behaviour or actions and the impact they have on other students and staff. Similarly, teachers use affective questions when reacting to situations. Questions include (Wachtel, 2012):

- Can you explain what happened?
- How did it happen?
- How did you act in this situation?
- Who do you think has been affected by this?
- How were they affected?
- How were you affected?
- What needs to happen to make things right?
- If the same situation happens again, what could you do differently?

Teachers in the current study reported that they used restorative dialogue to build clear expectations for students in their classrooms and to explain the consequences of not adhering to those expectations. As one female primary school teacher said:

> to have our circle and to calm down and say, okay well here, this is the group you're with now and this is the expectations and blah blah blah, was good for them to have that at the beginning of the day so we could set the tone for the day.

The teacher went on to say, "They know the rules, they know what's going to happen".

Circle time

Another key component of RP is the use of 'circles' or 'circle time' and formal conferences. These can take either a reactive or a proactive approach. Circle time can involve a small group of students or a whole class of students. When used in a reactive manner, the purpose of circle time is to bring students together with their teacher in a circle to discuss issues, conflicts or problems, or as a means to communicate in a supportive environment (Kaveney & Drewery, 2011). When used in a proactive way, this method allows the teacher to establish expectations for the classroom and offers students the opportunity to speak and listen in turn, thereby increasing pro-social skills (Wachtel, 2012). At the commencement of the school year, individual classroom teachers use a proactive approach by establishing acceptable behaviour with their students. Teachers use this as a way to encourage acceptable behaviour and co-operation. One primary school girl explained: "We have like school norms and then as classes we make—every year at the start of the year we make a list of our classroom norms, of what is important to our class". She continued, "I think it's good because it suits the people that are there, like it's not just a general thing". Another benefit of circle time was that it offers students and their teacher the opportunity to express their thoughts and ideas from their own perspective and in their own words.

Circle time and restorative circles were a regular key aspect used by the schools in the current research. Both students and teachers identified several benefits of this approach. Students felt that when teachers used proactive measures such as regular circle time, it built healthy relationships with their peers and allowed issues to be dealt with in a respectful, non-judgemental way.

> Yeah, and we'll all go around [in a circle] and talk and then sometimes it was like your feelings and then you go around and say what you're feeling and ... nothing can leave the circle, no one can judge. (Female primary student)

In addition, students identified the importance of circle time to promote self-reflection and empathy for others: "You need to just remember—you need to be considerate of everyone ... you need to be aware everyone has different feelings" (Female secondary student).

Teachers in the current study also identified similar benefits, such as taking turns, listening, sharing, and building empathy, trust and harmony within the safety of the classroom environment. As one female primary school teacher explained:

> By the teachers doing regular circle times, I believe it's going to give the children an opportunity to have a voice in their classroom with their teacher listening to them, building trust as well with their teachers. (Female primary teacher)

When restorative circles were used to address issues as they occurred, teachers felt that, on occasions, the students found this confronting. One female secondary teacher described her experience with a student:

> I remember having a conversation with her and it was one of many that we'd had—many restorative conversations that we'd had ... I'd pulled her out of the classroom and I started to ask the questions and she just goes, 'Oh, can you please just give me a detention and stop asking me these questions?' She was just like, 'Oh, you're draining my life away!' It was hard work, because she had [to] stop and think about what she was doing and she just sort of thought she'd actually rather just be on detention.

This type of scenario was used by teachers in the current study to address student behaviour by offering the student the opportunity to reflect on behaviour and allowing the student the opportunity to consider how he/she could do things differently. Addressing behaviour using verbal communication was one aspect identified by schools in the current research. Another aspect was through the use of written communication.

Teachers using affective language to 'write the wrong'

All of the schools in the research study used a consistent and structured method to deal with issues as they occurred. The purpose of this was to build student understanding of what behaviour was expected of them and give teachers confidence in the approach they were using. The methods used were consistent with the RP philosophy and approach and involved using restorative dialogue to address issues. Teachers, particularly in the initial stages of implementation, used "prompting cards" to remind them of the affective questions (described previously). The cards were attached to a lanyard and worn around the teacher's neck. Many teachers saw this as beneficial: "We have all these lanyards also on our duty bags outside. so it's a gentle reminder all the time".

The use of this process had a two-fold benefit, since not only were the teachers using the same language to address the issues as they occurred, but the students also became familiar with the expectations and the need to consider and reflect upon the incident or behaviour at the time of the incident: "I think all teachers should learn restoratives and ... they should have a book, like Mrs 'P' does at the office where she writes everything down" (Female primary student).

When dealing with specific incidents, teachers described how they wrote down the conversation: "I always write it down, they see me writing it down, I read it and get verbal recognition that that's okay" (Female secondary teacher). Students reported that when their teacher took time to listen to their side of the story and write this down, it gave them confidence that their issues were being understood and dealt with in a positive way:

> I could actually trust and tell them and that is Mrs B because I had to talk to her sometimes and she would understand what I was saying.
> (Male primary student)

> I just spoke to Miss T and it just felt like it was just me and her. I could say whatever I wanted to because I knew that she would help.
> (Female primary student)

The schools in the current study identified the importance of listening and using affective language in various situations, both reactively and proactively. As mentioned, the proactive approach provided students with the skills and language to consider their actions and their impact upon others. When used in a reactive manner, affective questions are used in a dialogue to remind students of the restorative philosophy and values.

Students writing the wrong

Another method schools in the current study used was written communication, known as 'reflections', to remind students of the restorative philosophy and values. As one male secondary student explained, "We had to write out what had happened and what we should have done … A reflection, behaviour reflection." Many of the schools who participated in the research study used written reflections to promote pro-social skills. A reflection was a written version of the affective questions (described previously), which encouraged students to think about their actions and the ways in which they could change their behaviour. Students were required to write down what they could do better and what needs to happen to restore relationships in order for the parties to move forward.

The use of reflection sheets by schools tended to occur following misbehaviour. In secondary school, reflections were used by teachers to gather "both sides of the story" from the students, prior to conducting a restorative conference or "chat". A restorative chat was an informal conversation using the same series of affective questions as described previously. Using the RP approach, students took time to reflect on the issues and write these down so that they could be discussed and then work out an appropriate way to resolve the issues with their teachers.

The students in the current study were able to identify the benefits of writing down their thoughts and reflections. As one male primary school student said, "It's good to make kids reflect on what they did". Both teachers and students did not consider that this was in any way an "easy" option since it challenged thinking:

> They do have to reflect more deeply on their behaviour and the consequences of it. (Female secondary teacher)

> You just do one before or one right after you do it and then the one the next day, and then you get to see how your attitude's changed a bit. Well, that's what I did ... I just realised that I was in the wrong. (Male secondary student)

In primary school the teachers initially had a restorative conversation or chat with students. They would then send the student home to complete a reflection sheet, which is signed by their parents. As one female primary school teacher explained,

> ... we also have behaviour sheets which we give to children, if they need to have that, but it's the same sort of restorative thing, so the questions on them are what you would ask them anyway, but it's just, I think, it's a bit more formal because it's written down and their parents have to sign it.

Teachers in the current study felt that it was an important aspect of the RP approach to keep parents informed about their child regarding social and emotional issues as well as academic achievements.

RP beyond the classroom

Schools in the current study believed that an important aspect of the whole-school approach to RP was engaging parents through written communication about their child and the school community's values. This communication involved the use of notes, emails, letters, newsletters, or students' written reflections that were sent home to parents. As one male secondary student said, "if it happens more than once in a row ... you get a note home".

School staff members in the study who had adopted a whole-school RP approach believed that the most effective way to address student misbehaviour was to involve the broader school community, in particular parents. One male secondary student explained: "Yeah, they can generally call your parents and have a meeting and stuff and work out what you can do to improve". Many teachers felt that involving the parents ensured there was transparency and the students were accountable for their actions.

> I think it's good that kids just can't try to get the easy way out of it … and just not tell anyone else and just cop it from one person, but they have to own up to, and tell their parents that it's happened too, and they've got to show them the facts because their parents have to sign it [the behaviour reflection sheet]. (Female secondary teacher)

In addition to written communication with parents, schools that had a whole-school approach to RP used policies, procedures and guidelines to reflect the restorative philosophy and practice. This maintained a consistent approach across the school community, including students, teachers, school administration, parents and the wider community (Blood & Thorsborne, 2005). The use of a whole-school RP philosophy and approach ensured the whole school community had clear expectations and guidelines to manage behaviour and encourage healthy relationships. One female primary school teacher described how, post-implementation, "We started doing a project to, like, rewrite the school's discipline policy and rein everything right in". The comment made by this teacher highlighted the value of planning and acknowledging the importance of school policies and procedures prior to implementation of RP in order to manage expectations.

Reactive uses of RP

A restorative chat

In addition to the proactive, preventive and planning aspects of RP, reactive approaches were also used to address behaviour and incidents as they occurred. These reactive measures were used in both formal and informal ways. When used in an informal manner, teachers and students in the current study described this as a "restorative chat' or simply a "chat". The idea was for students and teachers to engage in an informal conversation about a particular situation or misbehaviour as it occurred. Many of the teachers identified that the use of a restorative chat meant that students felt "out of their comfort zone". At times, it appeared that students preferred their teachers to adopt a punitive approach as a consequence. The students' comments suggested that they found the punitive approach less confronting rather than working through the restorative questions, reflecting on their behaviour, and working out what they could do differently.

Despite the challenges identified by teachers and students in addressing issues through restorative conversations, one primary school student saw this as positive: "I think it's a good way to resolve them because it just works". Another student felt regular circle time was "kind of fun … you sit there and it makes you happy." Teachers felt as long as they followed the "script" using the affective questions when responding to issues, and wrote down what they saw and heard, then the outcome was "really powerful".

Restorative conferences

A similar method was used for conferences, either informal (with just the students and teachers) or formal (involving parents or members of the broader school community). The use of conferences by schools was usually in response to a wrongdoing or misbehaviour. In a restorative conference, those involved were brought together in a circle, allowing each person to discuss in turn what had happened and how they had been affected. The culmination of the conference occurs when all parties have agreed on a way forward in order to heal the harm created by the wrongdoing (Wachtel, 2012). In the current study no teacher identified an incident occurring which was severe enough to warrant a formal community conference. This was consistent with prior reports that have found that the use of formal community conferencing in schools tends to be used for a small percentage (between 1 and 5 percent) of the population (Morrison et al., 2005). These findings suggest that the schools in the current study were successfully using preventive/proactive RP approaches along with restorative dialogue and/or circle time to reduce or minimise escalation of behaviour.

Challenges to using the RP approach

The current research study found many positive aspects and benefits of the use of RP in schools. However, there were also challenges. The two main challenges teachers described were a lack of time and resistance from other staff. A lack of time to use RP due to an overcrowded curriculum was the greatest concern expressed by teachers. A female primary school teacher explained:

> if you're doing a little bit of restorative and the language then you've lost 30/45 minutes every day and that's a lot when you've only got 25 hours in the week and the Government says you have to do your five hours of maths and your five hours of language and your five … you know, it doesn't add up. (Female primary teacher)

In contrast, other teachers felt that RP was a way of managing relationships and it was important to spend time to build those relationships and pro-social skills. A male secondary teacher advised:

> work on the concept of getting a rapport with students so that you have a working platform to deal with issues … spending time on friendship issues and issues where relationships had broken …. building resilience and taking responsibility. (Male secondary teacher)

One key purpose of RP is to educate students so that they communicate more effectively and develop the skills to reflect on their own behaviour (Blood, 2005). When RP are adopted as a philosophy within the school environment, they offer students the opportunity to change and create a greater sense of community (Blood, 2005). When change occurs within the school environment, teachers no longer consider time is a barrier. One female secondary teacher described how RP is a philosophy the school has adopted:

> Just time and just realising it is an ongoing thing, otherwise it just sort of, yeah, in such a way as another idea, and sort of making it not just a project or a thing but just the way we do things. (Female secondary teacher)

The other major concern expressed was a lack of consistency in how RP was implemented and used. In the current study, the inconsistency was evident within the same school and across different schools due to different approaches adopted by teachers. Teachers identified a struggle between those who embraced the RP approach at a whole-school level and those who were unable to effectively implement RP in some situations. Those teachers who struggled with the use of RP would tend to resort to punitive discipline approaches. A secondary teacher explained:

> When you come across teachers who are resistant to restorative practices, because, you just have a conversation [and] it's all right. They don't understand about sitting there, having eye contact with the person, having that conversation … It is so much easier to sit in a room for an hour and have a detention. (Secondary teacher)

Teachers suggested that, at times, they struggled to find an appropriate way to use restorative practices, especially regarding school uniform breaches. The teachers spoke of how it appeared pointless or meaningless for the student to 'reflect' on their behaviour when it was only a question of wearing the correct uniform. The comments suggested a lack of understanding of the underlying philosophy of RP, in that the focus should be on building effective, respectful relationships and not just as a means of behaviour management. One secondary school teacher explained:

> I don't think we've explored restorative practices in those issues properly as a system, not just a school. Every restorative school would have similar issues like lateness and uniform, and I don't think any of us have really got into depth in how to use restoratives appropriately for those issues.

However, consistent with an RP approach, encouraging students to reflect on why schools may need to have rules requiring that students wear a school uniform may assist students to understand the rationale behind what may seem to them to be trivial rules, and could result in a change in students' behaviour.

Punitive discipline and the restorative school

Some teachers felt it was important to use a restorative conversation prior to taking any disciplinary action. A female primary school teacher explained:

> They're [the detentions] sort of for uniform infringements and— they still exist. They exist within the context of there's always a

conversation first and so on. So we've sort of had to reconcile it—that—you know, element of our practice.

Overall, teachers explained that in the event punitive discipline was necessary, such as a detention or suspension, then it occurred within a restorative context. Teachers used a restorative conference both prior to and/or following the detention or suspension, so that the student was able both to reflect on behaviour and to calm down. Students were offered the opportunity to agree to a "consequence" and then "have a restorative conversation" so they could "think about what they had done". Although teachers acknowledged the use of punitive discipline occurred when "all else fails", they firmly believed that RP was "more confronting than the punitive stuff". All schools mentioned that they used expulsions from school rarely; for example, "I can't think when our last expulsion was".

The use of punitive discipline, even in the restorative school, was still used and some of the schools in the current study suggested that this could, at times, have a place. However, a restorative school ensured the use of any form of punitive discipline was preceded or followed by a restorative conversation. Despite these findings, one interesting comment was made by a secondary teacher, who said, "I got one of the secretaries to bring up all the detention data … the kids that turn up to detention are repeat offenders. So it's not working".

Her solution to this issue was to change the detention to regular restorative circle time. This teacher recognised that the punitive approach was not working and the solution was an RP approach. For schools adopting a whole-school approach to RP it was vital that their use of sanctions such as detentions and suspension reflected a relational approach. One female secondary teacher described such an approach: "Yeah detention on a Thursday night for things such as lateness and uniform again, but they changed it and called it community service."

Although teachers in restorative schools reacted to situations as they occurred, these situations were used as learning opportunities. Such opportunities enabled students to understand, reflect on and learn from their mistakes, giving them the opportunity to address their behaviour and change. Hence, despite the use of either preventive or reactive approaches, the overall aim was a whole-school philosophy for dealing with issues in a consistent manner in order to increase pro-social skills.

Implications for schools adopting RP

Using a whole-school restorative philosophy and practices had obvious benefits for student learning, a key aspect of entry into adult society. The results of this study indicate that students embraced the concept of restorative practices, and although they also found it challenging to reflect on their own behaviour, they recognised that this could have a long-term benefit for them in the future: "like this you can use in your whole life, every life situation, like restorative practices is [a] really helpful thing to use" (Female secondary student).

The comments made by both students and teachers from this study offer a valuable insight into the broad perceived impact of RP; in particular, the ability to reflect on one's own behaviour and consider the long-term benefits of developing pro-social skills. Perhaps as a community we need to support schools by acknowledging that they are educating the next generation of adult citizens, and therefore making time for restorative practices is important to ensure we have responsible, well-adjusted adults in future years. As a result, this may then place pressure on education systems to adjust their own expectations, thereby allowing schools the resources and time they need to adopt the use of restorative practices.

For school leadership teams, despite the initial challenges of addressing difficult behaviour, there was also a need to address and challenge the perceptions, and concerns, of teachers when implementing a whole-school philosophy and approach such as RP. It would appear that despite growing recognition of the value of using social and emotional learning approaches such as RP, there is still work to be done to ensure the education system can support schools adopting such approaches. The current issues identified, such as a lack of time and an overcrowded curriculum, highlighted teacher concerns when adopting the restorative philosophy and practices approach. Yet it seemed that with adequate professional development other teachers can overcome these challenges. In order for schools to successfully implement and sustain such programmes, policy makers need to be aware of the demands placed on teachers. There needs to be support provided to teachers through additional training and professional development days.

Finally, one female primary school teacher summed up the value of using the restorative philosophy and practices approach:

you know, parents drop their children here and six hours later they pick them up. They need to know in that timeframe you're doing the best job and that doesn't just mean educating them, it means making them a well-rounded child.

Conclusion

The use of RP has shown positive results in managing student misbehaviour and reducing punitive disciplinary measure in schools in New Zealand, Scotland and Australia (Drewery, 2007; Kaveney & Drewery, 2011; McCluskey, Lloyd, Stead et al., 2008; Shaw, 2007). This research indicates that the use of RP allowed students to become more aware of their own behaviour and the impact their behaviour had on others. It has further been suggested that this reduces the need for the student to be removed from the classroom since the classroom environment is calmer (Kaveney & Drewery, 2011; McCluskey, Lloyd, Kane et al., 2008). In addition, students tend to feel they are being listened to, which improves the student–teacher relationship, thereby reducing the need for teachers to control and discipline students (McCluskey, Lloyd, Kane et al., 2008). However, the implementation and successful use of restorative practices is still dependent upon the individual schools and local authorities to support the approach.

The findings of the current study described here suggest that the use of RP was not only perceived as an effective means of managing student behaviour, but is also a philosophy and approach that builds healthy relationships and increases pro-social skills in students. However, both students and teachers acknowledged that punitive discipline can, at times, be considered the easier option. Despite this, the current study found the use of punitive discipline did not deter or alter student behaviour. As a result, many of the teachers were questioning and reflecting on this situation. That is, how do they address the challenges they face that can hinder broader change within the school environment? It would seem that school leadership and policy makers seeking to implement RP need to consider their use of punitive measures such as detention and suspension in the broader sense. If they choose to continue using punitive discipline approaches, they need to ask, "How will these approaches integrate into the RP framework within their school?" Schools need to consider how they can adapt their current approach to reflect one that is relational and incorporates the use of restorative practices as a part of this process, in a meaningful and problem-solving way.

There is no doubt the schools using RP in the current study reported a perceived positive impact on student thinking and behaviour. The extent to which RP had an effect on teachers is mixed. Similar to students, teachers acknowledged the positive outcomes that RP had on student thinking, behaviour and relationships. However, the main issues teachers described were competing demands for their time and inconsistency in the application of RP.

The issues raised by the teachers in the current study suggest there is a need for policy makers and governments to re-examine the importance of prevention, building pro-social skills, social and emotional learning, and community values. Without the implementation of a broader holistic approach, such as a whole-school RP approach to manage student behaviour, individual teachers, students, school administrators and parents will continue to face challenges. One female primary school teacher summarised the importance of effective behaviour management as follows:

> I think it's a no brainer ... I watch the news and I think for goodness' sake, what we need here is a restorative process, they [people] need consequences that are meaningful and ... [consequences that] teach somebody and not put them in prison so they'll come out criminals. (Female primary teacher)

References

Armstrong, M. (2007 November). *Building and repairing relationships the restorative way*. Paper presented at the National Coalition against Bullying conference, Melbourne, VIC.

Blood, P. (2005 August). *The Australian context: Restorative practices as a platform for cultural change in schools*. Paper presented at the XIV World Congress of Criminology, Philadelphia, PA.

Blood, P., & Thorsborne, M. (2005 March). *The challenge of culture change: Embedding restorative practice in schools*. Paper presented at the Sixth International Conference on Conferencing, Circles and other Restorative Practices: Building a Global Alliance for Restorative Practices and Family Empowerment, Sydney, NSW.

Daly, K. (2002). Restorative justice: The real story. *Punishment & Society*, *4*(1), 55–79. doi: 10.1177/14624740222228464

Daly, K., & Immarigeon, R. (1998). The past, present, and future of restorative justice: Some critical reflections. *The Contemporary Justice Review*, *1*(1), 21–45.

Drewery, W. (2007). *Restorative practices in schools: Far-reaching implications: Restorative justice and practices in New Zealand: Towards a restorative society.* Wellington: Institute of Policy Studies.

Kaveney, K., & Drewery, W. (2011). Classroom meetings as a restorative practice: A study of teachers' responses to an extended professional development innovation. *International Journal on School Disaffection*, *8*(1), 5–12.

McCluskey, G., Lloyd, G., Kane, J., Riddell, S., Stead, J., & Weedon, E. (2008). Can restorative practices in schools make a difference? *Educational Review*, *60*(4), 405–417.

McCluskey, G., Lloyd, G., Stead, J., Kane, J., Riddell, S., & Weedon, E. (2008). "I was dead restorative today": From restorative justice to restorative approaches in school. *Cambridge Journal of Education*, *38*(2), 199–216. doi: 10.1080/03057640802063262

Morrison, B., & Ahmed, E. (2006). Restorative justice and civil society: Emerging practice, theory, and evidence. *Journal of Social Issues*, *62*(2), 209–215.

Morrison, B., Blood, P., & Thorsborne, M. (2005). Practising restorative justice in school communities: The challenge of culture change. *Public Organisation Review*, *5*(4), 335-357.

Shaw, G. (2007). Restorative practices in Australian schools: Changing relationships, changing culture. *Conflict Resolution Quarterly*, *25*(1), 127–135. doi: 10.1002/crq.198

Wachtel, T. (2012). *Defining restorative*. London. UK. International Institute for Restorative Practices Graduate School.

Zehr, H., & Mika, H. (1998). Fundamental concepts of restorative justice. *Contemporary Justice Review*, *1*, 47–55.

Chapter 8 A stitch in time: Clues to mending the home–school relationship after a crisis event

Patty Towl

Key points

1. Effective communication assists a positive return to school following stand-down.
2. The key features of effective communication in crisis situations like stand-down are defined
3. Schools would benefit from supporting and promoting the active participation of the child's parent.
4. Teachers and parents provide hints and tips for effective communication in crisis situations.

Introduction

This chapter argues the case for developing guidelines to promote inclusive conversations during and following a stand-down event. These guidelines would focus on enhancing the role of the parent in these crisis environments. Stand-down is the Aotearoa New Zealand term for a short-term fixed-period suspension from school (i.e. temporary removal from school). Currently, school exclusion guidelines for schools and boards of trustees (Ministry of Education, 2009) set the parameters within which the legal requirements under sections 13–19 of the Education Act 1989 are met. Recent research (Towl, 2012) suggests that however well the legal requirements are met, standing a student down from school creates a difficulty which may increase the child's risk of further exclusion events, early exit without qualifications, and subsequent and well-documented poor life outcomes for young people (Fergusson, Swain-Campbell, & Horwood, 2002; Hemphill, Toumbourou, Todd, Herrenkohl, McMorris, & Catalano, 2006; Sutherland, 2007; Towl, 2012).

The difficulty with stand-down arises because it sets up the expectation that parents can successfully resolve at home an incident that occurred at school. Wenger's (1998) communities of practice model is useful for understanding why this is a problem, because the stand-down event creates a crisis interface between two communities of practice—the school and the family—and neither protagonist—the principal nor the parent—can operate effectively within the conventions of the other. Although principals do not have a role within the family, parents have a role within the school as a community of practice, albeit a passive one in many respects (Towl, 2012). Research (Towl, 2012) shows that it was active intervention by parents during and following stand-down events that resulted in an enduring return to school. These parents, however, activated their role within the expectations of the school rather than the family.

In Aotearoa New Zealand, as in many countries that employ the market-driven model in education, the number of school exclusion events of all types rose sharply in the 1990s. Although considerable effort has gone into reducing stand-down, suspension and exclusion from Aotearoa New Zealand schools, the number remains stubbornly high: for stand-down at just under 3 percent of the total school population each year. A research study (Towl, 2012) of 10 students stood down from school in one provincial area of Aotearoa New Zealand revealed the barriers to returning to full school membership following an exclusion event. The study showed that while there are particular actions schools and families can take to mend the rift that opens up between the child and school at stand-down, they have to work together within an agreed communication-rich space. The problem for the students who did not settle back into school was that the opportunity was not taken up because, for various reasons, the structure was not in place to enable it to happen.

This chapter constructs the parameters for a working space within the school–home interface at stand-down. The first section presents a view of school membership through Wenger's (1998) modes of belonging to communities of practice. The discussion then proceeds to presenting the barriers to school personnel and parents working together. The final section presents those actions that prove useful for re-engaging a child with school following an exclusion event, with an emphasis on inclusive communication and enhancing the role of the parent. Comments used for illustration in this chapter were all drawn from Towl's (2012) study. Students chose a name to protect their privacy and their parents and teachers are referred to through that name. Principals and senior management teachers were numbered in the order they were interviewed.

School membership: a complex concept

Wenger's (1998) theory of situated learning in communities of practice is a useful way to understand what has to be achieved in a productive relationship between school and family at stand-down. Schools are communities of practice, as are football clubs and families, because, firstly, membership is ongoing and, secondly, each member contributes to an understood single enterprise. In the case of a school, that enterprise is learning to demonstrate the skills necessary for entry to adult society (Laluvein, 2010). The majority of children manage to maintain membership of their school, but at crisis points, such as an exclusion event, for some children their ongoing membership is in question. A successful and enduring return to school after an exclusion event is difficult, because it requires a renegotiation of school membership (Towl, 2012). Wenger's (1998) modes of belonging to a community of practice suggests there are three interrelated elements to membership, as shown in Figure 8.1.

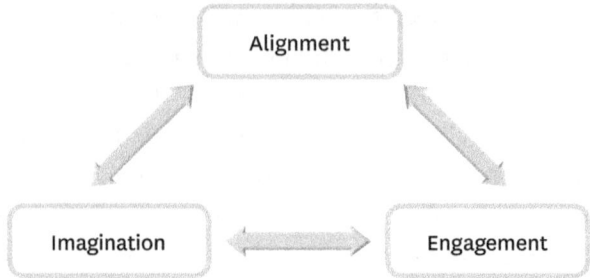

Figure 8.1: Modes of belonging (Wenger, 1998, p.174 abridged)

Unlike most school experience, where membership is covertly expressed and taken for granted, following a stand-down event the child—like any person seeking membership of a football club, for example—must overtly demonstrate their readiness for membership. They must present their closeness of fit with the conventions of the community (alignment), through perceiving and being perceived as part of the past, present and future stories of the community (imagination), and through engaging in the community's everyday business (engagement) (Towl, 2012). The purpose of the suggested working space is to put in place the rules and conditions that would enable the child to overtly express membership.

At stand-down or any exclusion event, two communities of practice—the school and the family—come into contact. Although both parents and children have specific roles within the school as a community of practice, the roles they take within a stand-down event currently tend to be based within the family as a community of practice (Towl, 2012). In Wenger's (1998) terms, parents and students at stand-down are outsiders to the school. The school owns the right to stand down and determines the process to be followed. The principal makes the decision; there is no requirement to consult the child or parent prior to that decision being made (Ministry of Education, 2009). The child has the right to speak, afforded by the Principles of Natural Justice under the Bill of Rights Act 1990; it is the principal who grants that right and the circumstances that enable it to occur. In the expression of rights, therefore, the child's and the parent's roles are essentially passive. Principal 2 (Towl, 2012) expresses clearly the passive as opposed to the active role of the parent and school following the decision to stand-down:

> The stand-down has been used in order to engage with the family and during that time we probably spend as much time with the student and their family in home visits and that sort of thing and how are we going to get this right when they come back. (Principal 2)

Parents in the study recognised their passive role when their child was stood down. Mara's mother, talking about an older son, expressed a feeling of being left out of the loop: "I was trying to get him back to school and they were throwing him out". Bob's mother blamed the school for what had happened: "He didn't have any problems until he went to that school". In the outcomes of the study, however, Mara's mother, like some others, demonstrated that it is possible for parents to have an active voice in the period that follows a stand-down. It appeared to be her active role in negotiating her daughter's school membership that enabled Mara's enduring return to school. Those parents who were successful within the parameters of the study initiated and constructed an opportunity to manage actively the communication space at school and work with school personnel on their terms. This structure is entirely consistent with the communities of practice model, though the taki[1] (challenge) is that school personnel could do more to enable this process to occur.

Wenger (1998) describes the interface between communities of practice, especially at times of crisis, as problematic. Communication within communities of practice may also be difficult, but is easier because the basic rules of engagement already exist (Towl, 2012; Wenger, 1998). The next section describes the main barriers to productive working relationships between parent and school during a stand-down event. Towl's (2012) study showed that these barriers to communication at stand-down reveal the deep-seated and hidden narratives of what we perceive as appropriate behaviour, and that these perceptions are expressed in class, race and social difference. Successful outcomes from the study showed that these narratives, while potent, did not have to complicate an active communication space.

Degrees of separation: What gets in the way of productive relationships?

It was obvious from the study (Towl, 2012) that school personnel and parents were talking from different perspectives, expectations and needs about the purpose and outcomes of a stand-down event. Most school personnel acknowledged the need to keep schools safe and tended to talk in terms of zero tolerance policies, a practice that allocates a specific response to any misdemeanour. Zero tolerance responses are expressly forbidden by the Ministry of Education (2009), though the practice continues (Towl, 2012). Parents, however, while they acknowledged their child's inappropriate behaviour, said that it was a consequence of school-based problems. Their expectation was that the school would resolve the context which they felt caused the behaviour. Within the parameters of the study, outcomes dominated by the language of zero tolerance and school safety overrode the parents' expectations of explanation, resolution and reconciliation. An enduring return to school, however, required the voices of parents to be heard, and the degree to which parents had a voice in their child's return to school was important (Towl, 2012). Furthermore, voice tended to be dependent on social and cultural factors. Middle-income and low-income parents certainly approached communicating with the school in different ways, and Māori parents expressed a cultural reserve that was not commensurate with active voice.

Statistics about who gets stood down from school also provide a clue to these social and cultural barriers to productive communication. The Ministry of Education (2013) reports that low-income, male, Māori and Pasifika children are most at risk of being stood down. Stand-downs are more prevalent in low-decile schools,[2] and both Māori and Pasifika children experience twice the number of stand-down events as their proportional representation in the school population. Towl (2012) suggests, too, that children with special education needs are more at risk of being stood down. Finally, Towl's (2012) research suggests that even in high-decile schools, the children stood down still tend to be low income, Māori, Pasifika and special education needs children. The risk of being stood down, therefore appears to be, to some degree, a question of distance between the child and the middle-class Pākehā[3] ethos of most Aotearoa New Zealand schools.

To improve the potential for an enduring return to school following stand-down, schools should acknowledge and reduce the impact both of zero tolerance policies and of social distance on communication between the school and the family. Zero tolerance policies can get in the way of productive communication, and going down that path makes it more difficult for effective communication, especially between school personnel and socially and culturally diverse families. Research (Black, 1998) suggests that social distance and degree of familiarity affect outcomes in fields of communication that decide issues of right and wrong. The more socially distant and less familiar the participants, the colder and more punitive the outcome (Black, 1998). Liu and Lásló (2007) found that negative attributes and expectations attach to individuals from groups whose identity is derived through the negative definition of the dominant majority. Research (Ogbu & Simons, 1998; Towl, 2012) suggests that this characteristic of relationships is particularly pertinent to those students who are perceived either to have a disability (especially a behavioural disability) or to belong to an involuntary minority (e.g. Māori students).

Barriers to communication

Zero tolerance: the language of blame

Managing behaviour is a normal part of school life. Principal 2 describes the school campus as a place where conflict occurs:

> The nature of kids is they will stuff up. Thirteen or fourteen year old boys are lippy; they will get it wrong, time and place, somehow with someone at least once or twice a week. Fifteen year old girls will be smoking somewhere; fourteen year old girls will be cat scrapping.
> (Principal 2)

A stand-down event happens when an incident occurs in this ongoing field of conflict that must be addressed, but the prevalence of zero tolerance policies in Aotearoa New Zealand schools limits the choices that can be taken when crises happen. The language of zero tolerance dominated the contributions to the study by principals and senior management team members, especially when they were asked about why and how they used stand-down as a response to challenging behaviour. A stand-down was used in the context of its potential to control the behaviour of other students rather than its intention to change and improve behaviour. Using punishment to send a clear message to other students is a recognised function of zero tolerance policy (Henault, 2001). When asked why he stood students down from school, one teacher talked about sending a message:

> My personal philosophy is that the stand down is a message ... and it is one of the few ways we have of actually sending a message to the student and his family or her family but just as importantly and more importantly actually to the other kids in the school. (Senior teacher 4)

Similarly, Principal 1 noted:

> Basically because of their behaviour, or because what they are doing is totally unacceptable in the school, and we want to send that message clearly to the school and the community. (Principal 1)

Most principals and senior teachers recognised the use of stand-down for set behaviours, which is another feature of the language of zero tolerance. Some, however, like Principal 4, recognised that this constitutes pre-judging an incident, and that this is illegal:

> They have a fairly strict process by which if someone swears at a teacher therefore ... and—even though that is probably illegal according to the prejudging thing—I think there is a little bit of that happens. (Principal 4)

Inappropriate behaviour is made to sound more serious by using para-legal terms for everyday behaviour, a practice also common to Ministry of Education policy documents. Swearing, for example, was called 'verbal abuse', and hitting, 'physical abuse or assault'. In the same way, any inappropriate use of a cigarette lighter was described as 'arson', and underage drinking as 'drug and alcohol abuse'. The use of such formal language not only makes a problem out of what actually is everyday school life, but also creates unnecessary distance between the teacher tasked with addressing the breach and the child accused of causing it. It establishes blame and confrontation where resolution and reconciliation may produce the best outcomes for the child (Towl, 2012).

Principal 1 stated the extreme position her board of trustees took in its zero tolerance policy. Her comment shows the confrontational relationship between the board of trustees and the family, the passive role ascribed to the family by the board, and an expression of limited options for the principal:

> Bring them to us and the family can face us and we will tell them that this school expects good behaviour, and if they don't want to do

that and they are harming other children's chances or the chance for teachers to teach, then best go somewhere else. (Principal 1)

School zero tolerance policies were most problematic when stand-downs occurred for children with behavioural special education needs (e.g. autistic spectrum disorder). For the most part the incident occurred as a direct result of the disability. The following comment by Ben's teacher reveals how zero tolerance policies restrict the options available to teachers. She recognises the difficulties inherent in having policies that require specific and advertised outcomes:

> Ben got really agitated and instead of letting it go somebody else came in and he told both of them in a very loud voice in front of the whole class to fuck off. Everybody saw and they all know the behaviour management programme, and they go home and talk to their parents and say that Ben can swear and tell people to F off and all the rest of it, and he doesn't get stood down but … so you have to be consistent, so that's how it happened. (Ben's teacher)

Social difference

Both school personnel and parents recognised that social and cultural differences get in the way of productive communication. School personnel particularly associated both inappropriate behaviour and the seriousness with which they regarded stand-down with low-income children:

> Principal 1: Always depends on the socio-economics status, doesn't it? For some families huge shame and it's a real wow for other families it … oh yeah well … do you expect me to look after them?
>
> Researcher: Is it the high socio-economic people who are ashamed?]
>
> Principal 1: Usually.

Some principals also made a connection between social class and the likelihood of stand-down being an effective tool. Principal 3's comment draws attention to the statistic that most students stood down are not middle class:

> Occasionally, for a nice, white, middle-class individual who has made a particular mistake and error … fine … probably works. For the majority of youngsters who are recidivistic in their approach to most

things that they do and are well entrenched in their behaviour traits it is just another punishment. As for the parents and families too, though parents really want their youngsters to do well at school they probably did the same things when they were at school. (Principal 3)

Most of the families in the study came from low-income homes. Some drew attention to their belief that their children were treated differently because of their social position in the school:

Missy's mother: I think that if it was Missy doing the bullying she would have got stood down just like that, no questions asked, basically because the parents of the three who are doing the bullying are in the elite. One whose father is the chairman of the board and one whose parent was the receptionist, and the girl who is a very high achiever is also the student representative on the school board of trustees. Missy's none of those but I'd like to think she is just as high.

Researcher: Do you think there is social strata within the school?

Missy's mother: Yes.

Cultural difference

Across the study, school-based participants associated Māori children with negative behaviour, and family-based participants noticed this was the case. (Ogbu and Simons [1998] suggested that, by association, the same is also likely for Pasifika children.) The nature of the study was that questions were open-ended and relaxed. As researcher I knew many of the school participants as colleagues. Myers (2005) found that in casual conversation people use race talk even though in more formal situations people say the right thing. The race talk in this research study was a surprising outcome of these conversations: it was embedded in the everyday ways of talking between familiar colleagues. For example, Principal 4 associated Māori words with negative behaviour:

Schools need to use a range of tools to have a good working environment in working with adolescents and their particular needs to feel success. Some students feel success by academic success, others get their mana[4] by being noticed by other students for being naughty and things like that. (Principal 4)

George's teacher is more direct:

He sits with other boys that aren't exactly the best influence on him
... they are not as naughty as him but they are just as unmotivated ...
they are all Māori kids in that group. (George's teacher)

While examples like this may be considered by some to be insignificant, Bishop and Berryman (2006) found that Māori students noticed even subtle negative references and attitudes to them as Māori, and that this affected their sense of belonging to school. George noticed that his being Māori affected the way teachers communicated with him:

Researcher: What do you dislike about school?

George: Teachers' remarks ... like sometimes I feel singled out in
classes because I am Māori ... just feels like they are singling you out.

In the context of talking about managing behaviour, too, another difference between Māori and European participants was the frequent references to shaming. Shame in a European and a Māori context has different meanings and connotations, and the consequences of this difference could result in a significant barrier to communication. Many principals and senior teachers referred to shame as a means to promote positive action in parents when their child was stood down. For Māori parents, however, shame or whakamā translates as shyness or loss of mana. Missy's mother expressed this feeling of loss of mana. When she was asked what she found difficult when working productively with the school she said, she was embarrassed that everyone knew. She said, "Perhaps not in front of everyone". One community youth worker said that some Māori parents, as well as being whakamā, also felt that going into school to resolve difficulties with their children was whakahīhī.[5] The associated cultural constructs of whakamā and whakahīhī suggest that school exclusion practices may not be an effective way for schools to manage unacceptable behaviour in Māori children.

Barriers to communication: summary and suggested actions

While zero tolerance policies are expressly forbidden by Ministry of Education policy, the language and practice of zero tolerance appears to be embedded in Aotearoa New Zealand school culture. Zero tolerance policies appear to trap teachers tasked with resolving incidents into specific actions and impede effective home–school communication. Also, because zero tolerance policies hold the child's behaviour and subsequent punishment as an example to control others rather than as an appropriate punishment to change behaviour, they may have a significantly more unproductive impact on students from identified at-risk school populations. Because stand-down is a school process, trustees and school personnel should be aware of the potential impact of social and cultural difference on fair outcomes. Principals, senior teachers and trustees, therefore, could initiate the following actions.

1. Listen for the use of language and actions associated with zero tolerance practices. Create the opportunity for a conversation about eliminating zero tolerance policies to resolve conflict.
2. Identify if race talk and embedded bias is a problem by listening to the everyday casual talk in your school community. Listen for associations between being low income, Māori, Pasifika—or any other ethnic minority—and negative behaviour.
3. Collect, record and report on demographic and special education needs data for your school's stand-downs, suspensions and exclusions.
4. Consult with local Māori about how to mitigate whakamā and whakahīhī at stand-down, suspension and exclusion.

Creating a communication space at stand-down

The purpose of this final section is to outline the features of a working communication space within the home–school interface at a stand-down event. Communities of practice theory (Wenger, 1998) suggests that communication between communities of practice, especially at crisis points, requires careful and structured management. Research (Towl, 2012) has found that a communication space at stand-down was highly effective at keeping students in school, but that the current situation in Aotearoa New Zealand is haphazard. Furthermore, when there is no effective communication between home and school at stand-down, students may be at greater risk of exiting school early.

Expectations of the role of parents in school (Kennedy & Cox, 2008) suggest that the child's parent should be a central actor in resolving any behaviour event. Research (Bourdieu, 2000) has found that parents with more social capital with the school find this resolution easier. In the present study (Towl, 2012) only four of the ten parents were successful in renegotiating an enduring return to school for their child, yet, of these, three were low-income Māori and Pasifika parents, groups whose children are identified as at risk of school exclusion (Ministry of Education, 2013). These three parents used very similar approaches to returning their child to school, while the other parent, from a middle-income family, used a different approach. It is the similarity in approach of these three parents that directs the first part of this section. Consistent with the communities of practice model and with evidence in the study, schools have particular expectations of the role of parents as members. The actions of those parents whose children had an enduring return to school demonstrated that parents have access to particular forms of power that are useful at times of crisis, and that exercising that power establishes an effective role for them within the school.

The second part of this section documents a series of techniques used by school personnel and family members to improve the communication between home and school. It was obvious in the study that, in each case, the incident that resulted in the stand-down was a very small part of a larger story, and that the best outcomes came when the participants took the opportunity to tell the whole story. A stand-down is a natural and also a legislated opportunity for communication to occur between home and school. For most of the students, their schools had been aware of difficulties for some time before the incident occurred. Principal 7, for example, commented that stand-down "brings the seriousness of the child's behaviour to the family's attention". Across the study, principals and senior teachers used specific techniques to assist communication and reduce the potential gap that arises during a stand-down event. In the same way, parents commented on the modes of communication they found useful, both in working with the school and with their children at times of crisis at school.

Mara's and Missy's mothers and Tui's father: constructing effective home–school communication spaces

Mara, Missy and Tui all returned to school following stand-down, had no further stand-downs and remained in school. Their parents' similar actions enabled a space to be created that highlighted their alignment with the modes of belonging to the school as a community of practice. Their actions confirmed their role within the school rather than within the family. The lessons for school personnel could be that enabling the role of parent within the school at points of crisis may enhance a more enduring return to school. These three parents took similar actions.

1. At the earliest opportunity they took responsibility for initiating contact. This is entirely in keeping with the communities of practice model, because membership has been restricted and their child seeks re-entry. In many ways these parents acted as a negotiator for their child, a process commonly used in traditional societies (Black, 1998). All three revealed their 'alignment' with the modes of belonging by making overt comments that they took responsibility for their child's behaviour.

I don't have any fear of doing the stand-downs time and time again. If that was the case then I am seriously not doing my job and somebody is falling over. So we don't have any real problems with school. (Tui's father)

2. All made contact with a member of staff who acted as an intermediary. While the middle-income parents dealt with the principal directly, low-income parents approached a staff member with whom they had positive associations, mostly through older children. Consistent with the communities of practice model (Wenger, 1998), high-status members—or in this case familiar members of staff—are effective at managing crisis interfaces. Furthermore, in traditional societies it was common for low-status members to approach someone of recognised higher status to petition on their behalf (Black, 1998). Through this action these parents showed their 'imagination' of belonging through associations with the past stories of the school.

3. All brought to the stand-down story the positive attributes of their children. For most of the children in the study the incident of inappropriate behaviour over-rode other evidence of their positive school lives. These 10 children sang, danced, played representative sport, made films and held responsible community positions. What was different in the cases of Mara, Missy and especially Tui, was that their parents, unlike the other parents,

continually emphasised their child's positive 'engagement' with school. These positive attributes infiltrated and, over 6 months, over-rode most of the negative stories. Tui's father talked about his strategy: "The good and the bad I guess with him … quit the bad and enhance the good ones" (Tui's father).

4. All used their power as parents to change their child's school environment. In each case they insisted on a change of class. Each parent recognised not only that conflict is context specific, but that they had the power to insist that their child was placed in an environment where they could realise their plans for school achievement. Tui went back into an academic stream where he could get the qualification he needed to be a builder. Mara went to an extension class where she could head to university, and Missy to a class where her friends were and where she was safe from being bullied. Unlike the six students who exited school early, for these three there were no further stand-downs or suspensions.

Summary

In these four common actions these three parents created a space where their child's membership could be overtly demonstrated. They recognised and confirmed the school's expectations of them as parents at points of crisis. They reminded the school of their child's membership, and they used established strategies to advocate on their, and their child's, behalf their right to membership. Finally, they used the power parents have to provide a safe and successful environment within which their child was able to flourish.

What of those parents who don't have the skills to intervene? Where the home–school relationship has broken down over a series of unresolved crises? Where the family does not have an existing alignment with the positive stories of the school community? Apart from the potential efficacy of the parent personally confirming their role in the community of practice, there is nothing in the actions of these three parents that schools cannot enable in order to promote, enhance and support the role of the parent within the school's expectations at times of crisis. They can ensure positive contact with the family at the earliest opportunity and can identify and promote a suitable, high-status, school-based and neutral intermediary to bargain on the family's behalf. They can emphasise the parent's and the child's positive attributes and promote existing stories of school membership. Finally, they can uncover the whole story of conflict the stand-down incident has identified, discover the nature of the conflict, and either resolve it or remove the child from it to a place where they can achieve.

Promoting and improving the communication space: hints and tips from teachers and parents

Across the study there were a lot of good ideas from principals who had managed to reduce their stand-downs, and from parents who had kept their kids in school. This section summarises a few of these. Most of the crises arose because the child was unable to access either the curriculum or the safety of a group of friends. The most serious and most difficult to resolve were those that combined both factors. It was interesting that all of the children in the study wanted to achieve well academically but needed the support of strong friendship groups to enable this to occur. The hints and tips that follow all promote positive communication as a way to improve membership of the school.

Both Principal 6 and Principal 8 had taken steps to reduce the number of stand-downs from their schools. Principal 6 was the only principal who had constructed an environment in her school that was more likely to produce an inclusive outcome at crisis points. She acknowledged that stand-down is a point where there is an opportunity to sort out the context of conflict. She also showed that making a statement about behaviour can coexist with resolution and reconciliation; for example:

> We are using restorative practices more and more. We made a decision to be quite deliberate about the use of stand-downs and we are trying to turn them into a much bigger deal that is really about making a statement, drawing attention to things and insisting that people come in. (Principal 6)

Principal 6 recognised that certain children are more likely to be stood down, and she set in place a communication environment to enable issues to be addressed before they occur:

> Our earliest thing is that we work quite closely with our biggest contributing schools on not just for learning needs but on behavioural needs. So for this year's Year 9s we knew who the red flags were, had already met with the families, already had behaviour management programmes of some form in place before the kids even started at the school. Instead of saying … fresh start, we are saying no no no no no … history of things not going well at primary, the likelihood is it won't go well at high school (Principal 6)

She also recognised the importance of ease of communication:

> It is good to negotiate with the individual parents how they want to be contacted. A large number, in particular our Māori community, really like emails so we find email a very quick and effective method. We will have quite a few at-risk students with whom there is daily email contact between the parents and the school, both ways. We find that very effective It is asynchronous: you don't have to both be there at the time. (Principal 6)

Finally, Principal 6 followed, explicitly, the Ministry of Education's (2009) rules for stand-down. In doing so she complies with the student's right to the principles of natural justice:

> If we believe that the incident may lead to a stand-down or suspension we halt investigations and contact the parents and ask them if they would like to be present. We believe that the student has a right to have their parents … that is part of their parents' right also to be present.

She also respects the child's right to privacy:

> We always give a print-out of the pastoral notes to parents. They have to have this so we are constantly saying to teachers anything that you write in an email, on paper, on the computer, the students and their parents have the right to see it

Similarly, Principal 8 recognises the importance of the principles of natural justice. His asking the student to plead guilty or not guilty may sound too formal or paralegal, but it gives the child both an opportunity to have their say and to participate in the decision making:

> I never stand the student down until I have heard their side of the story … Generally I try and hear their side of the story, hear the

teacher's side of the story, and then corroborate that with other
students who might have been in the company at the time and
then ask them how they plead, guilty or not guilty, before I decide.
(Principal 8)

By using the following strategy, Principal 8 eases the communication space between home and school, and forces the child to take a role in the stand-down and discuss the consequences:

One thing I do use a lot is I've got the speaker phone on the desk
and I ring the parents and get the kid to tell the parents what they've
done. I use that as a bit of a wee tool and they hate it. Then we talk
about what they did and the consequences and how to make it right
and they go on their merry way again. (Principal 8)

Finally, Principal 8 recognises that incidents occur within a context. He acknowledges that children may not be aware of how others perceive their behaviour and that drawing attention to this may avoid more serious consequences. He creates an early communication space with clearly identified consequences, which includes all of the protagonists:

Last year we had two boys in Year 10 who were allegedly harassing
other students. They pleaded guilty. I pulled out the file and showed
them their student management profile and they sat with amazement
when they read the incidents of harassment they had been involved
in and I said if it happens again you will be stood down and rang
the parents and told them ... we never had another problem all year.
(Principal 8)

Across the study, parents and teachers commented on the use of monitoring and home–school communication tools used on the return to school. These tools mostly took the form of contracts and the 'daily report'. While school personnel found contracts useful, parents and students did not. The main problem was that they were standardised and not negotiated. Parents and students who commented, therefore, did not express ownership of the contract. The daily report, however, gained a big tick from both students and parents. It enabled students to prove their membership in terms of good behaviour. Some teachers whom the students thought disliked them wrote positive comments, and this had the side-effect of improving that relationship. On the other hand it gave parents an opportunity to monitor their child's progress and to be involved. Daily reports used positively were a powerful communication tool. Parents, however, would have liked a say in how long their child remained on daily report. For the most part the schools made an arbitrary decision to finish the report, whereas the parents would have liked it to continue.

Most of the parents found most communication with school, including the letters about the stand-down itself, difficult to follow and keep track of. Because half of the students in the study had some form of special education need, often associated with reading level, it might be reasonable to assume that their parent also struggled to make sense of complex documents. A proportion of the parents, however, said they read well but still found the documents difficult and hard to organise. Despite their enthusiasm for daily reports, parents found them difficult to follow, keep track of and administer. Tui's father not only summarised the frustrations of many but also came up with a novel solution:

> All these ones and twos and signatures of teachers and period ones and twos. I don't know what's going on. I don't know what period's what. I need another table at the bottom to fit that set of numbers to that class and that time so I know where he is finding it hard. So in the end they didn't take it on board so I drafted up my own table.
> (Tui's father)

It would be useful to parents if schools reviewed their documentation for stand-down. The use of reading age and reading ease scales would make the documents easier to follow. Using coloured paper would delineate between different documents. One school in the study provided a clear file for parents to keep the documents in. Finally, the regular use of an intermediary or coach from the school would help guide parents through a complex process, which, potentially and with good communication, might only happen once.

Final comments

Enhancing the existing role of the parent within the school as a community of practice is far easier, more reliable and less confrontational than trying to manage the communication interface between two different communities of practice. To achieve this, school principals and trustees who own the process need to be very clear about what that role is and how to activate it for the benefit of the child. Supporting and enabling an active communication space in exclusion events may not only improve outcomes for children at risk of early exit, but may also prove a useful management tool at other points of crisis.

References

Bishop R., & Berryman, M. (2006). *Culture speaks*. Wellington: Huia.

Black, D. (1998). *The social structure of right and wrong*. San Diego, CA. Academic Press.

Bourdieu, P. (2000). *Distinction: A social critique of the judgment of taste* (R. Nice, Trans.). Cambridge, MA: Harvard University Press.

Fergusson, D., Swain-Campbell, N., & Horwood, L. J. (2002). Outcomes of leaving school without formal educational qualifications. *New Zealand Journal of Educational Studies, 37*(1), 39–55.

Hemphill, S., Toumbourou, J., Todd, I., Herrenkohl, T., McMorris, B., & Catalano, R. (2006). The effect of school suspensions and arrests on subsequent adolescent antisocial behavior. *Journal of Adolescent Health, 39*, 736–744.

Henault, C. (2001). Zero tolerance in schools. *Journal of Law and Education, 30*(3), 547–553.

Kennedy, S., & Cox, S. (2008). *The case of Emily: A focus on students as they transition from primary to secondary schooling*. Wellington: Ministry of Education.

Laluvein, J. (2010). Parents, teachers and the community of practice. *The Qualitative Report, 15*(1), 176–196.

Liu, J. H., & Lásló, J. (2007). A narrative theory of history and identity: Social identity, social representations, society and the individual. In G. Moloney & I. Walker (Eds.), *Social representations and identity: Content, process and power*. New York, NY: Palgrave Macmillan.

Ministry of Education. (2009). *Guidelines for principals and boards of trustees for managing behaviour that may or may not lead to stand-downs, suspensions, exclusions and expulsions: Part 1: Legal options and duties*. Wellington: Author.

Ministry of Education. (2013). *Stand-downs, suspensions and exclusions from school*. Retrieved from http://www.educationcounts.govt.nz

Myers, K. (2005). *Racetalk: Racism hiding in plain sight*. Lanham, MD:

Rowman & Littlefield.

Ogbu, J., & Simons, H. (1998). Voluntary and involuntary minorities: A cultural-ecological theory of school performance with some implications for education. *Anthropology and Education Quarterly, 29*(2), 155–188.

Sutherland, A. (2007). *Classroom to prison cell*. Wanganui: Stead & Daughters.

Towl, P. H. (2012). *"I am bad apparently": The role of stand-down to manage behaviour in communities of practice*. Unpublished doctoral thesis, University of Otago.

Wenger, E. (1998). *Communities of practice learning, meaning and identity*. Cambridge, MA. Cambridge University Press.

Notes

1 Taki: Māori word for challenge.
2 In New Zealand a calculated socioeconomic status (SES) is allocated to each school on the basis of a 1 to 10 or decile scale. A decile of 10 means the school has a high SES.
3 Pākehā: a Māori word that means not Māori but usually refers to European New Zealanders.
4 Mana: Māori word for integrity, prestige, charisma.
5 Whakahīhī: Māori word for boastful.

Chapter 9 The McAuley Champagnat Program: A community response to a local problem

Kevin Quin and Katrina Mohammed

Key points

- Committed leadership is essential to the introduction of an innovative educational programme.
- Recognition and respect are essential to indigenous community participation.
- All programme curricula activities and processes should reflect indigenous contribution.
- Schools have a responsibility to promote the successful participation of all students.

Introduction

This chapter describes a working model for educating indigenous Australian youth in the context of providing for the educationally rejected. Mainstream educational systems often find themselves incapable of accommodating students with seriously challenging behaviours. These students are subject to disciplinary procedures, and are repeatedly suspended or transferred to other schools, where the pattern is repeated. The students, often among the most disadvantaged, frequently abandon the educational system.

We describe problems confronted by mainstream schools and their communities. The recognition of the problem in the large regional city of Shepparton led to a determination to assist disadvantaged students, and we describe the successfully operating programme designed to help these students. Because indigenous Australian students are disproportionately represented within the ranks of the seriously disadvantaged, the programme makes a special effort to work collaboratively and respectfully with indigenous Australian families and organisations to seek their guidance in providing educational assistance.

Committed leadership

In 2004 Peter White, the principal of Notre Dame College, Shepparton, was faced with a dilemma. The principal of a neighbouring secondary school contacted him to enquire whether Notre Dame College would accept enrolment of a troubled and disruptive student. The enquiry was a routine matter—indeed it had become too routine. This was the ninth such request White had received during the year. His middle-school programme at the College was straining to accommodate requests to cater for students who had been expelled, threatened with expulsion or were on a 'second chance' transfer from adjoining schools.

White raised the problem with the executive officer of the Local Learning and Employment Network (LLEN), Jennifer Hippisley. The LLEN was a useful forum for discussing educational issues confronting educational providers in the area. White and Hippisley discussed the dilemma posed by having an inclusive policy encouraging acceptance and support for all students, and the difficulty presented by severely disruptive and challenging students who had the capacity to impair the learning opportunities of others. Further research into the Shepparton community revealed more than 180 students of school age who were no longer enrolled in any school. The problem was clearly systemic and widespread.

White then convened a meeting of local educational providers and other agencies interested in youth affairs, including representatives of the local indigenous Australian community, the Department of Employment, Education and Training, Brayton Youth and Family Services, the Department of Human Services, and the police. The meeting quickly recognised the challenges presented by widespread truancy and prolonged absenteeism, and the limitations of the current responses from conventional educational providers.

This discussion had particular salience for Mark Rumble from Brayton Youth and Family Services. Rumble's organisation provided accommodation for young people, many of whom were clients of the Department of Human Services and had been removed from their homes because of safety concerns. While Brayton could provide welfare support and accommodation, it struggled with the educational needs of its clients. Rumble offered the use of a number of disused buildings on the Brayton site as a potential location for a school programme devoted to the needs of young people who had become disengaged from the mainstream educational system. White accepted the challenge of providing an educational programme. The McAuley-Champagnat Program (MCP) was born. In February 2006, MCP opened with its first students.

This brief summary of the genesis of the programme reveals several of the key components of what was to become a successful educational programme for a unique cohort of students and a relational pathway for indigenous Australian families. The programme originated in:

- inspired and committed leadership
- the identification of genuine need
- determination to provide positive outcomes
- a real responsiveness to community consultation.

The advisory board: recognition and respect

The programme was established and administered by an advisory board. From its inception it was decided that the advisory board would have particular emphasis on participation from the indigenous Australian community as well as wide community representation. A list of the board members and their affiliations are presented in Appendix A, and includes representatives from the following indigenous Australian organisations: Academy of Sport, Health and Education (ASHE);

Victorian Aboriginal Education Incorporated Association; and Rumbalara Aboriginal Football and Netball Club.

Representation from the indigenous Australian community was considered to be important for several reasons.

- The indigenous Australian community is an important component of the Shepparton population, and Shepparton is home to a significant number of Victorian Indigenous Australians. The Australian Bureau of Statistics reported a population of 2,080 from the 2011 census (Australian Bureau of Statistics, n.d.).
- Indigenous Australians have suffered from generations of neglect, and their participation in social networks has been discouraged, both directly and indirectly. It was considered important not to repeat this pattern.
- As a result of their dispossession and generations of disadvantage, Indigenous Australians are among the most impoverished members of the Australian population. The Australian Bureau of Statistics reported that Indigenous Australian families in the municipality of Greater Shepparton have a median household income only 77 percent of that of the wider population. In Greater Shepparton the median weekly household income is $980: for Indigenous Australian families the median weekly household income is $755. (Australian Bureau of Statistics, n.d.)

The advisory board was constituted in a manner designed to ensure that Indigenous Australians were represented in a programme expected to have the capacity to provide educational opportunities for Indigenous Australian youth as well as providing for other students experiencing social disadvantage.

The nature of disadvantage

> The Indigenous Australian education disaster is a subset of a wider problem: a persistent failure to close the achievement gap between disadvantaged students and disadvantaged schools on the one hand and the wider school population on the other. (Pearson, 2011, p. 23)

Pearson's observation provides a pithy summary of the origin of educational disengagement. Educational disengagement is both a consequence and a cause of social disadvantage. The educational participation of many Indigenous Australian students is characterised by high drop-out rates and intermittent attendance. In 2011, 66 percent of Indigenous Australian students completed Year 10 and 22 percent completed Year 12, compared to 84 percent of the wider population completing Year 10, and 51 percent completing Year 12 (Steering Committee for the Review of Government Service Provision, 2011). It has been reported that Indigenous Australian children have lower kindergarten participation, are less likely to attend maternal and child health services, are more likely to be suspended in primary and secondary school, and are more likely to move between schools, than non-Indigenous Australian children (Department of Education and Early Child Development, 2014). Because indigenous Australians are disproportionately represented among the disadvantaged, and because of the specific nature of Indigenous Australian disadvantage and deprivation, Indigenous Australians are disproportionately represented in any programme designed to assist the disadvantaged.

A service to mainstream schools

While conventional schools are committed to providing the best possible educational opportunities for their students, there are inevitably some students for whom the programmes and procedures are unsuitable. Though these schools have laudable intentions, they lack the resources, capacity or flexibility to provide the support and assistance for a minority of students. In particular, they lack a culturally sensitive curriculum and an environment capable of nurturing the Indigenous Australian identity. It is common for programme managers to find that a relatively small number of students require a large amount of time and effort. An organisational churn of detentions, suspensions and disciplinary hearings frequently occurs. Arrangements with neighbouring schools for second-chance transfers often means that the student is treated in much the same way in a different location. As a consequence, the student's behaviour is not improved, punitive methods of dealing with disruption lead to more hostility and resentment, and as the student becomes increasingly disengaged, truancy increases. A more flexible, targeted programme is essential if the situation is to be ameliorated.

This process and its consequences are embodied in the following personal account of one student's experience.

Learning from life

Hi, my name is Wendy*, just an average 15-year-old who messed up her school life.

When I started secondary school in Shepparton my attendance was good, I did my work and was respectable. I went to all my classes every day, I was always on time and was always on top of my work. Never once did I fail a class or disrespect a teacher, or even wag school. I was a good little girl.

But then there was Kate. She bullied me from Grade 5. She had jealousy issues about our friends. Kate and I were best friends for almost two years before the bullying started. Kate would hit me, throw things at me and also say nasty things to me. I was young, about 10 years old, so I thought it was normal. As I got older and started learning about bullies I realised it was wrong.

The day finally came when Kate and I had it all out. We thought that we would just have a fight and get it over it, and we did. The fight broke out at lunch time on the oval. I knew this fight was going to happen so I begged mum to let me stay at home that day but she told me "You're my little princess, you can do this Wendy, stand up for yourself for once". My self-esteem was always low. I never thought positive about myself. I constantly thought I was better off gone and that no-one cared, but I realise now that people need me just as much as I need them. I listened to my mum and stood up for myself. But back to the incident, Kate came running at me out of nowhere and had started hitting me. In self-defence I hit her back and then a couple of seconds into the fight the teacher came running out of nowhere and broke up the fight.

Everything got out of hand and turned into a really big mess. My brother got involved and some really terrible things happened. I got expelled because of that incident. After the fight my brother and I sort of did a runner from the teachers because we thought we needed to hide so we wouldn't get in trouble, but we got caught by teachers anyway.

As my brother and I waited in the principal's office, the police arrived and took us to the police station for questioning. The look on my mother's face shattered my heart when she came to pick us up. I love my mum and there is nothing I ever want to do to hurt her.

I got a new start at another secondary school in Shepparton. My first day was simply the worst. It was like I was made to feel like absolute crap. My life turned to worst and I started losing everything I had ever loved.

I was labelled a 'second-chance-student'. Every day I attended school I would always be reminded that I was a second-chance-student. I had enough so I started being negative about absolutely everything. I always felt like nothing would ever go right and I was trapped in my own little bubble where no one listened to me or even noticed me.

I always felt left out. I felt like an outsider … as if I went there to be left out? It felt that no-one cared about me and no-one seemed to ever notice me at all so I gave up and just left. I couldn't cope anymore and I still can't. It hurts so much being like that.

I wagged pretty much every day. Things weren't the same anymore. I rarely attended school. I was so negative about school and my life. Things were getting serious and I started self-harming and attempting suicide but gladly failed every time.

My school decided it was time for me to move on to another school and so did I. I had my first visit to the McAuley Champagnat Program and I could say it was pretty scary because everyone looked at me weirdly like, "Who is that?"

I was very nervous on my first day and I was a little awkward but then I fitted in quite easily. Being at a school campus that has about 50–60 students is just so much easier because you only have about eight to ten students in a class, which makes it so much easier to work as a team and get work done.

I do more work at MCP than I ever did at my previous school. I attend school every day. I've had the opportunity to have a lifetime experience and go to the snow. I've made new friends. I've become more confident and I have done some voluntary work at Verney Road School.

MCP has given me an opportunity to change my life and become happy and confident again. I get great support from the staff and they really care about the students. They work hard to help us in all areas of our life, not just education.

I have new goals now. I want to transition back to mainstream school and at the moment that's exactly what I'm working on. I have some goals I need to achieve so I can work my way to mainstream school and my teacher and welfare officer are helping me do that. Beyond school I'd like to be a drug and alcohol counsellor.

I never thought my life would turn out like this. In a way I don't regret what's happened over the past two years because it either turned out to be a blessing or a good lesson to learn.

I have a new life ahead of me now. I have a life filled with hope and I am way more positive.

* Please note the names of students have been changed for privacy reasons.

Responsive services

From its inception the MCP had a pastoral care orientation towards the nurture of students. In this orientation it reflects indigenous Australian tribal and family culture. Care of students was not an afterthought, or a part of the programme crammed into an already overcrowded curriculum, but essential to the successful functioning of the programme. Fundamental to the nurturing orientation was the principle that each student had individual needs and personal circumstances that led to the predicament of school disengagement, and the way to increased engagement was to assist with those needs and circumstances. MCP was designed to be welcoming and supportive of students and their families in recognition of the fact that disengagement is a social problem that requires a culturally and socially supportive response.

Staffing reflects this orientation. MCP has a staff of welfare workers and teachers working within each class group (referred to as a 'team'). In addition, the programme employs two part-time psychologists, ensuring students have access to psychological help on most school days. Nurturing students is the role and responsibility of all staff members. Teachers are responsible for delivering an educational programme with an emphasis on literacy, numeracy and vocational preparation; welfare workers monitor attendance, liaise with families and assist in the social integration of students into the programme; psychologists evaluate intellectual ability and social-emotional adjustment, provide individual counselling, and advise teachers and welfare workers. This interdisciplinary approach ensures that the educational programme is delivered within a supportive, proactive welfare network.

Foundational principles

The programme has developed foundational principles based on *acceptance, inclusion* and *persistence:*

acceptance: MCP accepts students without reservation in spite of any previous experiences they may have had

inclusion: MCP includes all students in its curriculum provision

persistence: MCP refuses to abandon any student or to give up in its efforts to assist students to complete their education.

These principles represent the approach of the programme to all the students entrusted to its care. Students disengaged from mainstream schools frequently feel rejected, discarded, demeaned and undervalued; they are often hostile, resentful, suspicious, guarded and defensive. It is essential to reassure students that they are safe, secure, and accepted. Once students realise they are in a safe and supportive environment, their previously hostile and defensive attitudes are disarmed. This is an essential prerequisite to any educational provision.

Positive behaviour principles

While it is recognised that students, welfare workers, teachers, ancillary workers and volunteers all have different roles, MCP recognises that it is essential that all be treated with equal respect. The following document was adopted by the programme and reflects its insistence that every person is entitled to feel valued, accepted and safe.

> # MCP
> ## A SCHOOL OF HOPE
>
> ### WE BELIEVE
>
> - Every person at MCP has an equal right to be treated with respect.
> - Every person at MCP has an equal right to feel safe.
> - Every person at MCP has an equal right to be encouraged and supported in their efforts to improve and to work.
>
> *Every person should be spoken to respectfully and politely. Every person has the right to be addressed by the name they prefer. Every person should be protected from degrading abuse. People should not be criticized for their race, colour, family, gender, age, shape, size, abilities or dress.*
>
> *Every person has the right to feel free from violence and the threat of violence. There is no place at MCP for weapons of any kind.*
>
> *People should be confident that their property will be protected and not be damaged, defaced or stolen. Our personal belongings, the buildings we share, and the environment we live in, should all be cared for and not damaged or defaced.*
>
> *MCP is a place safe from the influence of illegal substances. No person will bring illegal substances to MCP; any person whose behaviour is affected by the use of illegal substances will leave the campus.*
>
> *Every person has the right to work to improve. Every person should cooperate with planned activities and those activities should proceed without interference or distraction.*

This document can be invoked by any person on the campus, whatever their role, to ensure they receive respect and safety. The foundational principles and positive behaviour principles inform all activities and procedures at MCP. The implementation of these principles distinguishes MCP from many conventional settings. While all are essential, MCP makes every effort to ensure that students know they will not be abandoned, and that the mission of the programme is to provide every opportunity for success.

Referral and intake

Secondary schools in the region refer students to MCP and participate in a carefully designed transfer process. The referring school prepares a comprehensive background information document on the student, including school reports, incident reports, suspensions, disciplinary hearings, and information about previous assessments and personal history. A representative from the referring school, the student and the student's parent/carer then visit MCP for an information-gathering orientation to the programme. A tour of the campus follows, and the programme and its objectives are explained. Students and parents visit classes and are shown the facilities. On this visit it is made clear that enrolment will depend entirely on the decision of the student and parent/carer. The family is then given a period of time to consider their decision. They are provided with application forms and told to contact the programme if they decide to proceed with the enrolment. If they decide to proceed, the next step is for them to ring the programme and make an appointment for a formal intake.

At intake, the parent/carer and student submit the required documentation and meet with one of the psychologists. The psychologist conducts an interview and collects a developmental and educational history. Both the parent/carer and the student complete the relevant forms from the Achenbach System of Empirically Based Assessments (Achenbach & Rescoria, 2003). On the basis of the information provided, the psychologist prepares a brief profile of the student for the information of the teacher and the welfare worker of the team to which the student is to be assigned.

The student is then assigned to a team. Teams are groups of 10 to 12 students, a teacher, and a welfare worker. Students are assigned to teams on the basis of team size, gender balance, any previous experience of current students the new enrolment might have, and any other factor considered relevant. The parent and student meet with the teacher and an individual learning plan is developed.

Individual learning plan and accountability

The individual learning plan (ILP) is fundamental to the experience of the student at MCP. On the basis of the documentation provided to the teacher and discussion with the family, social and educational goals are determined and strategies devised to implement them. Parent/carer and student contribution to the ILP is essential. An evaluation date for progress towards the goals is set. The aim of the ILP is to design a programme to suit the needs of the student and family; it is not assumed that the student is at any 'level', and the goals are tailored to individual needs.

The length of time the student will spend in the programme is one of the goals for discussion. For some students a goal will be to return to a mainstream school as soon as possible; for others, work preparation is a priority and they will plan to leave after they have identified a desirable job and have completed the necessary prerequisites. Still others will remain with the programme to complete the Victorian Certificate of Applied Learning (VCAL), an accredited Victorian school certificate emphasizing literacy, numeracy, and industry-specific skills, work-related skills, and personal development skills.

The ILP is subject to regular assessment and revision. At the end of each semester, parents meet with teachers and welfare workers to review the progress of the student against the desired goals. This important information for parents and carers provides the opportunity to decide on or refine goals. If it appears one goal is proving to be too difficult to attain, it can be modified so it can be achieved in stages or over longer time frames. While the ILP is designed to suit the individual student, every ILP has goals for attendance, behaviour, social co-operation, literacy and numeracy. The ILP provides regular accountability processes. Once the intake process and the ILP are completed, the student can begin work with the team.

Daily programme

Because the MCP campus is on the outskirts of Shepparton, most students arrive by bus. Each morning the bus is met by rostered teachers and welfare workers, who walk with the students to the campus buildings. This process of escorting and walking with the students is supportive and protective. It reflects tribal practice, where any group of youngsters is escorted by a responsible adult when on a journey. On arrival the first task is for all students to secure their belongings in a locked room. Students bring little personal property to the programme, but security is assured if all property is safely stored.

The students then proceed to the campus kitchen and dining-room, where they prepare themselves breakfast. A range of cereals, spreads, bread and fruit is provided. Milo is a popular beverage. Students sit at tables, often joined by teachers and welfare workers, and chat about recent events, incidents and matters of personal interest. Breakfast provides an opportunity for a graduated entry to the events of the daily programme and provides essential, healthy nutrition to fuel the day's activities. Conversation can provide welfare workers with important information about the student's preparedness for study. Once again, this communal sharing of food is a reflection of tribal and family practice. Respect for the place of eating and the care of this environment is a shared responsibility.

All teams then proceed to their rooms and the morning is devoted to learning activities designed to maximise literacy and numeracy. Students complete work consistent with the goals established in their ILPs. Visitors to the programme often comment on the calm, quiet and industrious manner in which activities are undertaken.

One team is slightly different to the others. Those students who have been with the programme for longer, or who are older, are assigned to the VCAL team. In this team, students complete a variety of certificate courses. Students might undertake:

- a Certificate I Vocational Preparation Course, including following workplace safety procedures, personal effectiveness and orientation to work
- a Certificate II in Engineering
- a Certificate III in Hospitality (Operations), including basic methods of cookery, organising and preparing food, cleaning and maintaining kitchen premises, and following workplace hygiene procedures
- a Certificate II in Building and Construction, including workplace safety and environmental procedures, carpentry and hand tools, bricklaying, and basic first aid
- a Certificate II in Hairdressing.

A number of students have completed the nationally recognised White Card, gaining the necessary skills and knowledge to operate safely in the construction industry.

In the afternoons students participate in an elective programme. An important feature of the electives is the emphasis on activities reflecting Indigenous Australian culture. Members of the Indigenous Australian community, in some cases relatives of students, provide cultural arts activities such as basket weaving, modelling of native animals, didgeridoo playing, and the recognition and gathering of bush foods. An important aspect of the programme is an emphasis on recognition of the importance of indigenous culture. Students have participated in expeditions to the Cummeragunja Reserve near Barmah with local Indigenous Australian men as escorts, visited the Rumbalara Aboriginal Cooperative and engaged in their health awareness programme, and participated in the annual Sorry Day to commemorate the National Apology.

These cultural activities assist in the transmission of traditional lore. While creating art works and discussing language, playing the didgeridoo, learning how to manage a budget in the My Moola classes and being escorted on a local river walk, students are also made aware of how such activities form part of traditional culture. Senior members of the Indigenous Australian community working with the students are able to preserve and create traditional culture, and transmit respect for and awareness of traditional values.

Of course the programme observes ceremonies such as Anzac Day, Remembrance Day or Harmony Day. On such occasions Indigenous Australian students are responsible for a 'Welcome to Country' and are aware of welcoming visitors to their country and providing traditional hospitality while expressing respect for their elders and traditions. Every day the indigenous Australian flag flies beside the Australian flag, and on ceremonial days this display is vitally significant. In addition, within the elective programme students choose from a range of activities such as woodwork, sewing, art/craft, life-skills, gym, or a variety of sports. The programme also operates a small farm in which the students can participate in animal handling and plant propagation.

MCP provides a meaningful and challenging educational programme. This is essential to the self-esteem of the students, who are aware of the importance of certification to their future careers. The programme is decidedly not a drop-in centre. It provides a purposeful way for students to plan for a productive future as functioning members of Australian society. Perhaps the best way to understand the integration of Indigenous Australian values and traditions into the school programme is through the eyes of the students themselves. The following is one student's affirmation of her experience of Sorry Day.

Sorry Day

I am ecstatic that the Australian government and the Australian citizens have finally presented an apology to all indigenous Australians, now known as 'Sorry Day'. The government brings all Australians together to recognise 'Reconciliation'. The 'Stolen Generation' were taken from their families, forced into slavery, taught white ways, and abused. After all these years the Australian government 'Finally' apologised, and 'reconciliation' has brought Australians together.

On the13th February, 2008, Mr Kevin Rudd (Prime Minister of Australia) presented an apology to all Australians. He wanted the indigenous people to know he, on behalf of all Australians past and present, were sorry for the removal of the indigenous children during the 1950-1960s. 'The Stolen Generation' were welcomed 'home'. Concerts, barbeques, reconciliation walks; flag raising events were held, morning teas and lunches and motivational speakers visited communities to celebrate this important event.

100,000 is a big number isn't it? Well, that's how many indigenous children were taken from their families. This was to teach them 'white ways' and to eventually breed out all of the indigenous people. These children were eventually known as 'the Stolen Generation'. What they went through has ruined and scarred them for life. Most of the indigenous children suffered from depression because of the removal, other children might have been sexually abused, mistreated and removed from their family and their home.

'Reconciliation' what does it really mean? It's about Aboriginal, Torres Strait Islanders and non-Indigenous Australians coming together. Each year between 27th of May - 3rd of June we celebrate reconciliation week by inviting motivational speakers to schools, workplaces and communities, Reconciliation walks or street marches and statements presented by politicians from federal, state and local governments. These events are organized to encourage Australians and the younger generation to celebrate reconciliation week and to remind Australians about 'coming together'.

> This essay is very close to my heart because I am part Aboriginal. I believe that no matter what someone has done in their past life I would never wish any of this to anyone, everyone deserves a chance to have/live a happy and safe life. I am proud to say that I am indigenous and Australian, and this is because the Australian 'white' citizens have finally done something.

Welfare support

The provision of an individually targeted educational programme is only one component of MCP; welfare workers are an essential part of each team and assist in the classroom in a number of ways. Welfare workers discuss with students in their team all elements of their socialisation on campus. The welfare worker becomes acquainted with the student's peer group, is aware of the activities and tensions that occur in each group, can intervene in incidents of bullying, and can monitor the student's application to set tasks and participation in class work. The welfare worker has an important mentoring role for students and is often the first to become aware of difficulties the student may be experiencing, and refers students to psychologists for counselling.

The welfare worker monitors the attendance of each student. If a student is absent, the worker rings the student's home to ensure the student will return as soon as is practicable. Importantly, the welfare worker can provide some family support. If, for example, a student is needed to babysit a sibling while the parent has another commitment, the welfare worker can assist the family to find support elsewhere to ensure the student's attendance. If the student's weekend social activities lead to regular Monday absences, the worker can also work with the family to reduce this problem.

The provision of welfare workers is recognition within the programme that much student behaviour is related to their social networks, and that the student needs assistance with regulating their social networks and activities to maintain their school commitments. Family and social events have significant impacts, and the programme recognises that student success relies on balancing these various, sometimes conflicting, demands. Parents and carers often struggle with this balance, and the welfare worker can help to ensure the programme can work in harmony with the home for agreed outcomes. In this way, welfare workers can help parents to include social goals in ILPs. In every respect, MCP strives to support families in their efforts to provide the best opportunities for the children in their care.

It has been the deliberate practice of the programme to ensure that the co-ordinator of the welfare workers is a senior Indigenous Australian woman. The welfare co-ordinator brings to her role her deep experience of Indigenous Australian family practices and understanding of community. She knows every child and every family, their circumstances, strengths and challenges. In her daily dealing with students she is able to embody the family values of her community to support and reinforce traditional relationships.

Meals

The programme provides breakfast, morning tea and lunch. There is a professional-quality kitchen with two catering staff. The provision of healthy food is an important supplement to the diet of all students and ensures that concentration and attention are not impaired by lack of nutrition. There are other equally important benefits from having a professional kitchen. Educationally there is the benefit of teaching the students food preparation. This is of particular assistance to the VCAL hospitality group, but it is also useful as other teams consider issues of diet, nutrition and health.

The kitchen supports families in several ways.

- Families do not have to provide food. This reduces the stress of preparation for school in the morning and can be an important financial support. Families can be confident that students will be able to face the day with sustaining, healthy food.

- One elective in food preparation involves parents attending for an afternoon with their student and preparing a meal. This meal is then taken home to provide for the family. This helps families to understand the programme and become more familiar with its procedures and culture.

- Each team is rostered for a week with responsibility for clearing tables, dishes, and vacuuming the floor. All students (and staff) participate in this duty. The sight of students performing a task that might be avoided at home sometimes bemuses visiting parents.

- There is clear social benefit in students sitting together at a table and eating a meal. In the absence of electronic media, students engage in conversation with their peers and staff members. There is inevitably discussion of appropriate use of cutlery and crockery, and basic table etiquette is observed.
- Birthdays and achievements are noted at meal times. If a student has excelled in some area, or a group of students has been awarded a certificate such as the White Card, meal times provide the opportunity to celebrate such events.

The provision of meals has enormous educational and social benefits, and fits within the welfare orientation of the programme.

Décor

The built environment is informed by an Indigenous Australian aesthetic. A local Indigenous Australian artist / landscape gardener was commissioned to design the serpent garden at the entrance of the campus. Students made the paving slabs and decorated them with native animals and designs, and they planted the garden with indigenous flora. The story of the garden is preserved in a plaque on a rock within the garden at the end of the path, which is designed in the shape of the traditional serpent. Inside the buildings, rich earthy colours have been chosen. Artwork based on traditional designs decorates walls, and even notice-boards follow sinuous lines. Efforts are made to ensure the environment reflects commitment to Indigenous Australian culture.

Skilled workforce

The teachers and welfare workers at MCP have undertaken a task that, while immensely rewarding, involves considerable challenges. Students involved in the programme can be very demanding of time and can present emotionally confronting situations and problems. Workers must demonstrate considerable flexibility and resilience in their daily tasks. Staff are mutually supportive and encouraging, and there are a number of ways in which they are supported by the programme.

All staff are entitled to external supervision and are expected to attend supervisory sessions at least once a term. Supervision provides the opportunity for staff members to discuss personally confronting problems in a supportive and independent environment. All staff participate in professional development. Staff can attend professional development days provided by external organisations covering matters such as dealing with children with special needs, specific conditions such as autism, or other educational issues and developments. Opportunity is also provided for MCP staff to meet with other providers of similar programmes to exchange ideas and experiences.

Local partnerships

MCP has made extensive efforts to be involved in the local community. Reference has already been made to its involvement with important Indigenous Australian educational, welfare and sporting groups. MCP survives with the support of individuals and groups in the local community. Foremost among these are the volunteers, who assist the programme. Local people who have heard of the programme and support its aims help in the kitchen preparing meals, assist in art/craft and practical classes, provide animal care on the farm, and volunteer technical help with specialised equipment. The generous support of volunteers keeps the programme functioning. In addition, there are numerous groups who provide essential support and services. A list of some partnerships is provided in Appendix B.

One noteworthy partnership is with Dr David Whelan and the Goulburn Valley Health Dental Service. This partnership has provided a dental service to all MCP students. Workers at MCP make appointments with the dental service and take students to the clinic, where a dental health assessment is undertaken and dental care is provided. All MCP students have participated in this service. Another example is Shepparton Foodshare, which generously provides much of the food prepared in the MCP kitchen, or the St Vincent De Paul organisation, which helps by providing clothing when required. The programme is helped by many generous organisations in the region.

Conclusion

The subtitle of this chapter is "A community response to a local problem". Following the committed leadership of a local school principal, the Shepparton community accepted responsibility for a perceived problem affecting local youth. If what Pearson calls "the Indigenous

Australian education disaster" (Pearson, 20011 p. 23), and the associated achievement gap evident between the socially advantaged and the socially disadvantaged, is to be improved, responsibility must be accepted. So long as governments and government departments at all levels, educational organisations, welfare organisations, communities and individuals do not accept responsibility, the problem will persist.

In 2014 the Victorian Department of Education and Early Childhood Development published *Garrin Garrin: A Strategy to Improve Learning Outcomes for Aboriginal Victorians*. In it are described seven "action areas", which are the foundations of system-wide success. These action areas are:

- committed and courageous leadership
- respect and recognition
- culturally accessible and responsive services
- strong and resilient families
- a skilled workforce
- partnership at the local level
- robust accountability.

MCP commenced long before these action areas were defined, but the programme provides a working example of these areas in action. Starting with strong leadership committed to community engagement and cultural recognition, a programme was devised and implemented to support local families with disengaged youth. The McAuley-Champagnat Program has been providing an alternative educational pathway for disengaged youth in the Shepparton region for almost a decade. Many of these young people are among the most disadvantaged and marginalised in the community. While MCP is not an exclusively Indigenous Australian setting, 26 percent of its students have an Indigenous Australian background and the programme has a strong indigenous focus. Since its inception, MCP has provided support for hundreds of young people who have not been able to be successful in conventional settings, but have been able to establish regular patterns of attendance, earn certification in nationally recognised courses, return to mainstream schools or other training organisations, or enter the workforce as valued employees.

There are undoubtedly many instances of outstanding success in the provision of services to disengaged students. MCP provides one model of an educational pathway that has been of significant benefit to a local Indigenous Australian community in a regional area. An important way for people interested in improving the educational opportunities for the socially disadvantaged is to have access to successful working examples of good educational practice: "Gathering and publishing stories of 'best practice' in Aboriginal education is a matter of urgency" (Nicholls, 2011, p. 151).

References

Achenbach, T. M., & Rescoria, L. A. (2003). *Manual for the ASEBA school-age forms & profiles.* Burlington, VT: University of Vermont, Research Centre for Children.

Australian Bureau of Statistics. (n.d.) *2011 Census QuickStats: Greater Shepparton.* Retrieved from http://www.abs.gov.au/websiteabs/D3310114.nsf/home/home?opendocument

Department of Education and Early Childhood Development. (2014). *Garrin Garrin: A strategy to improve learning and development outcomes for Aboriginal Victorians.* Melbourne, VIC: Department of Education and Early Childhood Development.

Nicholls, C. (2011). Responses. In N. Pearson (Ed.), *Radical hope: Education and equality in Australia.* Collingwood, VIC: Black Inc.

Pearson, N. (2011). *Radical hope: Education and equality in Australia.* Collingwood, VIC: Black Inc.

Pearson, N. (2014). A rightful place: Race, recognition and a more complete Commonwealth. *Quarterly Essay, 55,* 1–55.

Steering Committee for the Review of Government Service Provision. (2011). *Overcoming indigenous disadvantage: Key indicators 2011.* Canberra, ACT: Productivity Commission. Retrieved from http://www.pc.gov.au/gsp/indigenous/key-indicators-2011

Appendix A: McAuley-Champagnat Program Inaugural Advisory Board

Monsignor Peter Jeffrey	*Canonical Administrator, Notre Dame College; Chair, Notre Dame College Council*
Martin Ellemor	*Juvenile Justice, Department of Human Services*

Julie Rolfe	*Chief Executive Officer, DOXA*
Justin Mohamed	*Director, Academy of Sports, Health, and Education*
Phil Guthrie	*epresentative, Academy of Sports, Health, and Education*
Geraldine Atkinson	*Victorian Aboriginal Education Incorporated Association*
Brian Collins	*Education Officer for North East Regional Office*
Mark Rumble	*Brayton Youth and Family Services*
Jennifer Hippisley	*Executive Officer, Goulburn Murray Local Learning and Employment Network (LLEN)*
Dallas Terlich	*City of Greater Shepparton*
Paul Briggs	*Rumbalara Aboriginal Football and Netball Club*
Peter White	*Principal, Notre Dame College*
Karen Fox	*Deputy Principal, Notre Dame College*
Tom Sexton	*Catholic Education Office, Diocese of Sandhurst*
Warren Roberts	*Mission Australia*

Appendix B: Community Partnerships

The following groups and organizations provide invaluable material support to our programme:

Catholic Education Office Diocese of Sandhurst

Opening the Doors Foundation

Goulburn-Valley Dental Health Service

Rumbalara Aboriginal Co-operative

School Focused Youth Service

Brayton Youth and Family Services

St Vincent de Paul

Shepparton Foodshare

Community Fund Goulburn Valley

Sportsman's Warehouse

Beechworth Correctional Centre

Shepparton Community Policing Squad

State Emergency Service

Shepparton Trades Hall Council

Chapter 10 Outside in: One school's endeavours to keep disadvantaged young people in school and engaged

Margaret Callingham

Key points
This chapter:
1. Contributes to answering the question, How can we keep young people *in* school and engaged?
2. Uses actual examples to examine how one school worked to reduce exclusion
3. Demonstrates a framework to help schools reflect on what works for student engagement.

Introduction
This chapter contributes to thinking about school exclusion contexts by flipping the viewpoint to examine how one school works to reduce exclusion. Student engagement is the central concept used to reduce exclusion as well as for improving equity. The key question is, 'How can we keep young people in school and engaged?' To answer this question the chapter draws on case study research in a Victorian government

secondary school. Although no school is perfect, the case study demonstrates what is possible in an ordinary secondary school in a context of disadvantage. An analytical framework that brings together the elements of meaning, control and connectedness was found to be a useful tool to reflect on the ways this school promoted student engagement.

Exclusion, engagement and equity

The constructs of exclusion and engagement both constitute equity issues and comprise a complex inter-relationship between school students and school contexts.

Exclusion and equity

The equity issue with exclusion is that very often there is a correlation between students' backgrounds and exclusion. Research findings have consistently identified the over-representation of excluded students who fall into one or more of the following categories: male, low socioeconomic background, non-dominant ethnic group, special education need (Fenning & Rose, 2007; Hemphill, Plenty, Herrenkohl, Toumbourou, & Catalano, 2014; Theriot, Craun, & Dupper, 2010). This categorisation, in schools and in research, can lead to an 'othering' of these students as 'dangerous', 'deviant' or 'deficient'. In a review of research on school exclusion and African-American males, Fenning and Rose (2007) argued for a shift in focus to pay attention to school factors as possible contributors. Theriot et al. (2010) agreed that very few studies attend to school characteristics, and they identified no studies that examined student and school factors together. Their own United States-based research, which addressed this gap, led to the conclusion "that school exclusion stems from a complex interaction between student and school-level characteristics" (Theriot et al., 2010, p. 17).

A cross-cultural study within schools in Australia and the United States (Hemphill et al., 2014) built on this research by extending the selection of student and school influences. Findings confirmed that both student and school factors were associated with suspensions. Of particular interest for this chapter was the inclusion by Hemphill et al. (2014) of the school-level characteristic of school climate. Consistent across the two states, the research revealed that low levels of student commitment aligned with high levels of student suspension. This led the researchers to emphasise "the importance of promoting a positive atmosphere in schools to reduce the need to use school suspensions in response to challenging student behaviours" (Hemphill et al., 2014, p. 192). I argue, along with Sullivan, Johnson, Owens and Conway (2014), that an increase in student engagement will contribute to both promoting a positive atmosphere in schools and the reduced need to use school suspensions. .

Engagement and equity

The equity issue with engagement is that there is a correlation between student engagement and more equitable educational outcomes. This was shown in a comprehensive Canadian study—with 93 secondary schools and 32000 students in grades 6 to 12—that revealed schools with higher levels of engagement were more successful irrespective of students' backgrounds, and differences in levels of engagement across schools had "less to do with students' family background than they do with school policies and practices" (Willms, Friesen, & Milton, 2009, p. 31). Two important factors of engagement are, first, that it "is not generated by students alone … engagement is highly dependent on the institution's contribution" (Wehlage, Rutter, Smith, Lesko, & Fernandez, 1989, p. 177); and second, it is an alterable state, amenable to change (Lawson & Lawson, 2013; Wehlage et al., 1989).

Engagement has many dimensions and conceptualisations, which makes it a problematic term without a commonly agreed definition (Christenson, Reschly, & Wylie, 2012a; Lawson & Lawson, 2013). However, a definition that resonates with this chapter is from the *Handbook of Research on Student Engagement*:

> Student engagement refers to the students' active participation in academic and co-curricular or school-related activities, and commitment to educational goals and learning. Engaged students find learning meaningful, and are invested in their learning and future. It is a multidimensional construct that consists of behavioural (including academic), cognitive, and affective subtypes. Student engagement drives learning; requires energy and effort; is affected by multiple contextual influences; and can be achieved for all learners. (Christenson et al., 2012a, pp. 816–817)

This definition clearly puts the focus of engagement on student participation. This participation is characterised by the involvement and activity of being 'in task' rather than mere school attendance (Ladwig, 2010), or the passive compliance of being 'on task' (Munns, Lawson, O'Brien, & Johnson, 2006). It also highlights that engagement and participation include the pursuit of non-academic passions, interests and activities that engender "a sense of 'school is for me'" (Munns et al., 2006, p. 10). Importantly, it reinforces a commitment to forging a connection—with school, learning and education—that will lead to improved achievement and attainment levels. The adjective 'meaningful' describes learning that is beyond abstract, sedentary and test oriented, to learning that is relevant, active and purposeful. The verb 'invested' is also pertinent because people invest with the expectation of reaping a return, and students invest effort into their learning when they perceive it as valuable and beneficial to their present and future lives (Munns et al., 2006). There are many facets of student engagement, and this definition identifies three that appear most consistently. The reference to multiple contextual influences is also important, because context matters (Christenson et al., 2012a), and influences include:

- family (e.g. resources in the home; homework support; support of school; learning expectations)
- peers (e.g. attendance; aspirations; opt-in of school values)
- school (e.g. school climate and culture; classroom and behaviour management; curriculum and pedagogy; support services; student participation)
- community (e.g. links with the local community; the school's reputation in the community; opportunities for work experience, training and service learning) (Reschly & Christenson, 2012).

The definition concludes with the categorical declaration that student engagement is attainable by all.

The dynamic, productive and inclusive nature of engagement articulated in this definition goes beyond compulsory attendance and school retention (Moher & MacGowan [1985], in Appleton, Christenson, & Furlong, 2008; Stehlik, 2011; Teese, 2006). Hence, in terms of the key question for this chapter, 'How can we keep young people in school *and* engaged?', I contend that success with the latter will positively influence the former. This is supported in the literature (Lamb & Rice, 2008; Levin, 2000; Reschly & Christenson, 2012) and explains why student engagement is strongly linked to school reform (Christenson, Reschly, & Wylie, 2012b), as evidenced in middle-school and school renewal initiatives that focus on transforming traditional school structures and pedagogies to promote engagement (Hayes, Mills, Christie, & Lingard, 2006). Despite this, secondary schools in Australia have had little success, overall, in producing more engaging educational experiences for students from disadvantaged backgrounds (Victorian Auditor-General, 2012), and this constitutes a critical equity issue. One tool to help schools reflect on the ways educational experiences can promote students' engagement in learning is a framework based on the elements of meaning, control and connectedness.

Analytical framework

For my analytical lens for this chapter I draw on a framework Wierenga (2003) used to conceptualise "*what works* for young people in decision making roles" (p. 5, emphasis in original). The framework has three key elements: meaning, control and connectedness (see Figure 10.1).

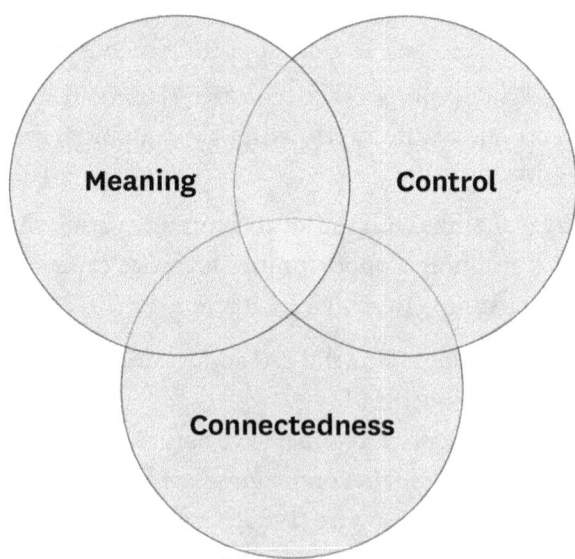

Figure 10.1: Wierenga's framework

Source: Wierenga, 2003, p. 64

Over the years this framework and variations of its three elements have been applied to developmental psychology (Phillips, 1990, cited in Holdsworth, Cahill, & Smith, 2003) and sociology, and in the fields of youth work (Holdsworth & Blanchard, 2006; Wierenga, 2003) and education (Holdsworth, 2004; Holdsworth et al., 2003; Stokes, 2003; Wyn et al., 2014).

Table 10.1 is my synthesis of the understandings that previous studies have associated with the three elements of the framework. I am particularly interested in the way Wierenga (2003) applied the framework as a reflective tool, and in its utility to reflect on "*what works for student engagement*". It is important to note that just as Figure 10.1 depicts the three elements as interconnecting, the understandings across each element in Table 10.1 also connect and overlap.

Table 10.1: Understandings of the framework elements

Meaning	Meaning is about educational experiences supporting students' active participation in learning that has relevance and purpose beyond the programme.
	Meaning involves structuring educational experiences so that students: contribute to something that is important and has value beyond the classroom; can make a real-life contribution; achieve practical outcomes in real-life situations; experience authentic work/community contexts; and experience direct involvement in real problem solving and decision making to produce a real product/outcome.
	Learning without the element of meaning = abstract &/or trivial
	To achieve meaning involves asking questions about how educational experiences can be structured to: draw on students' community and cultural knowledge; identify issues that are meaningful to students; and position students to make a difference or worthwhile contribution.
Control	Control is about educational experiences equipping students with the skills, resources and strategies to take ownership of their learning.
	Control involves structuring educational experiences so that students: are listened to; have authentic choices; set goals; devise plans; make decisions; manage their time; and are supported to resolve problems and conflicts.
	Learning without the element of control = teacher directed/dominated
	To achieve control involves asking questions about how educational experiences can be structured in order to: give students more input and authentic choices as opposed to teacher choices; give students more opportunities to show initiative, take responsibility, organise activities and manage projects; build students' capacities and strengths; support students rather than direct them; and focus on process rather than product.

Connectedness	Connectedness is about educational experiences developing students' learning relationships: within the programme, in the school community, and beyond the school.
	Connectedness involves structuring educational experiences so that students: develop social roles, social relationships and social connectedness; develop team skills, including communication, co-operation, collaboration, conflict resolution and problem solving; experience working with and alongside others; learn how to help others without doing things for them; network; and develop leadership and mentoring skills.
	Learning without the element of connectedness = disconnected &/or alienating
	To achieve connectedness involves asking questions about how educational experiences can be structured in order to: enhance relationships; build relationship and team skills with adults and students; be more accepting of individuality, difference and diversity; provide social support and affirmation; gather people around to work alongside; and enable peer mentoring, coaching and leadership.

Using this framework I will explore what works for young people's engagement in learning by looking at a case study of one particular school. Before moving on to the thematic analysis, I provide some background about the school. The leadership team at the school preferred that it be named in this publication, and permission to do this was granted by the Victoria University Human Research and Ethics Committee. Pseudonyms have been used for the young people in the vignettes.

Exploring McClelland College

McClelland College is a government years 7–12 school with an enrolment of 870 students. It was recommended to me because of its investment in programmes to engage students who, typically, would be disenfranchised in the education system. Three programmes in particular feature in this article: Hands On Learning; Connect; and the McClelland Academy Program.

The school is not held up as a model but as a case for critical and reflective debate. This is in line with the well-established tradition of case studies within schools (Black-Hawkins, 2010). The college is not perfect, but it is continuously seeking to improve. Exclusion has not yet been eliminated, but the school is working to counter both exclusion and disadvantage.

McClelland College is situated in an aging housing estate. Changing demographics in the estate have led to declining enrolments at the College and its feeder primary schools. The modern buildings and well-kept grounds of the College sit in contrast to the tired houses and overgrown gardens that surround it. My first impression was of a private school, and because my research is specifically focused on what schools are doing to engage young people from backgrounds of disadvantage I became concerned that the College was marketing itself to middle-class families in preference to local families. When I voiced this at my first meeting, the immediate response from the principal was, "Yes, we do need to attract more students, but not at the expense of pushing out local students from low socioeconomic backgrounds." With confirmation that the school was committed to catering to its local students, arrangements were made for the study to commence in July 2013.

The remainder of the chapter is organised around three themes that were identified as contributing to answer the question 'How can we keep young people in school and engaged?' Although discussed separately, these themes are closely connected. The themes are:

- a personalised learning approach
- a community approach
- an in-school approach.

Each theme includes a vignette of a real student at the College to make the discussion about how we can keep young people in school and engaged more authentic. The analytical framework discussed above is applied to each vignette to reflect on student engagement across the elements of meaning, control, and connectedness.

A personalised learning approach

Figure 10.2: McClelland College open day flyer.

The image in Figure 10.2 was used on the 2013 College open day flyer. The school devised this image to symbolise its personalised learning approach to schooling. The relevance of a personalised learning approach to this chapter is that it is the flipside of more homogeneous forms of schooling that tend to explicitly and/or implicitly exclude young people who, for whatever reasons, do not 'fit' a school. The personalised learning approach of the College is highlighted through a vignette on Dawn (see Box 10.1).

Box 10.1: Dawn: A personalised learning approach

Dawn was 13, in Year 7, and living in residential care when I first met her at the College in 2013. At one stage Dawn completed a timeline of her past and she wrote that she had been to 14 primary schools. Dawn's perception of the amount of times she had moved is indicative of the lack of stability during her formative years. It is not surprising, therefore, that there was very little regularity in Dawn's school attendance. The same erratic pattern applied to her living circumstances.

At one stage Dawn was living in a squat in Melbourne's inner north for periods of time, and then arriving at school (in an outer south-eastern suburb) reeking of the squalid conditions where she had been staying. When she arrived at school, staff would forage for a school uniform for her to get changed into. The supply of school uniform items had been a regular occurrence due to the lack of consistency in Dawn's life. There was even a time, before she was enrolled in the school's Connect programme, when one of the assistant principals brought an additional sandwich to school, just in case Dawn turned up.

In Connect, food items are available to students. For Dawn, this multi-age programme, with an average of 12–18 students and an adult:student ratio of approximately 1:9, offered a supportive, trauma-informed approach to teaching and learning. As part of this programme, Dawn helped to devise her own individualised learning plan (ILP), which allowed for flexible attendance and off-campus study via self-paced learning units. When Dawn was once again in school uniform, she looked no different from any other student. The homogeneity of the school uniform, however, belied the heterogeneous approach of the college to its student population.

> A key component of the College is the opportunity for young people to contribute to their community. Several Connect students, including Dawn, volunteer at City Life (a charity café/food bank) on a weekly basis. Although Dawn is often the recipient of charity, the College gives Dawn the opportunity to flip that around and make her own contribution back to the community.

Dawn's complex life and individual needs do not 'fit' into the conventions of very many secondary schools. For example, a common school response would have been to discipline Dawn for being out of uniform. In contrast, the College rallied to support Dawn rather than add to her marginalisation (Garrett, 2014). The College demonstrated a commitment to counter exclusion and—importantly—to counter the disadvantage in Dawn's life by promoting her positive participation in school and the community. In 2013 Dawn wrote about her opportunity to contribute: "I love volunteering down at City Life … I enjoy that very much." Of her interpersonal relationships and support she wrote, "I like the people that are in Connect and the staff that work in Connect and the way they help us out." Dawn's optimistic reflections about her experiences in the College are consistent with the findings of Gilligan (2006) about the conditions under which vulnerable young people can thrive: "[g]rowth, healing and development in children come from two sources: key social relationships and key social roles" (p. 42).

In this vignette the personalised learning approach of the College works to keep Dawn in school and engaged. When the analytical framework is applied, it is clear that the three elements of meaning, control and connectedness are represented, with connectedness rating the highest. The meaning element is involved through Dawn's contribution to City Life café, where she helped to prepare and serve food to homeless and disenfranchised people in the community. Dawn's end-of-year reflection indicated the value she placed on making this real-life contribution.

In the element of control, Dawn had quite a say in the level and pace of her learning through her ILP. She made decisions regarding her timetable. She also made choices regarding her involvement in community outreach programmes and volunteer work.

In terms of connectedness, the school represented a safe environment with extensive networks that included strong one-on-one support and people who worked alongside and helped Dawn, academically and personally. Overall, Dawn experienced the school as somewhere she was welcomed, wanted and valued in all of her individuality. Within Connect, Dawn had developed trust relationships and she expressed connection with the adults and her peers in this programme. Dawn also worked productively as part of a team at City Life, and this helped to increase her social roles and social relationships, as well as developing her co-operation skills.

The next theme examines more closely the community approach of the College and the developmental opportunities this fosters for its students.

A community approach

The relevance of a community approach to this chapter is that it is the flip side to insular forms of schooling that cater to a narrow range of students. A community approach to schooling engages young people via resources both within and beyond the perimeter of the school, "because family, peer, and neighbourhood ecologies exert powerful influence on students' educational opportunities and interests, as well as their aspirations for the future" (Lawson & Lawson, 2013, p. 433). The role of this community is not to hand responsibility over to others, but to share responsibility with others in order to support and add value to young people's educational and life experiences. At times these community contacts contribute with/in the school, while at other times the school contributes with/in the community of these contacts. The community approach of the College is highlighted in a vignette on Colin (see Box 10.2).

Box 10.2: Colin: A community approach

Colin transferred to the College part-way through Year 7 because he was having trouble fitting in at his previous school. This manifested in broken relationships due to his refusal to participate and unwillingness to work. After discussions about options, Colin and his family decided he would give the College and the Connect programme a try.

The Connect programme works to maintain a high adult to student ratio. As a minimum, all of the Connect classes have a teacher and a support worker. The current support worker is an older, grandmotherly person whom the students refer to as 'Nan'. Other positive adults include: youth workers accessed through community programmes; volunteers with various expertise; and young people on work experience placements, including trainee-teachers, doctors, youth workers and psychologists. An example of a volunteer in Connect is the Year 9 co-ordinator, who volunteers to work one-on-one with Colin on his reading.

The community programmes that Connect links into offer students a diversity of applied learning experiences, from artistic to health and fitness related. Colin particularly enjoys the latter. Colin also signed up to participate in the 'Big Brother Big Sister Mentoring in the Hood' programme. This is a group initiative, where mentors meet weekly with a group of young people to participate in activities that build relationships and resilience. For his input into the community, Colin chose to volunteer at the City Life café / food bank, and in this role his positive adult network expanded again to include the café co-ordinator, the food bank co-ordinator, the cook, and a team of other volunteers.

Within a short period of time it became clear that Colin enjoyed and had skills in practical activities. It transpired that Colin had a shed at home where he designed and built tables, and so he was also offered a day per week in Hands On Learning (HOL). HOL is a programme where two adults and up to 10 young people work on practical activities involving building, gardening, and maintenance. Two members of the student team in HOL also volunteer as cooks for the day, and this involves checking for food allergies, planning what to prepare for morning tea and lunch, shopping, cooking, and, after the meals, washing dishes and cleaning up. In this holistic programme, relationships and social skills are developed in the process of working on practical activities and sharing meals. Like Connect, this is a multi-age programme in which more experienced participants, regardless of age, take on leadership roles with novices to HOL.

Colin derived yet another social network through his involvement in the McClelland Activity Program (MAP). MAP is a multi-age programme that runs for half a day across the whole school, and it is an opportunity for students and staff to pursue their passions. Colin's chosen MAP was 'Design for the Environment', and in 2014 this began

> with skill development in designing and building an outdoor area within the College. It then progressed to the College students leading primary school students to build an outdoor mathematics area in their school. This programme also utilised peer leadership roles, so Colin once again experienced peer mentoring.

In this vignette, the community approach of the College works to keep Colin in school and engaged. Considered and timely supports that are put in place with/in the College recognise "that getting the right support at the right time can help young people lead healthy lives and stay connected, engaged and participating in their communities" (Grogan, Colvin, Rose, Morstyn, & Atkins, 2013, p. 12). Grogan et al. (2013) compare these supports to scaffolding that "can be increased, reduced or removed as needs change" (p. 13). Once again, the conceptual framework provides a tool to reflect on the ways the College and its various programmes promoted Colin's engagement in the school and with learning.

In terms of meaning, Colin contributed practically to the authentic work context of City Life café. In HOL and MAP Colin also produced practical outcomes in real-life contexts within the school and community. The control element is represented by the decisions Colin made in his ILP, where he elected which areas he needed to study one on one, in small groups and via self-paced units, and about his involvement in practical, hands-on approaches to his learning. Colin also made choices about involvement in community-linked programmes and volunteer work. Even within programmes such as HOL Colin had a choice of activities to pursue.

In terms of the element of connectedness, at his previous school Colin did not fit the role of a conforming, print-oriented student and this caused broken connections. In contrast, the College demonstrated that Colin was welcomed and accepted in his individuality, and he was surrounded by networks, mentors and peer supports to increase both his social connections and his social roles. Colin obtained one-on-one support with his reading; he gained the satisfaction of completing work in a supportive environment with a low student-to-adult ratio; and he worked semi-independently on self-paced modules that had a practical orientation. Colin also worked productively as part of the City Life team. In addition, he learned together with and alongside other practically oriented students in HOL and MAP. Colin had come from a school where his practical skills were not recognised or valued, and the College worked to flip that around so that Colin could make his own contribution, within school and in the community.

Next is a vignette showing the in-school approach of the College in relation to a behavioural incident. The analytical framework is also applied to it as a reflective tool.

An in-school approach

Exclusion has not been eliminated at the College, yet the following vignette (see Box 10.3) illustrates how an in-school approach to a behavioural incident involving Noel and Trent did facilitate engagement.

Box 10.3: Noel and Trent: an in-school approach

Noel and Trent were given a modified learning arrangement after a behavioural incident in Connect that involved allegations by a teacher of their refusing instructions, swearing and throwing things at her. The boys refuted many of the allegations, and in his initial investigation the assistant principal (AP) could not be certain about the details of what had transpired. According to the AP, the modified learning arrangement—in the form of an in-school suspension—was the best way to support the teacher and the Connect programme while there was unrest. It also gave him time to personally monitor the situation in Connect. In addition, the modified learning arrangement was considered the best way to support the boys and their families while this monitoring was conducted.

At the College, in-school suspensions are often spent in the administration area. At times students work in the meeting rooms, and when these are booked they work in the space between the offices of the principal team. An advantage that I have observed with this arrangement is that the principal team, and other staff who passed, had opportunities to interact with students, to help them with their work, and to encourage them in that work. With Noel and Trent, I and others were able to offer lots of encouragement because they usually had their heads down and were getting on with their work. One of the APs had a particular interest in maths, and during this time he found that Noel also enjoyed maths, so they spent snatches of time discussing Noel's work. Through these interactions Noel seemed to consolidate a sense that he was good at maths.

As a result of his assessment of the entire context that led to the incident, the AP made some adjustments to the staffing in Connect. This indicated that the modified learning arrangement was not simply 'punishment by exclusion', which would send a message to the boys that they were the problem. Rather, it confirmed that the modified programme created space for the AP to assess the entire situation and to make modifications that would benefit all of the students in Connect, including Noel and Trent.

Upon his return to Connect, Noel transitioned into the Year 9 mathematics class. An important point to note about this transition is that, procedurally, the Connect classes are consistent with the rest of the school. For example, all classes commence with expected learning or focus plans, which are written up, and all classes finish with reflections. Procedural consistency such as this helps to set the Connect students up for success within the school, whichever programmes they transition into.

This vignette contrasts with behavioural incidents that place full responsibility on students, that punish them through exclusion, and that return them to the same situation without making adjustments or providing them with support to re-engage (Quin & Hemphill, 2014). When the analytical framework is used as a tool to reflect on student engagement in this exclusion event, it is no surprise that the elements of meaning and control do not feature. Regarding control, however, it is worth noting that it was within the boys' control to disengage from the school by choosing not to attend, or to disengage from the learning by choosing not to use the time productively.

Paradoxically, connectedness rated highly because the in-school suspension facilitated maintenance of the boys' relationships: with the school, with learning and with staff. Connectedness with the school was retained because the boys continued to attend every day. Connectedness with learning continued because the Connect co-ordinator discussed and supplied the boys with work. Connectedness with other staff was maintained because the modified learning arrangement was located in the office area. For example, it was because of this location that one of the APs began to work with and encourage Noel and Trent with their maths. This had a positive impact on Noel's confidence and self-esteem and facilitated his transition into the Year 9 mathematics class. Further, a relationship of trust was maintained with the boys as a result of the changes that were made in Connect. The boys saw that the time they were out of Connect *was* used to make modifications as a result of the AP's assessment of factors that contributed to the behavioural incident.

With student engagement as the central concept for reduction of exclusion, the themes of 'a personalised learning approach', 'a community approach' and 'an in-school approach' were identified as contributing to answer the question 'How can we keep young people in school and engaged?'

Summing up

The chapter argues that when a school is more engaging for students, it is less exclusionary and more equitable. The commitment by the College to engage rather than exclude was demonstrated in its personalised learning approach, which wrapped around to include academic, social and personal support. Such an approach is important for all students, and is especially crucial for students with backgrounds of disadvantage, trauma and neglect (Smyth, Down, & McInerney, 2010; Te Riele, 2012). For example, Dawn was not the only student to receive items of school uniform: the College has cupboards of spare uniform items and a shelf full of new school shoes, so that when a student attends school the focus is on their learning, not excluding them due to uniform issues. This is because when young people like Dawn become estranged from school, they are vulnerable, "with a narrower base of positive role models on whom to draw for guidance, inspiration and encouragement" (Gilligan, 2006, p. 37). As was reflected using the analytical framework, the College worked proactively to flip this around to promote student engagement as a bridge to counter exclusion and ameliorate disadvantage.

The commitment to engage rather than exclude was also demonstrated in the community approach taken by the College. This was shown in its investments to provide supportive learning spaces, comprising high adult to student ratios, committed to building students' academic abilities in conjunction with their interests and talents. Colin's story illustrated that the greater a student's needs, the greater the number of role models, resources and social roles the school sought to put in place. This investment is consistent with the equity principle that disadvantaged students must be targeted if their educational outcomes are to be improved (Gonski et al., 2011). Many schools do not invest in the education of students who do not fit into traditional models of schooling, especially students who may be deemed to be detrimental to the school's test results (Slee, 2014). As was reflected using the analytical framework, however, the College worked proactively to flip this around to promote student engagement as a bridge to increase access to learning.

A further commitment to engage rather than exclude was demonstrated in the College's in-school approach to behavioural incidents. This approach is consistent with Garrett's (2014) contention that in-school suspensions can be a way for schools to take advantage of time in school to work with young people rather than add to the problems of those already affected by adverse life experiences. As this book highlights, school suspensions have potential long-term negative impacts on suspended students. However, as was reflected using the analytical framework, the in-school approach of the College worked to promote student engagement as a bridge to increase connectedness to school and learning.

This chapter has contributed to thinking about school exclusion contexts by flipping the viewpoint to examine how one school worked to reduce exclusion. The chapter has also demonstrated the practical utility of applying a framework as a tool to map student engagement across the elements of meaning, control, and connectedness. Overall, the purpose of the chapter has been to make a contribution to critical and reflective debate about the ways in which schools can increase engagement and reduce exclusions of young people from backgrounds of disadvantage.

Acknowledgements

This research is supported through the Australian Government's Collaborative Research Networks (CRN) programme. I acknowledge the support of both the Victorian Department of Education and Early Childhood Development for approval to conduct research in a government school, and McClelland College, whose staff and students have been a pleasure to work alongside. Further, I would like to thank Ani Wierenga and Roger Holdsworth for providing information regarding the framework; Kitty te Riele for her wise counsel; and colleagues at the Victoria Institute for Education, Diversity and Lifelong Learning for their input.

References

Appleton, J. J., Christenson, S. L., & Furlong, M. J. (2008). Student engagement with school: Critical conceptual and methodological issues of the construct. *Psychology in the Schools, 45*(5), 369–386. doi: 10.1002/pits.20303

Black-Hawkins, K. (2010). The framework for participation: A research tool for exploring the relationship between achievement and inclusion in schools. *International Journal of Research & Method in Education, 33*(1), 21–40. doi: 10.1080/17437271003597907

Christenson, S. L., Reschly, A. L., & Wylie, C. (2012a). Epilogue. In S. L. Christenson, A. L. Reschly, & C. Wylie (Eds.), *Handbook of research on student engagement* (pp. 813–817). New York, NY: Springer.

Christenson, S. L., Reschly, A. L., & Wylie, C. (2012b). Preface. In S. L. Christenson, A. L. Reschly, & C. Wylie (Eds.), *Handbook of research on student engagement* (pp. v–ix). New York, NY: Springer.

Fenning, P., & Rose, J. (2007). Overrepresentation of African American students in exclusionary discipline: The role of school policy. *Urban Education, 42*(6), 536–559. doi: 10.1177/0042085907305039

Garrett, K. (2014). Childhood trauma and its affects on health and learning. *Education Digest, 79*(6), 4–9.

Gilligan, R. (2006). Creating a warm place where children can blossom. *Social Policy Journal of New Zealand, 28*, 36–45.

Gonski, D., Boston, K., Greiner, K., Lawrence, C., Scales, B., & Tannock, P. (2011). *Review of funding for schooling: Final report.* Canberra, ACT: Australian Government. Retrieved from http://foi.deewr.gov.au/node/30439/

Grogan, P., Colvin, K., Rose, J., Morstyn, L., & Atkins, C. (2013). *Building the scaffolding: Strengthening support for young people in Victoria.* Melbourne, VIC: Victorian Council of Social Services.

Hayes, D., Mills, M., Christie, P., & Lingard, B. (2006). *Teachers and schooling making a difference: Productive pedagogies, assessment and performance.* Crows Nest, NSW: Allen & Unwin.

Hemphill, S. A., Plenty, S. M., Herrenkohl, T. I., Toumbourou, J. W., & Catalano, R. F. (2014). Student and school factors associated with school suspension: A multilevel analysis of students in Victoria, Australia, and Washington state, United States. *Children and Youth Services Review, 36*(1), 187–194. doi: 10.1016/j.childyouth.2013.11.022

Holdsworth, R. (2004, 23 June). *Good practice in learning alternatives.* Paper presented at the Learning Choices Expo, Sydney, NSW.

Holdsworth, R., & Blanchard, M. (2006). Unheard voices: Themes emerging from studies of the views about school engagement of young people with high support needs in the area of mental health. *Australian Journal of Guidance & Counselling, 16*(1), 14–28.

Holdsworth, R., Cahill, H., & Smith, G. (2003). *Student action teams: Phase 2: 2001–2002: An evaluation of implementation and impact.* Melbourne, VIC: Youth Research Centre.

Ladwig, J. G. (2010). Beyond academic outcomes. *Review of Research in Education, 34*(1), 113–141. doi: 10.3102/0091732x09353062

Lamb, S., & Rice, S. (2008). *Effective strategies to increase school completion report.* Melbourne, VIC: Department of Education and Early Childhood Development.

Lawson, M. A., & Lawson, H. A. (2013). New conceptual frameworks for student engagement research, policy, and practice. *Review of Educational Research, 83*(3), 432–479. doi: 10.3102/0034654313480891

Levin, B. (2000). Putting students at the centre in education reform. *Journal of Educational Change, 1,* 155–172.

Munns, G., Lawson, J., O'Brien, M., & Johnson, K. (2006). Student engagement and the Fair Go Project. In NSW Department of Education & Training and University of Western Sydney (Ed.), *School is for me: pathways to student engagement* (pp. 7–14). Sydney, NSW: NSW DET.

Quin, D., & Hemphill, S. A. (2014). Students' experiences of school suspension. *Health Promoting Journal of Australia, 25*(1), 52–58. doi: 10.1071/HE13097

Reschly, A. L., & Christenson, S. L. (2012). Jingle, jangle, and conceptual haziness: Evolution and future directions of the engagement construct. In S. L. Christenson, A. L. Reschly, & C. Wylie (Eds.), *Handbook of research on student engagement* (pp. 3–20). New York, NY: Springer.

Slee, R. (2014). Discourses of inclusion and exclusion: Drawing wider margins. *Power and Education, 6*(1), 7–17. doi: 10.2304/power.2014.6.1.7

Smyth, J., Down, B., & McInerney, P. (2010). *'Hanging in with kids' in tough times: Engagement in contexts of educational disadvantage in the relational school*. New York, NY: Peter Lang.

Stehlik, T. (2011). Conclusion: Moving forward to more equitable educational outcomes for all young people. In T. Stehlik & C. Patterson (Eds.), *Changing the paradigm: Education as the key to a socially inclusive future* (pp. 157–168). Mt Gravatt, QLD: Post Pressed.

Stokes, H. (2003). *Engaging young people in school through the arts*. Melbourne, VIC: Youth Research Centre.

Sullivan, A. M., Johnson, B., Owens, L., & Conway, R. (2014). Punish them or engage them?: Teachers' views of unproductive student behaviours in the classroom. *Australian Journal of Teacher Education, 39*(6), 43–56. doi: 10.14221/ajte.2014v39n6.6

Te Riele, K. (2012). One size does not fit all: Belonging and marginalised youth. In N. Bagnall & E. Cassidy (Eds.), *Education and belonging* (pp. 71–84). New York, NY: Nova Science.

Teese, R. (2006). Condemned to innovate. *Griffith REVIEW, 11*, n.p.

Theriot, M. T., Craun, S. W., & Dupper, D. R. (2010). Multilevel evaluation of factors predicting school exclusion among middle and high school students. *Children and Youth Services Review, 32*(1), 13–19. doi: 10.1016/j.childyouth.2009.06.009

Victorian Auditor-General. (2012). *Student completion rates*. Melbourne, VIC: Victorian Auditor-General's Office.

Wehlage, G. G., Rutter, R. A., Smith, G. A., Lesko, N., & Fernandez, R. R. (1989). *Reducing the risk: Schools as communities of support*. Lewes, East Sussex, UK: Falmer Press.

Wierenga, A. (2003). *Sharing a new story: Young people in decision-making*. Melbourne, VIC: Youth Research Centre.

Willms, J. D., Friesen, S., & Milton, P. (2009). *What did you do in school today? Transforming classrooms through social, academic and intellectual engagement*. Toronto, Canada: Canadian Education Association.

Wyn, J., McCarthy, G., Wierenga, A., Jones, M., Lewis, A., O'Donovan, R., et al. (2014). *Enabling spaces for learning: A knowledge archive and shared measurement framework*. Melbourne, VIC: Youth Research Centre.

Chapter 11 The Ministry of Education's Behaviour Crisis Response Service: Helping educational facilities to manage crisis situations and keep students engaged in learning

Mike Crosby, Grant Malins and Terry Carter

Key points

1. The Behaviour Crisis Response Service (BCRS) is a Ministry of Education initiative from the Positive Behaviour for Learning (PB4L) Action Plan 2010-2014.
2. BCRS provides a structure to implement the provision of programmes and initiatives to turn around problem behaviour in children and young people.
3. The BCRS engagement with an educational facility is a collaborative exercise
4. Some 2 to 3 years after they were referred to the BCRS, the vast majority of the students were still attending an educational facility.

Introduction

In the first part of this chapter you will learn a little of the history and purpose of the New Zealand Ministry of Education's Behaviour Crisis Response Service (BCRS) as it operates within the Northern Region, and of the process followed in responding to a request for BCRS support from an educational facility within its boundaries. The second part of the chapter contains an example of the information gathered by a BCRS lead worker in his meeting with school staff. Information about the student and the crisis, along with a co-constructed interim management plan, are provided, with accompanying commentary on the data collection and the planning process to give insight into how the former was gathered and how the latter evolved. The third and final part of this chapter gives a brief synopsis of the BCRS's intake and outcome data for the 2014 academic year, which will inform you of our referral sources and those they seek support with.

Background

The BCRS, now in its 6th year of operation, is an initiative that came out of the Ministry of Education's Positive Behaviour for Learning (PB4L) Action Plan 2010–2014. This was to be implemented through the provision of programmes and initiatives for parents, teachers and schools across the country to turn around problem behaviour in children and young people and encourage pro-social behaviour.[1] Within the PB4L initiative all educational facilities were to have access to a BCRS, which would provide quick support from the Ministry to stabilise a crisis situation. The criteria for a response from the BCRS have two dimensions: the incident or event itself and the level of disruption associated with it.

Incident or event

The crisis will usually involve *high* levels of one or more of the following behaviours:

- violence and/or aggression
- intimidation and/or threat
- dangerous behaviour
- self-harm
- problematic sexualised behaviour.

Level of disruption
The school is insufficiently prepared to deal with the degree of disruption the incident or event has evoked, and this has affected staff and/or students to the extent that their normal level of functioning has been *significantly* disrupted.

Focus
On each occasion the BCRS's engagement with an educational facility is a collaborative exercise, where the focus is on the development and implementation of an intervention plan that will lower the *immediate* levels of risk and stress associated with the incident or event. This undertaking has the four goals of the BCRS as its focus:

1. ensuring the safety of staff and students
2. stabilising the school environment and preventing further deterioration of the situation
3. identifying and linking to other resources and/or services
4. collaborating in the formulation and writing of a plan for the interim management of the situation.

Setting the scene
Finally in this section, and primarily for the benefit of our overseas readers, we provide a brief overview of selected geographic and demographic characteristics of the Northern Region covered by the BCRS. It stretches 150 kilometres, from Wellsford in the north to Maramarua in the south, and from the east coast to the west coast along that stretch of countryside. Within the nearly 5,000 square kilometres of its confines there are 87 secondary schools, 401 primary and intermediate schools, and 1,224 early childhood education centres, with a total of 324,174 students[2] on their combined rolls.

Part 1: What we do

The initial call
Typically a facility will make a phone call to the BCRS's dedicated number and relay to the co-ordinator facts about an incident that is causing much concern, along with identifying details related to the educational facility and the student. There are two response options at this point of contact: acceptance, or advice and guidance:

- acceptance: the referrer is advised that a BCRS team member will contact them and make arrangements to meet, discuss their concern in more detail and collaborate in the writing of an interim management plan
- advice and guidance: the referrer is given information that will help him/her to:
  - manage the incident internally, or
  - communicate with the appropriate Ministry of Education service manager and/or assigned lead worker, or
  - make contact with the most appropriate service and/or agency to meet their needs.

The decision to accept or give advice and guidance is made after the BCRS co-ordinator and the referrer complete an Access Guidelines Checklist over the phone. This checklist guides the gathering of specific details about the incident triggering the referral, along with information about the student and his/her behaviour in general. At this time the co-ordinator will also check the Ministry of Education's database to determine the student's status with the organisation. If the student is, or has recently been, a client of the Ministry, the referrer may be directed to contact the lead worker and/or the service manager associated with the team concerned. The rationale is that there is a case worker who is well informed about, and known by, the student, the facility and his/her family, and as such is perhaps best qualified and positioned to respond to the facility's call for assistance.

Once the BCRS co-ordinator has conveyed to the referrer that their call for assistance has met the team's criteria, he tells the referrer the name of the BCRS team member assigned to respond and to expect a phone call very soon. The appointed lead worker makes contact with the referrer as soon as possible to set up a meeting time that suits the availability of both parties. Given that arrangements will need to be made for the appropriate staff members to be released from their teaching duties so as to take part in this meeting, it is not always possible for the referring facility's management to settle these arrangements on the day of the call. So saying, with the majority of referrals to the BCRS, a meeting is scheduled so that all parties meet within 24 hours of the request for support being lodged. On the part of BCRS personnel, it is unlikely that one of its four team members cannot get to the referring facility the day the referral is received, if that is what is needed and/or requested.

Meeting with school staff

Just who meets with the BCRS lead worker is a decision made by the senior management of the facility involved, but ideally this will include those individuals who know the student concerned best, along with a senior management person who has the power to authorise and implement the important decisions that will be made in the 'co-authored' response to the crisis situation. This recommendation is conveyed to the referrer by the BCRS lead worker when s/he makes the initial call to the facility, as is information about the role of the BCRS lead worker, an overview of what a BCRS response looks like, and an indication of how long the meeting will run.

Typically, but bearing in mind that no two crisis situations are the same, given the array of settings, concerns and individuals involved it takes approximately an hour and a half for a BCRS lead worker to orchestrate the gathering of background information and facilitate putting together the components of an interim intervention plan. Templates developed within the BCRS are used to guide lead workers in this undertaking. Using a template that best suits the crisis event, the BCRS lead worker acts as 'minute taker', facilitator and co-contributor in the data gathering and planning process. The objective of the BCRS lead worker is to leave the facility assured by staff members that they are feeling more confident in dealing with the immediate crisis and knowing they have documented how they will do so over the short to medium term.

One task flowing from the BCRS lead worker's contribution to the meeting is the commitment to write up the notes of the meeting and present these in the form of data gathering and intervention planning notes.[3] This document is emailed to the school by the next school day, at the latest. If the BCRS is experiencing a 'spike' in the number of calls it is receiving at the time, it is judicious to provide the school with a photocopy of the template on which all the background data and planning notes were recorded during the meeting.

If it is agreed by those at the meeting that the student concerned will require ongoing support from a Ministry of Education psychologist or special education advisor, the facility is supported with lodging a referral for such support with the appropriate Ministry service manager. If such a referral is lodged, the BCRS lead worker will continue to work with the school to meet the student's needs until a lead worker is appointed by the relevant service manager. At that point the two lead workers will co-ordinate the transition of the student from one team to another.

Part 2: How we do it

An example of the information gathered from school personnel and the co-constructed interim intervention planning, as recorded by one BCRS lead worker, is presented in Appendices 1 and 2.[4] When referring to these two appendices it is important for the reader to recall that the BCRS lead worker concerned had 60–90 minutes with school staff members in which to get the background information and develop the interim management plan that has been presented here. Rarely do the educational institutions we are dealing with have more than an hour to meet with us, though there has been the rare occasion when 2 hours have been made available.

Given the prescribed tasks and the ever-increasing demands educational facilities have to cope with each day, BCRS members have, of necessity, refined their data gathering and co-planning of an interim intervention plan to the point where they maximise the time each educational facility says they can spend with them on the day they meet. This parameter is established at the start of our meeting, and those present are informed that the available time will be divided so that one-third is spent looking back at the crisis and the student concerned, and the remaining two-thirds of the time to looking ahead through the development of an interim intervention plan.

Setting the scene

Once the formalities of introductions and the clarification of an end time for the meeting have been dealt with, the BCRS lead worker explains to all present the procedure s/he will follow in helping the facility to develop an interim intervention plan that sets out how the crisis they are facing will be dealt with. That conversation may go something like this:

> I acknowledge that there is likely to be a long and detailed history associated with the referred student and his/her behaviour that has brought you to the point where you have asked the BCRS to become involved. My objective in the 60 minutes you said we have available today, is to co-develop with you a plan that will guide you in the management of this student's behaviour over the short to medium term and/or until the appropriate ongoing support becomes available.
>
> For the first 20 minutes we will look back at the behaviours of concern and devote the remaining 40 minutes looking ahead by way of setting behaviour goals for the student and specifying what will be done to help him/her achieve them.
>
> Given such tight time constraints, it is important that we remain focused on our ultimate goal of writing an interim management plan. To this end I will assist you by providing a structure and process, which I will now describe.

At this point, the BCRS lead worker shows staff members an A3-sized data collection and planning template (Appendices 1 and 2) s/he will use, briefly describing each section within its two phases. Then begins the process of questioning staff members to elicit background information on their major concerns about the student under discussion, and their thoughts and ideas for the interim management plan.

Analysis of behaviour: Looking back

The BCRS lead worker sets the scene for this phase with a script that goes something like this:

> As I said earlier, there is likely a long and detailed history that 'sits' around the referred student and his/her behaviour, and I do not want in any way to trivialise or minimise your stories about this. However, given the time we have available to us, and our goal of co-constructing an interim management plan, I am going to request that each of you limit what you say so that what you present is a distillation of the key message around each of the sections we will be covering in our data collection and co-planning exercise today.

The BCRS lead worker goes on to say:

> I will be asking each of you a series of questions. Each time I ask a question I will give you all time to consider it, and request that you present your answer in a short phrase that conveys your considered opinion—no 'ands' or 'buts', just a short phrase that crystallises your knowledge of, or opinion on, the matter I ask about. I realise this is no easy task; as I said before, you could give me much detail about this student and his/her behaviour, but the approach I adopt will keep us focused and make writing an interim-management plan achievable within our timeframe.
>
> There is one other strategy I will inform you of before I commence my questioning. I order my questioning in some sections by asking the person here who has least knowledge of the student to contribute first. This avoids the next person questioned having to say they have nothing more to add because it has all been said. It increases the likelihood of obtaining information that might not get presented if we asked those who know most about the student to give their opinions and views first.

Now the BCRS lead worker sets about asking questions to solicit answers to each question, moving from left to right across the template (Appendix 1) and from the top line down to the second; for example, beginning with a question about the 'Behaviour of concern', on to 'Antecedents', and through to 'What works best'. Other information of importance that does not neatly fit into any of the preceding categories is recorded in the section headed 'Notes'.

There are times when a staff member has to be reminded of the protocol around brevity and 'putting into a nutshell' their response without elaborating upon it. Being reflective and then precisely and concisely responding to each question is no easy task, especially given that our meeting is often the first time all those present have had the opportunity to sit together and discuss a student whose behaviour is now presenting them with a serious challenge. Naturally there is a desire to 'download' personal thoughts, issues and wants at these times, and this has to be pre-empted by the BCRS lead worker so that these matters are acknowledged while not side-tracking all present from the task we are gathered for. Most staff members quickly demonstrate a remarkable talent for getting to the very nub of the matter under discussion when the conditions outlined above are placed upon them. Most importantly, this approach counteracts long monologues from any given staff member with the accompanying 'focus drift' it generates in their peers, and thus facilitates the achievement of our goal to conclude the meeting with a workable interim management plan.

While the gathering of information proceeds in the manner described above, there is frequently information provided by those present which is best recorded under a section other than that being addressed at the time. There is flexibility, so the process is fluid and expedient in order not to overlook recording other important information from the participants.

Intervention plan: moving forward

Before describing this phase of the meeting in detail, look at Appendix 2. You will note that while there are a number of 'thoughts' or suggestions recorded in the section headed, 'Intervention planning—moving forward', there is little detail associated with each entry. There are two reasons for this.

- The 'thoughts' and ideas most often relate to what school staff are familiar with and using with other students in the school. There is therefore common understanding among those at the meeting about these matters—what they look like and how they are implemented. A brief comment is all that is needed to bring to mind much that is already common knowledge and practice for the participants.
- The BCRS lead worker simply does not have the time, nor the space, to record specific details within the timeframe we are working to.

Appendix 2 is in fact a concept design for a management plan, and staff will refer back to it when developing more detailed plans as they move from crisis management towards a more formal and systematised approach to managing the day-to-day care of the student under discussion. A BCRS response is in a sense much like the actions of the fire service responding to a house fire: the blaze is put out and the firemen leave. The householder, however, has much to do as they consult architects, obtain permits from local council officials, settle claims with their insurance agents, engage and liaise with builders, plumbers and electricians, and in time rebuild the family home. Immediate threats to safety and wellbeing have been attended to, but there is still a great deal of work to do to normalise the situation.

In this second phase of the meeting, 'Intervention planning—moving forward', goals are set and strategies to attain them specified. The BCRS lead worker reminds those present of how much time we have to devote to the co-development of this management plan and then begins this process with a script that goes something like this:

> In this part of our meeting we are going to decide on the goals you want to help the student to achieve; we will state what you will do in class and in the playground to facilitate the achievement of those goals, then look at what part parents could be asked to play in helping their child achieve the goals you have set. Consensus on how difficult times will be managed must be reached also, and finally we have to consider what resources are required to carry out this plan.

Eliciting two to four goals is the first task to be undertaken here, and having the most important of these broken down further by looking at 'First steps towards our goal' is a simple way of putting a goal into a more specific statement of desired behaviour and/or an achievable, measurable action.

The section headed 'Managing difficult times' is where the reactive strategies are laid out, and this is often an important matter to deal with early in the process. A crisis event can generate a feeling of helplessness in those who have experienced the event, so making sure there is an agreed plan for dealing with subsequent crises can be very empowering. Knowing you have a planned response for the most difficult of times gives you more confidence to try less 'drastic' approaches first. As a teacher you may remind yourself that "There is a way out of this [crisis] situation, a way to end it, but let's stick on in there and use some of the other strategies I have at hand first."

The focus now shifts to identifying what strategies there are within the school's general student management approach and the teacher's personal classroom management style that could usefully be applied to achieving the agreed goals for the student. Additional strategies may well need to be considered, because in extraordinary times extraordinary measures are called for. To that end this is a point in the meeting where people may need to 'step out of the box' to reflect upon their long and varied experiences, to draw on what they have read and heard from colleagues that may be of value in this current set of circumstances. The BCRS lead worker has much to offer in this discussion and reflection. His/her experiences in other such meetings, his/her knowledge and his/her professional training are drawn upon to present other perspectives and options for consideration.

Strategies agreed upon by staff participating in the meeting should be guided by the following three principles; the strategies should:

- be compatible with school-wide and classroom management practices
- match the student's needs and capabilities
- be manageable for all concerned.

Knowing whether or not your intervention is having the desired effect is important, so agreement on a recording system is necessary. BCRS lead workers have examples that other teachers have used and recommended as being time efficient and user friendly, collating sufficient detail to draw sound conclusions while using a plan and language that parents can also understand.

The final section of 'Intervention planning—moving forward' has as its focus deciding the resources that will be required to implement the plan. This includes professional input by way of specialist assessments or treatments, and teaching programmes and resources. The former will require a referral being made to an external agency, while the latter calls for the production or gathering of materials to be used when teaching new skills.

Part 3: How we've done

In the 2014 academic year there were 220 requests from educational facilities for BCRS support: 156 (70.9 percent) were accepted and 64 (29.1 percent) were classified as receiving advice and guidance support. The majority of students involved were males (79.1 percent), but the trend of an increasing percentage of females to be involved has continued for a fourth successive year. Table 11.1 gives a breakdown of the ages of the students referred.

Table 11.1: Ages of students referred to the BCRS (2014)

Age	Number of students	Percentage
2	1	0.5
3	2	0.9
4	10	4.5
5	31	14.0
6	19	8.6
7	14	6.4
8	16	7.3
9	16	7.3
10	17	7.7
11	28	12.7
12	23	10.5
13	16	7.3
14	10	4.5
15	5	2.3
16	2	0.9
Not known *	5	2.3
Facility response**	5	2.3
Total	220	100.0

* We were unable to establish the age of the students who received an advice and guidance service, which meant we did not have the opportunity to get the kind of accurate details which a school visit affords.

** No individual student was referred. This facility's concern was of a general nature.

The only limit that in any way relates to the age of a student the BCRS will support is that they be in a registered educational facility with a ceiling of Year 10[5] at the secondary level.

There was a range of inappropriate behaviours identified by the referrers when making a request for BCRS support. We have read through each descriptor provided by these referrers, identified the inappropriate behaviours they reported, and then categorised them under a series of general headings, which we present in Table 11.2.

Table 11.2: Behaviours of concern reported by referrers

Behaviour	Comments
Physical and/or verbal violence	Intimidating peers or staff, assaulting peers, hitting or pushing staff
Non-compliance	Continual disobedience and refusal to comply with school expectations with respect to academic engagement and/or behaviour
Sexualised behaviour	Showing or exposing one's private parts, touching other's private parts, coercing others to engage in inappropriate sexual activity, accessing pornographic sites
Damaging property	Damaging school property or property that belongs to peers
Personal risk	Leaving the classroom or school grounds; climbing trees to a precarious height or getting on top of school buildings
Self-harm	Attempting or threatening to hurt or to kill oneself
Threatening use of a weapon	Bringing a knife or a gun to school to harm another. Using an object such as a weapon to threaten and/or hurt peers

Table 11.3 gives the end-of-year educational placement of students referred to the BCRS in the 2014 academic year.

Table 11.3: End-of-year educational placement of students referred to the BCRS in 2014

Placement	Number	Percentage
Attending the same facility	153	69.5
Attending a different facility	34	15.5
Attending preschool	9	4.1
Left school for other educational opportunities	1	0.5
Not enrolled at a facility	10	4.5
Not known	8	3.6
Facility response	5	2.3
Totals	220	100.0

Follow-up in February 2015 revealed that seven of the ten students not enrolled at a facility had been taken off the roll of that facility due to continuous absence.[6]

We have calculated the number of different educational facilities that have sought support from the BCRS from its inception in 2010 through to the end of the 2014 academic year. This information is presented in Table 11.4.

Table 11.4: Number of different referring facilities, 2010–2014

Facility	Number of facilities	Percentage[7]
Preschool	27	[2.2]
Primary and intermediate	342	[85.3]
Secondary	40	[46.0]
Total facilities	[409]	

By the end of the 2014 academic year just over 2 percent of the region's 1,224 preschools had on at least one occasion sought assistance from the BCRS with the management of one of their students. Of the 401 primary and intermediate schools in the Auckland region, just over 85 percent have now sought such support, as have 46 percent of the region's secondary schools.

Finally, at the end of the 2012 academic year we looked back over the referral data gathered in 2010 and checked it against ENROL[8] to establish whether or not each of the 158 students referred in that year was enrolled in an educational facility. The whereabouts of those students is presented in Table 11.5.

Table 11.5: Educational placement of students referred in 2010 at the end of 2012

Placement	Number	Percentage
Attending the same facility	40	25.3
Natural progression*[9]	30	19.0
Attending a new facility	70	44.3
Gone overseas	3	1.9
Not enrolled at a facility	5	3.2
Not known	10	6.3
Totals	158	100.0

* Natural progression refers to the normal movement of a student from preschool, to primary, then to intermediate, and finally on to secondary

Some 2 to 3 years after they were referred to the BCRS, the vast majority of the students were still attending an educational facility. Over the past 4½ years BCRS personnel have worked with educational facilities to meet the needs of more than 900 students whose behaviour was severely disrupting the routines of a school's day. It continues to amaze us that there are so many people prepared to work so tirelessly to make school a place some of our most troubled young people want to be. What is even more astounding is that we have yet to come across an educational facility where there has been so much as a passing comment given to excluding or expelling a very difficult student. We admire you all, and it has been a pleasure to have been involved in the work you just get on and do every day.

Appendix 1: Data collection notes

Analysis of Behaviour—Looking Back
Behaviour of concern
What the student is doing that is a concern
Peter [Senior teacher: head of department]
Wanting to do what she wants to do when she wants—wants her own way. There is total non-compliance at these times. This creates difficulties for the teacher and disrupts the learning of other children in the classroom.
Sue [Classroom teacher]
Can be very aggressive. Hits, punches other children and adults. Very non-compliant with adult/teacher requests/directives. Not mixing with other students is a worry.
Maria [Teacher aide]
Not able to control her frustrations. Gets very angry. Very non-compliant. In class she does not work with other children. She will take things off other children.
Pauline [Principal}
I agree with what the others have said.
Non-compliance. Aggression at school—I think she might be aggressive at home too. Safety is a big worry because she runs away and doesn't seem to show fear for her own safety. There is verbal and physical aggression. Other children have been threatened by her ... and staff too.
Getting her into class when the bell goes is problematic.
Spending more time out of class than in class.

Chapter 11 The Ministry of Education's Behaviour Crisis Response Service: Helping educational facilities to manage crisis situations and keep students engaged in learning

Antecedents

What triggers the behaviour?

Peter

There are days when she is good and days when she is not. A teacher asking her to do something can be a trigger. There are times when she arrives at class wound up: a school or a home issue?

Sue

She arrives at school wound up: is it school or has something happened before she gets to school?

She reacts when you ask her to do something she has decided she doesn't want to do.

Other children close by or moving around a lot.

Not being first—first in line. Not being picked for something.

Maria

When she was not well things seemed to be worse.

She gets upset when other children do not agree with her or do what she wants then to do.

Doesn't like it when others who have a 'sense of justice' say what they think about what she is doing.

If someone doesn't want to play or share.

Pauline

When her 'personal space' is crowded.

When asked to share—she likes to keep things to herself.

Becomes oppositional if you ask her to do anything in a direct way.

Where the behaviour occurs

In the classroom and in the playground.

Consequences

How the student's inappropriate behaviour is responded to by staff

Not attending school each day or for a full day yet. On the 3 days a week she is attending school she remains for 1 to 2 hours a day.

A teacher aide (TA) is assigned to be with her throughout her attendance at school. One approach used by the TA to avoid defiance within the classroom when a task has been assigned is to use distraction.

It has been found that giving a choice by saying, "Do X and then you can do Y", has not been effective.

She will leave the classroom and go to the library to get away from others. Reduce stress? Avoidance of work? A combination?

Hypothesis or our theories
Thoughts on what the student is trying to achieve with this behaviour
Peter
I think there has been some trauma in her past and she has not recovered from it.
Sue
She is very anxious—there is a very high level of anxiety. I think she is a girl who has been traumatised.
Maria
I think she has great difficulty in making friends and forming social bonds with other people.
Pauline
It seems that her caregiver is central to her world, and if that person is not with her or nearby then she seems upset.
There is a mental health agency diagnosis of post-traumatic stress disorder.
What works best or exceptions
Times when the behaviour has been successfully dealt with
Times when the behaviour does not occur
Peter
OK with me when we are doing physical exercise. [Is it the person or the activity?]
Sue
What works changes—something will work once or one day but there is no consistence or predictability to it.
1:1 with an adult is something she really likes and is on-task with.
Maria
Knowing how much you can 'push' is important. You have to make new judgements on this on the run ..... it changes from moment to moment.
Moving other children away or her away from other children. Giving her space ..... she will tell me she wants to be on her own.
Pauline
She loves attention.

Notes
Agencies that have been engaged to support the student MOE Behaviour CYF CAMHS Police
Not sure that Child Youth and Family have been involved in the past when she may have been a witness to trauma.
There is an Individualised Education Plan. School + Family have met to discuss and review it.
There has been a Strengthening Families meeting this week.
Communicates with others clearly and at an age-appropriate level.
Understanding of language problematic with concern to taking things literally.
Will hide under furniture. Has special interests to the point of developing a fixation. This fixation can be on an object but it may at times be a person.
Will join in with others but likes to have her own way and do her own thing rather than taking cues from what others are doing and fitting in with the group.
While others coming into her 'personal space' upsets her, she will invade their personal space and not notice.
She seems to be very, very focused on something or completely inattentive—no in-between.
When stressed or upset she will become quite rigid; will flap her arms and hands.
Wants to come to school. There is no problem getting her to come each day.

Notes

Each teacher is asked in turn to give in his/her own words their answer to the question under each column heading. When all staff members have done so we move on to the next column across the sheet and down to the next level where the procedure is continued. Each question within the different sections in APPENDIX 1 contains a separate focus and as such the responses given by any staff member to a question in one section may not necessarily relate directly to their response in the preceding section though there will of course be a relationship between the two. Each staff member is responding to the student's behaviour within the context of their own opinion and with the knowledge of what others in the meeting have also put forward.

Appendix 2: Interim management planning notes

Intervention Planning—Moving Forward
Goal(s) for this student
What we want the student to do instead of the inappropriate behaviour
What new skills will be taught + modelled + rehearsed
How the 'reinforcers' of challenging behaviours will be minimised
Extending the time at school—longer hours and more days.
Being in the right place at the right time.
No hitting.
Presence + participation: at school and interacting socially with peers.
The first step towards our goal
Setting the first steps towards our ultimate goal
Stage 1   [now] 3 days a week to break time.
Stage 2   4 days a week to break time
Stage 3   5 days a week to break time
Stage 4   5 days a week as in Stage 3 but spending break time in the playground with peers before leaving
Stage 6   As in Stage 5 but remaining through to lunchtime 1 day a week.
The ideal is to have her at school 5 days a week within a school term.
Classroom
(Get a copy of the school rules + class rules)
Re-teaching + practising class rules
Reinforcing desired behaviours + teaching replacement behaviours
Using 'direct' instructions, requests, directives.
Using repetition—broken record. Short phrases.
Social stories constructed to introduce protocols and expectations around what happens in a classroom (e.g. what adults do and what children do).
Visual timetable—each day she will assemble this with the TA, who will explain what is going to be happening in the day and what she will be doing.
Produce a short script setting out the school rules—limit to four. Relate to our goals for her.
Sitting with one or two specified peers in a work setting.

Playground + school wide
Playing in restricted areas
Supervision + teaching new skills
Identify a place in the playground as a 'safe place': somewhere she can go where she is within school boundaries,' viewable' to staff and where she feels safe.
A TA focus in break time is to facilitate positive peer interactions—coach resolving 'disagreements' (i.e. not always getting her way).
Monitoring
Record 2 weeks of data
Use *goal card*. (BCRS lead worker to send template to school.)
Keeping track of the achievement of set goals on a period-by-period, day-by-day, week-by-week basis.
Behaviours recorded are:
being in the right place at the right time + keeping hands and feet to self—no hitting
2 points: No instance of not achieving goal
1 point: One instance of not achieving goal
0 points: More than one instance of not achieving goal
Home + community
Soliciting the support of parents and their roles
Share with caregivers the goals, strategies discussed to achieve them, and the role they can play in achieving the goals.
Send goal card home at the end of the week. Parents return with comment (email to parents).
Set up a time to review progress with family.
Resources
What support will be enlisted and how it will help
Paediatric appointment through family GP.
Social stories (send sample to school for adaptation)
Make a small booklet with scripts on the expectations, rules and routines associated with school. She could be a central character in the 'stories' as in a social stories approach.
Referral to Ministry of Education for ongoing support from a psychologist. (Email contact of service manager provided along with a referral form.)
The ECLIPSE model. Sherry Moyer. (Lend copy to school. Include recommendations on units to use.)
Ministry of Education booklet provided: *Autism Spectrum Disorder: A Resource for Educators* (June 2012)
Send school copy of *meet + greet* protocol to guide them in setting X up for a successful day.

> **Managing really difficult times**
>
> *Level 1: regular teacher management; Level 2: personalised teacher management; Level 3: formalised management: teacher + senior teacher; Level 4: teacher + senior teacher + principal*
>
> Misbehaviour to be dealt with when she has calmed down. Say what she did, how it affected the other person; specify what we do/don't do.
>
> Level 1: Told what the rules are (four rules to be written—related to our goals; e.g. "X is in the right place at the right time." "X does not hit, punch, push, kick or hurt other people.")
>
> Level 2: Daily reminders and practice. This takes place on arrival at school and at regular, scheduled times through the day. Positive comments when behaving as expected.
>
> Parent to have copy of the rules and can remind her of the school rules before leaving for school each morning. The same rules might be used at home too.
>
> Level 3: Use the *thinking spot* that is in the classroom.
>
> Level 4: Senior teacher involved. Parents informed. Meeting involving school and family.

Principle 1: Establish a safe learning environment for all: the school's behaviour management policy.

Principle 2: Communicate and enact clear, appropriate and consistent expectations and consequences through implementation of the school's behaviour management policy: school and classroom rules.

Principle 3: Teach, model and practise new skills for appropriate behaviour.

Notes

1 Ministry of Education. (2011). *Positive Behaviour For Learning Action Plan*. Wellington: Author, p 4.

2 All figures provided by the Ministry of Education are current for the start of March 2014.

3 A completed example is shown in Appendices 1 and 2. These are elaborated on in Part 2 of this document.

4 Some of the information, along with the names and other identifying information, have been changed to ensure anonymity for the individual and the institution involved.

5 New Zealand educational facilities are funded to self-provide services for students in Year 11 and above.

6 When a student is absent for 20 consecutive days without a reasonable explanation, the educational facility he/she is enrolled in has to take that student off their roll and notify the Ministry of Education of the student's non-attendance so that it can be followed up on.

7 This is the percentage of the total of THAT TYPE of facility in the Northern Region. 1 224 Preschools, 401 Primary/ Intermediate Schools 87 Secondary School

8 ENROL is the Ministry of Education's national database of a student's enrolment status.

9 Natural progression refers to the normal movement of a student from preschool, to primary, then to intermediate, and finally on to secondary.

Chapter 12 Narrative therapy as a guide for responding to unacceptable actions

Donald McMennamin

Key points

1. Unacceptable actions at school can be seen as a young person's attempts to achieve something, and/or a young person's understanding and expression of 'how one ought to act round here'.
2. These attempts and expressions flow from a young person's storied sense of self—their identity stories.
3. Developing alternative identity stories can significantly change the way a young person acts at school, including making restoration for harms done.
4. Developing alternative identity stories is a social achievement requiring the support of key people in a young person's life over time.

Introduction

Young people's actions at school can be seen as an expression of the storied identities that shape both their sense of who they are and guide how they feel they ought to act. In response to unacceptable actions, the practice of re-authoring young people's identity stories allows alternative life stories and ethical hopes for life to be explored and taken up. In order to respond effectively to identity stories and the sometimes unacceptable actions that flow from them, it is necessary to include young people's significant peers, teachers, and family and community members in a process of re-authoring. This chapter outlines a theory and practice of re-authoring identity stories.

In her exploration of students' experience of being stood down from school, Towl (2014) writes of seven students whose "narratives revealed that the stand-down was a consequence of their unsuccessful strategies to resolve the isolation that put them at risk of being bullied" (p. 3). Towl goes on to note that "the students in the study were making rational, albeit unacceptable, decisions about keeping themselves safe and resolving isolation through managing friendships" (p. 4). In this chapter I develop this theme to propose that young people's actions—in school and in communities—can be usefully thought of either as an expression of a desire to improve their situation in some way (action as intent or desire to achieve something), or as an expression of a young person's understanding of how their sort of person ought to act in these sorts of situations (action as an expression of identity stories). I propose that in exploring the hopes and intentions implicit in young people's actions (rather than focusing initially on their unsuccessful strategies for expressing such hopes and intentions), and developing alternative identity stories in keeping with young people's hopes and intentions, schools and community workers can make a significant difference to young people's actions as these young people are invited to develop and enact new and preferred identity stories.

I further propose that the identity stories that emerge from such inquiries must be enriched, confirmed, supported and maintained as much as possible by networks of relationships at school, at home, and within the community. As such, it is important that appropriate teachers, peers, family and community members are invited to co-develop and support preferred identity accounts with young people over time.

At those times when unacceptable actions at school or in the community lead to suspension or exclusion (or other punitive measures) being considered, I suggest that workers ask a series of questions, including: 'What might these unacceptable actions be in response to?', 'What might the young person be hoping for or trying to achieve in these unacceptable actions?', 'What do these hopes and intentions suggest about this young person's aims in life?', 'What do they say about the sort of person this young person hopes to be?', 'Does this young person have alternative reputations in other times and places—school, home, community—which fit with or complement their hopes and intentions, implicit in their (unacceptable) actions at school or in community?', 'Where appropriate, how might those alternative reputations be made more visible and available?', and 'How might support people recruit significant people (at school, at home, and in the community) to support a young person in developing, taking up and enacting different and preferred identity stories?'

In this chapter I demonstrate one such inquiry (see also McMenamin, 2014) through a process of re-authoring identity stories with Peter, a young person at risk of suspension or exclusion from school for "continual disobedience".

Peter's new stories

Peter was a 14-year-old Pākehā boy from a 1,200-pupil, multicultural, co-ed state secondary school in New Zealand. In response to his unacceptable actions at school, Peter had been spoken with, sent out of classes, removed from and changed all his classes and referred to deans and the counsellor. He had had letters sent home, and had been stood down from school for several days a number of times. I describe here an exploration of alternative identity stories which made a difference to how Peter understood himself, and to his subsequent actions at school.

My aim with Peter was to develop alternative accounts of his identity through stories about what he cares for and how he prefers to live his life. We would do this through exploring the effects of his current actions and reputations, and through exploring alternative reputations he might have, both at school and in other settings. If together we could re-author Peter's sense of self, his subsequent actions might reflect those preferred stories rather than the stories of 'troubled and troubling', which dominated at school at this time.

As we spoke over a period of weeks, accounts of Peter as being able to decide, as caring for children, and as being reliable and honest emerged in response to my questions and Peter's reflections. In the light of these identity stories, Peter saw himself as capable of acting differently at school, and wanting to do so. Previous to these counselling conversations these identity conclusions were available but had not been foregrounded sufficiently to influence Peter's actions at school. The work I describe here foregrounds alternative ways Peter might be known, and Peter reflects about whether those alternative ways of knowing him fitted with his hopes for himself and his future.

In offering these brief extracts from our counselling conversations—two concentrating on troubled stories and six concentrating on emerging preferred stories—my purpose is to show how practices of narrative therapy, such as externalising the problem and storying alternative descriptions of Peter's hopes for himself and others (White, 2007), make available different ways for Peter to think and speak about himself. I demonstrate how, as alternative descriptions are invoked, new possibilities for Peter to know himself emerge, allowing for different ways of acting to become available.

First extract: Externalising troubling reputation

Before beginning to explore the various influences that might be shaping Peter's actions, and before looking more widely within his life experience for alternative ways of speaking about him, guided by narrative therapy's Statement of Position Map One (White, 2007), in this extract I propose to Peter that he has reputations in the school that affect the way his actions become interpreted by others. I then interview Peter in front of three peers chosen by him as supporters, exploring the role and effect of prevailing reputations in his life.

I invite the reader to notice how we speak of Peter's reputation as a separate entity whose effects can be seen and reviewed. This externalising of reputation and its effects reflects a central narrative therapy understanding that the problem is the problem; the person is not the problem (White, 2007). Such a separation of the person and the problem positions Peter as an observer and critic of his reputation at school and its effects in his life. This separation represents a first step towards Peter declaring he would prefer things to be different.

This first extract is part of a counselling conversation in which I asked Peter why he thought his school dean referred him to me, as a school guidance counsellor, for discussions about his behaviour at school.

Peter: Ah, some classes I don't like so I tend to play up.

Donald: Oh yeah?

Peter: Like, I just can't help it [lost words] pencils and I bang them around and stuff. And like, I don't know, I just want to get teachers angry sometimes.

Donald: Do you?

Peter: Yeah, I just want to push their limit. I don't know why, but...

Donald: Yeah? How do you push their limit?

Peter: Yeah just like, I don't know, they just seem to like, you know how I told you about that reputation?

Donald: Yeah, tell me about that.

Peter: Some people don't even give me a chance. They just, 'He won't even be good. We will just kick him out of this class.' Like drama. I didn't like drama, so I was playing up and stuff, and I wanted to go to another class. There was a teacher that I didn't even know. I hadn't seen her or whatever. It was sport science. I hadn't even met her, or spoke to her or anything, and she said, 'No.' Because she has heard about me: the reputation!

Donald: So one of the effects your reputation has in school is that teachers don't even want you in classes. Is that true?

Peter: Yeah, they don't even give me a chance, because what if I want to be good in that class? Maybe it's because I don't like drama, but if I get put into something I do like I will be good. But they don't even give me a chance.

Donald: Yeah. So when that reputation, that idea of reputation … what sort of reputation do you have about the place?

Peter: Like my reputation?

Donald: Yeah

Peter: I think my reputation is quite bad because last year I was, like, pretty bad.

In this extract I seek to separate Peter's identity from that of his reputation. I use the externalising language of narrative therapy to speak of Peter's reputation as separate from him. From this stance Peter can reflect on the effects of the reputation he has due to the actions he has taken. In this 'observer and critic of reputation' conversation, Peter can speak of his knowledge of the effects of reputation as something apart from himself. It is this separation of his identity from his reputation that begins a process of Peter reviewing that reputation and its effects.

Second extract: Re-telling the troubled reputation to peers

In this extract from a later conversation Peter's three friends join us in conversation as an audience to my interview with Peter about his experience of his school reputation. Here I show how telling and re-telling his stories with peers as an audience develops Peter's school reputation as something external to him and as something having undesired effects. The importance of the peer audience lies in their joining with Peter in his desire to see himself differently. I invite the reader to notice Peter's developing awareness of the effects that his reputation is having in his school life, and as a result, his developing sense of self as an observer and critic of that reputation and its effects.

> Donald: Peter, what sort of reputation did you have when we first started working together?
>
> Peter: Um, I had a bad reputation.
>
> Donald: Yeah?
>
> Peter: Yeah, like, naughty, from last year.
>
> Donald: Did you? From last year. How come from last year?
>
> Peter: Cos I got stood down seven times and that ...
>
> Donald: Yeah, yeah, for what? I know this stuff, but I'm just doing it for these guys.
>
> Peter: For like swearing at teachers, and like, trying to push teachers, and tagging, and that stuff.
>
> Donald: Yeah, and all that stuff. And that reputation came through with you to this year?
>
> Peter: Yep.

Donald: How did that reputation affect you this year?

Peter: Oh, I didn't have much privileges, teachers thought I was like, all naughty as and stuff, so they didn't let me have a real chance.

Donald: They didn't give you a real … ?

Peter: They didn't give me a real chance to start over new…

Donald: And what other things did that reputation do for you around the classroom?

Peter: Everybody wanted me to play up and make them laugh.

Donald: Oh, your mates wanted you to play up and make them laugh … so that reputation had teachers not wanting to give you privileges, and people around you wanting to make you play up and stuff … ?

Peter: Yeah.

Donald: Anything else that reputation was doing for your work at school?

Peter: Ruining my concentration in class and stuff.

Donald: True? And what effect might that have had on the way you were learning in the classroom?

Peter: Like, I would have got sent out a lot.

Donald: Yeah? Did you get sent out a lot?

Peter: Yeah!

Donald: Yeah?

Peter: Out of every class.

Donald: In fact you got sent out of all your classes, eh?

Peter: Mmm, I got sent out of all my classes.

Donald: Into a whole new set of classes.

Peter: Mmm.

Throughout this conversation I am speaking of Peter's reputation as external to him, as something we can name, explore the effects of, and take a stance for or against. My practice invites Peter into an understanding that the problem (named here as reputation) is the problem: he is not the problem. The more clearly the reputation is seen as having undesired effects, the more likely it is that Peter will look for alternative ways of being known and of acting; that is, the more likely it is that he will take up alternative stories about himself as they become available through our explorations. My work here is shaped by the maps of narrative practice drawn from White (2007) and White and Epston (1990), among others, which offer guidelines for exposing the undesired reputation and its effects, as well as an exploration of any preferred reputations and their effects.

Looking for alternative stories

Much of narrative therapy guides counsellors in looking for and expecting to find people "living out their lives according to intentions that they embrace, in pursuit of what they give value to in life" (White, 2007, p. 103). I enter these conversations with Peter (and his peers) assured that, within his actions, there will be evidence of what Peter cares about (his intentions). In the six brief extracts presented in this next section, Peter and I search for alternative reputations that have been either implicit in Peter's stories or waiting to be explored in other areas of his life.

In these extracts I demonstrate how language practices of narrative therapy make alternative descriptions available for Peter; descriptions that are drawn from his real experience and might be preferred by him. Having taken a stance against the effects of his previous reputation, Peter reviews these alternative descriptions. It is within these redescriptions, and in the peer endorsements that follow, that preferred stories about who he is are developed for Peter to consider and take up.

In the first of these six extracts I begin to explore with Peter alternative reputations, starting with a summary of Peter's ability to decide and his desire to learn. Next I explore with Peter alternative descriptions that arise from his community. In the third extract I invite Peter to evaluate these emerging reputations, and in the fourth Peter takes a stand for these emerging reputations. In the next extract Peter outlines some of the effects of the new and preferred reputations. Finally, I interview Peter's peers, with Peter as an audience, for their responses to Peter's tellings of his new and preferred reputations. I invite the reader to notice the way these tellings and re-tellings make Peter's hopes for himself more visible and available to be taken up by Peter.

First extract: A summary of emerging school reputation

In a previous conversation I had asked Peter, "How did you make that change?" He replied, "I don't know. I just decided. I got sick of my old behaviour." Later in that conversation Peter commented, "I think it is just because, you know how I said that I can decide? I think it is commitment, I need to be committed to something and then I can do it."

Following a narrative therapy practice of naming emerging character traits in order to review them (Morgan, 2000), in this interview I asked Peter about the word 'decide' as a possible name for an action he had taken to make a difference for himself. I wondered if we might begin to develop a story of Peter as someone who *can decide*. I went on to explore Peter's desire to learn: is this learning a character trait he would include in his preferred identity accounts? This is an example of Peter and me exploring alternative descriptions and character preferences implicit within Peter's actions. The conversation continued as follows:

> Donald: So in the middle of all this I'm hearing you say two things: one is you can, if people speak to you properly, you can decide to just do things differently...
>
> Peter: Yeah, get respect back from the teacher.
>
> Donald: So that is the first thing: you can just decide. That's the first thing right? And the second thing is—forgive me if I have got this wrong—it sounds like you are quite interested in learning stuff?
>
> Peter: Yeah, most of the time. But it depends like the teacher, because last year Miss W., like she is such a cool teacher and I love English, and this year I absolutely hate English. I look at my timetable and I would be like, 'Oh yeah, I got English first' and then like. ..
>
> Donald: But apart from teachers and all that sort of stuff, are you quite interested in learning stuff?
>
> Peter: Yeah.
>
> Donald: Can you say something about why?

> Peter: It's just good cos, like, you know something, right, and then next lesson you can just write it down, just be like, do the work. And sometimes I like producing, like, neat work and stuff.
>
> Donald: Do you?
>
> Peter: Yeah.

In this extract, in response to an enquiry that focuses on potential alternative descriptions, Peter begins to make preferred identity claims: *I can decide, I like producing neat work*. These self-descriptions are spoken in Peter's own words and reflect his hopes for himself. From here it begins to be possible to invite Peter to choose these emerging descriptions as potential guides for future actions at school. As I highlight below, such emerging identity claims require the involvement and support of significant community members.

In the next extract, guided by my interest in how people in his community might describe him, Peter describes further possible identity claims.

Second extract: Community-based reputations

In this interview Peter has been answering my questions about how the mother of his friend, Tama, would describe him. He has also described how a local internet cafe owner hired him to deliver pamphlets for the business. I highlight here that implicit within an account of Peter being hired to deliver pamphlets is the possibility that others may see him as reliable, as honest, as a worker. The transcript begins with me recalling what Tama's mother had previously said about Peter, and how a local internet cafe owner had employed Peter to deliver pamphlets.

> Donald: So can you see what we are doing here, like, together we are working out a different kind of reputation for you! So far we have seen that Tama's mum speaks about you in ways that are cool as, like good, you know, 'I like this guy.' And Nick [the internet cafe owner] has trusted you with this whole thing, and paid you for this whole job, even though, you know, some guys would just chuck it [the pamphlets] off a bridge; but he knows something about … does he know that you are honest or reliable, or some sort of words like that? Or nah?
>
> Peter: Oh yeah, he does. Because one time I was at the internet cafe,

and he gave me more money than he should have given me, and I was like, 'Oh bro. Look, you gave me about $2.50 extra.' He was like, 'Oh. OK. I will just take that back.'

Here a tentatively offered description of Peter as "honest or reliable" is taken up by Peter and further developed with an example of honesty in action, shaping an emerging description of Peter as an honest and reliable person. I emphasise here that this is not simply semantics: Peter's sense of identity is being re-shaped within these re-descriptions. I propose that the actions Peter takes in response to such emerging descriptions are likely to be very different to those actions shaped by his previous school-based reputations.

In the next extract I invite Peter to evaluate the emerging identity claims he has made thus far. Not surprisingly, Peter takes up these preferred descriptions with some enthusiasm.

Third extract: Evaluating emerging reputations

Within practices of narrative therapy it is important that the emerging stories told about Peter are ones that fit with his preferred sense of self. Just as Peter was active in evaluating and rejecting earlier reputations, here he is invited to evaluate emerging new descriptions. As an active observer and critic of these emerging accounts, Peter enthusiastically takes up the alternative versions. Here, rather than being described by others, Peter is positioned as author of his own identity claims.

> Donald: So how is it going for you, in the sense of this idea of we can tell a different story about you, Peter? How is it fitting? What are you hearing about yourself? What have we been talking about so far?
>
> Peter: Good things. I realised that I can be good if I were to be committed, and get a good reputation, and like eyeing up, decide what ... things now for my future ... all those reasons.
>
> Donald: You are hearing all that stuff, eh? See all that stuff there? [Shows notes collected earlier of various affirming things people have recently said about Peter.] What sort of a guy, what name would you give to a person who has all that stuff going on for them? How would you describe a person like that?
>
> Peter: Happy ... on to it.

Donald: On to it! Happy ... on to it!

Peter: If I was all those things, all those things all the time. Oh, maybe not occasionally ... even if I be myself, I would be a good person I reckon.

Here I ask Peter to evaluate the explorations of stories from different parts of his life. Peter is positioned as editor of the emerging accounts of his identity, and describes such a person as "Happy ... on to it"—"I would be a good person I reckon."

Fourth extract: Continuing to take a stand on new reputations

In the previous extract Peter expresses liking what is being said about him, and he begins to describe a future living that way. In the next extract Peter expands on the effects of a new reputation, and together we reflect on how he has made such a shift in reputation. In response to my questions, Peter talks about how new reputations are making a difference for him, and that he prefers these reputations. My use of preferred descriptions makes them increasingly available for Peter to take up.

Donald: When you think about that reputation, what do you think about it now? What, are you for it, or ... ?

Peter: It's changed a lot I reckon.

Donald: Yeah? How has it changed?

Peter: I've been getting A's, and House Cards and stuff.

Donald: OK.

Peter: And like, it's fun being good, cause you get privileges, and you can still play up a little bit.

Donald: You play up a little bit?

Peter: And still get A's!

Donald: And still get A's!

Peter: Mmm.

Donald: So you found the balance between good reputation and a bit of fun?

Peter: Yeah.

Donald: How did you make that change—from one to the other?

Peter: I don't know—I just decided—cos I was sick of my old behaviour.

Donald: How come did you decide?

Peter: Because I felt like it.

Donald: Yeah?

Peter: And I had consequences if I didn't.

Donald: Yeah—you saw those consequences. What consequences were they man?

Peter: Um, going to [another local school].

Here Peter re-uses an earlier description of himself as "a person who can decide." That description, previously tentatively offered and taken up by Peter, appears here as an established part of his preferred self-description. Although I did not pick up on it in this interview, implicit in Peter's account is an ability to weigh up consequences and make decisions. In keeping with a re-authoring project, such a description of Peter as someone who can weigh up consequences and make decisions could be offered tentatively and, if taken up, explored for other times when it had been of use to Peter, and for what it might say about what Peter holds to be important. Through the practices of telling and re-telling of these accounts, Peter is able to hear, evaluate and take a position on these new ways of describing him.

Fifth extract: Reflecting on differences noticed

In this extract I discuss with Peter the effects of his new ways of being described and add yet more vocabulary to the descriptions available. Peter reports that his new reputation has preferred effects in the present, and it appears it may have preferred effects in the future as well.

Donald: So, have you noticed any difference since you have been bringing this new reputation to school?

Peter: Yep.

Donald: What difference have you noticed?

Peter: Like that I'm good and stuff, and that I get House Cards and get privileges.

Donald: And I know it's kind of an obvious question, but what difference do you think it might make to your exam results at the end of the year?

Peter: Quite good, cos I am learning more and I'm enjoying it. I'm learning more.

In this extract Peter and I have grown his preferred account to include future possibilities, and Peter has again evaluated those possibilities as positive. Through these carefully layered enquiries a vocabulary for a re-description of Peter has become available through which to make sense of himself. As we shall see in the extract to follow, significant others are invited to join Peter in these preferred vocabularies and to add their own descriptions to a growing pool from which Peter's alternative identity stories can be written.

An originator of narrative therapy, Michael White (1995) writes that "if the stories we have about lives are negotiated and distributed within communities of persons, then it makes a great deal of sense to engage communities of persons in the negotiation of identity" (p. 26). Throughout this re-authoring project, the ongoing re-storying of Peter's identity is first negotiated with Peter, then with his peers, and subsequently with his teachers and family. In this way Peter is supported throughout this work by those who are an audience to his actions. In this way, too, these people are recruited into the description-of-self language that Peter prefers, further supporting the presence of the preferred identities.

In this final extract I invite Peter's three peers to respond to what they have heard of Peter's account. When I invoke an audience of teachers through the written comments they had provided in response to my request, Peter responds with delight. My purpose in including this extract is to yet again demonstrate the emergence of preferred identity stories, this time through the eyes of his peers and teachers.

Sixth extract: Peers' response

After several weeks of meeting together and exploring Peter's preferred accounts, I interviewed Peter again in front of his peers and invited them to respond. In the following transcript, Peter's peers, Andrew and Tama, make comments, while Jason has nothing to add at this point. I ask Peter to evaluate what he has heard, and he responds.

Donald: You three—what did you just hear about Peter?

Andrew: He has a good reputation in class.

Tama: He's been concentrating a lot.

Donald: He has been concentrating a lot. [To Jason] Did you hear anything in there, man? What did you hear what I was reading out to Peter?

Jason: He was …

Donald: Oh, sorry man—I didn't mean to put you on the spot—you might see something as we go along … So this guy has improved over the last week. Is that true, or not true?

Peter [calls out]: Yeah!

Tama [joking]: Mmm … not really sure about that … Mmm.

Donald: So how does it fit for you—being the guy who's improved in the last week?

Peter: Awesome!

Donald: Yeah?

Peter: It feels good.

Donald [shows Peter the paper with the teachers' names and comments recorded]: See all these teachers? Every single one of them said some stuff about you that was sweet.

Peter [singing]: I feel good!

Peter is clearly delighted with the descriptions he is hearing. The rich language that has emerged over the weeks from Peter's own tellings, and those of his peers and teachers, has developed an account of Peter that he prefers.

In these extracts I have shown how language developed through explorations of Peter's intentions and alternative reputations can provide new descriptions. These new identities describe Peter as a reliable worker, a determined student, a valued cousin and an interested learner. In the presence of these new possibilities Peter hears and evaluates what is being said about him, takes up a preferred stance and begins to act differently at school.

Practices of narrative therapy

Within narrative therapy, the premise "The problem is the problem; the person is not the problem" (White, 2007) is a central tenet. This stance emphasises problems as being external to a person, leading to conversations about people's relationships with the problems that beset them and their preferred directions in life. Conversations that seek to expose the effects of the problem, and the ways it works in a person's life, are central to this way of working (Morgan, 2000; White, 2007; White & Epston, 1990). Such externalising practices are seen throughout my conversations with Peter in sentences such as, "This idea of trouble; that reputation came through with you to this year?", "What other things did that reputation do for you around the classroom?", and "Anything else that reputation was doing for your work at school?"

In this context, the language separates Peter from the reputation he is known by, positioning him as an observer of his own actions and their effects. In this conversation the effects of his school reputations no longer contribute to Peter's character—Peter can decide to what extent he wants to align himself, and the ways he is known, with these reputations.

Also within narrative therapy is the idea that identities can be developed through exploring alternative stories. Here, stories of identity move from familiar accounts of life to the "not yet known, but possible to know" (White, 2007, p. 276) accounts of preferred identity. This idea shapes much of the conversation above; for example: "So can you see what we are doing here, like together we are working out a different kind of reputation for you!" and "Forgive me if I have got this wrong, it sounds like you are quite interested in learning stuff? How is it going for you in the sense of this idea of we can tell a different story about you, Peter?"

In narrative therapy terms, Peter's sense of self is shaped by the ways he is described. Through my questions, which focus on alternative and preferred descriptions, Peter has access to more choice about how he wants to be described and act in the world. Through the externalising of his previous reputation and its effects, and an exploration of the many alternative descriptions implicit within his actions and offered by significant others, Peter is able to review how he is described and re-author his preferred identity claims, and to evaluate these claims. As such, Peter exercises ethical agency, which is the hoped-for outcome of these practices.

In response to these enquiries, Peter makes a number of identity claims: "I was sick of my old behaviour"; "[I am] polite and stuff, funny, good to get along with"; "I'm good and stuff"; "I am learning more and I'm enjoying it"; and "I feel good!" These identity claims have become available to Peter through explorations into his hopes and intentions, and into other places and relationships where he may be known differently, and through paying attention to Peter's small claims, thus adding to their credence. In light of these preferred identity claims, Peter is less likely to act in ways contrary to the school's hopes for him, and as a result, suspension, exclusion or referral to an alternative education site become less likely.

Gathering the community

Although not recorded in this chapter, during the weeks of our meeting together to explore alternative descriptions of Peter and his actions, Peter's peers, teachers and family had been reported to and invited to contribute to Peter's developing accounts through conversations and emails, and through listening to Peter's stories. In consultation with Peter I invited his supporters—peers, teachers and family—to a gathering to further tell and re-tell his preferred identity stories which had emerged. In the final section I present a letter I sent to the participants of that gathering. This letter served as a record of the event, as well as yet another telling of the shared identity project.

Dear all,

Thank you again for the support you show for Peter in stepping into a new reputation at school. While for us all it is only ever an 'on the way' report, what we heard on Tuesday seemed to most of us to be a pretty good step in the right direction!

Chapter 12 Narrative therapy as a guide for responding to unacceptable actions

Coming out of a project looking at how schools can respond to young men in ways that avoid exclusion, we have all been working in our own ways to support Peter, and through his story, to support others in getting the most out of these years at school.

As we heard, Peter was heading for Alternative Education, or a course, or looking for another school. Now he's saying that he gets second chances, privileges, rewards, trust, good attention, food, house cards, and compliments.

To achieve this, Peter decided to get things better for himself at school. He did this by deliberately bringing his out-of-school reputation for reliability, kindness, good work etc. into school.

But he could not do that on his own, because old reputations stick quite closely. To make the change he had some very real help.

- Mr Mac helped clarify his preferred reputation.
- Tama, Andrew and Jason supported Peter by being there with him, and adding ideas.
- Peter's teachers knew of his efforts and supported them by noticing them, and by acknowledging them with attention and rewards.
- Peter's Dad has always and continues to lead Peter and support him with trust and encouragement.
- Huia and Brent from another school supported Peter with their keen interest in his story.

I know too that D, the RTLB,[1] has supported Peter and his teachers. And I know that Mr B, Mr S, and others have supported Peter with clear guidelines and consequences.

Here are some quotes from Tuesday's meeting:

Peter:

> I don't have to be bad.
>
> Instead of getting bad attention I can get good attention.
>
> Ms B said I am becoming one of her top students and I can get into good classes in the future.

The friends said:

> It was a bit of a surprise because he had a bad reputation, but now he thinks about his consequences.
>
> He used to get E's in class and now the blue book is filled with A's. [Teachers record daily in the 'blue book' with grades for behaviour, attendance and so on.]
>
> He didn't used to be like that!

And the teachers said:

> He's been paying more attention to what you say; he's listening, taking what you say and using it.
>
> In PE, and from a dean's perspective, the switch has been a major one. His manners, his ability to be attentive, doing what is asked of him, offering to help; there's high energy and positive energy. I've seen a major shift. There is more of an ability to reason with Peter. He will listen and try and change things. It's a lot nicer because it's not negative, so much nicer.
>
> Peter is more open to my ideas, he's listening a lot better. Success is coming from wanting to learn. I've noticed Peter doing better, and the work he is doing.
>
> I've seen a big change after the first two days where he had to be removed, then, when he came back, he didn't do that stuff again. In the last 3 weeks I've noticed a real improvement, a huge difference. It makes me want to pay more attention to smaller things, because I know he is not playing with mates. He is higher in my attention for help when asked. This is really noticeable.

Peter's father said:

> Getting notes about trouble in school is hard. Without those there is no drama happening. Now he brings his blue book home, and mostly it is all A's! Now there is no need for that terrible feeling of taking away from your child the very things you want to give him—he gets more trust, and I am not needing to restrict him. It's more peaceful!

And in the community? From the other school involved in the doctoral project which gave rise to Peter's story, Huia said that Peter had given her so much hope!

She said, 'I see doors to futures of brilliant young men flying open all over the place!' Huia described the process as simple: 'The most important is about doing the relationship differently, focusing on the small and positive. This has definitely made a difference. There is one boy in particular who is hearing about these things, and now I have more insight into possibilities for him and for others.'

And these stories will be sent out to South Africa, and the people there will respond to what it's like for them to hear it—the echoes bouncing out all over the place!

So it's been great working together on this project. It's only a step along the way, but it's a good step.

A genuine thank you to you all.

Donald

I'll leave the last word to Peter:

> What's it like to hear all this Peter?
>
> "It puts a smile on my face! It's pretty cool! Thanks! And the teachers probably appreciate that I'm not bad in class!"

Conclusion

The process of re-authoring identity stories with young people described here winds through a range of individual and community conversations, all aimed at bringing to light preferred identity conclusions for young people, and enriching those preferred identity conclusions with the contributions and support of people who care for them. Although not linear, a process of re-authoring identity conclusions includes: naming problem reputations and their effects for the young person and others; offering restorative practices, as appropriate; identifying preferred identity claims for those involved; searching for and developing alternative accounts in keeping with preferred identity claims, together with key support people; and circulating preferred identity accounts among a community of support, including efforts to make a difference for others, where appropriate.

In this chapter I have described young people's actions as an expression of the identity stories that shape their sense of who they are, and guide how they feel they ought to act. The practice of re-authoring young people's identity stories as described here allows for alternative life stories to be explored and taken up in ways that change behaviour and reduce the need for responses such as suspension and exclusion to be considered.

References

McMenamin, D. (2014). Supporting reputation and behavior change at school through exploring and retelling preferred identity stories. *Journal of Systemic Therapies, 33*(3), 69–86.

Morgan, A. (2000). *What is narrative therapy?: An easy-to-read introduction.* Adelaide, SA: Dulwich Centre Publications.

Towl, P. (2014). Would the real bully please stand up? *New Zealand Journal of Education Studies, 49,* 2.

White, M. (1995). *Re-authoring lives: Interviews and essays.* Adelaide, SA: Dulwich Centre Publications.

White, M. (2007). *Maps of narrative practice.* New York, NY: Norton.

White, M., & Epston, D. (1990). *Narrative means to therapeutic ends.* New York, NY: Norton.

Note

1 RTLB: resource teacher of learning and behaviour.

Chapter 13 Conclusions

Sheryl Hemphill and Patty Towl

This volume suggests a way forward to reduce the harm of school exclusion in Aotearoa New Zealand and Australia. While it is acknowledged that there is no support in theory and research for school exclusion, the practice is well embedded in Australian and Aotearoa New Zealand schools. School exclusion disproportionately affects vulnerable children from at-risk groups, and there is ample evidence of the negative associations between school exclusion and poor education, health, employment and justice outcomes for young people. It is the obligation, therefore, of those who promote school exclusion as appropriate practice, those who make the decision to exclude and those who encounter the negative outcomes for excluded children, to take responsibility to manage and reduce harm.

The contributors to Part One of this volume asked you to interrogate the policy and practice behind your use of school exclusion. Where does your school sit in an environment where inclusive practices and the child's right to advocacy are paramount in law and policy but often questionable in practice? How do you define and enable inclusion, and what do you really understand by inclusive practices? Part One presents some challenges to current practices for children who are unlikely to fit a narrow definition of educational delivery. Perhaps it is the mode of delivery that needs to change; that is, the practice of setting up provisions designed to fit underserved children as closely as possible to a system that has already excluded them. There was a strong theme in Part One that all those involved in education decision making, especially those relating to exclusion practices, need to listen to the voices of the children and families affected. It is reasonable to assume that through our knowledge and experience we know what is best for children, but through our practices of excluding children—either in or outside school—we not only stigmatise and deny opportunities; we also deny diversity and restrict the possibilities for conversations that will enrich our schools and the educational experiences of all children.

Part Two of this volume provided clear guidance on those factors that resolve exclusion environments to reduce harm and help retain students in mainstream education. The outcomes of even short-term exclusion events may place children in marginalised contexts where they may find themselves either in partial or full withdrawal, or in alternative educational environments both in school and in the community. A dominant theme in Part Two was that children do not choose exclusion pathways unless there is no other viable and safe option.

We have presented a variety of approaches resolving exclusion across a number of different education providers. The common theme to all of these approaches is that each provider made a commitment to inclusion, and that commitment came from within. Each provider had stepped away from current practice, chosen a more diverse pathway, taken the opportunity to educate, and broken the habit of punishing behaviour through exclusion. The positive outcomes for all children were clearly evident.

The common themes to resolving exclusion contexts were robust, inclusive communication, and flexible, multidisciplinary problem-solving approaches. Children in trouble at school are either in crisis or in ongoing trauma, or both. It is essential that plenty of time and resources are allocated at these crisis points to ensure the whole story is told and all options are investigated. Communicating expectations to children was a key element in many chapters. It was clear, too, that expectations are often misinterpreted. Schools could take a first, easy step to resolving and reducing exclusion by interrogating the communications they have with children and their families. The authors in this volume firmly support restorative practices. It was clear that children want to be included and do things right. We strongly support the view that when things go wrong, children must be given the opportunity to put things right. Nor do we believe that there is any point in a child's school career where there is no going back. There was clear evidence in this book that even the most difficult situation has a resolution that retains the child in education.

These children in trouble at school, however, are in crisis and they require more resources at this point in their lives than the majority of children on the school site that day. Some children are in trauma and require ongoing time and resources to help them get their lives in order. The approaches presented in this book are in operation in Aotearoa New Zealand and Australia, so the philosophies, policies and resources already exist in the current environment. Retaining troubled children in school requires multidisciplinary problem solving. The approaches suggested in this book place the child at the centre of resolution. They recognise and account for the multi-faceted nature of marginalisation. These flexible and creative approaches acknowledge, value and take into account cultural and social diversity, physical and intellectual disability, and the overabundance of trauma some children are required to manage in their lives.

To make a start to move away from exclusion and towards inclusion, providers would find it useful to identify the resources already available in their school and community. You could contact the authors in this book, who have provided contact details. Some of the programmes arose from school–researcher partnerships. Making the commitment to include, then working it through a research partnership, could be a positive and financially viable way to include your whole community and address the issues in a robust and reliable way.

Finally, completing our first Aotearoa New Zealand and Australian book on resolving school exclusion has raised more questions than it answered. There are many more conversations that need to be had around what is meant by inclusion and whether inclusive practices are anathema to school safety. Why is it, for example, that there appears to be an increasing trend in excluding very young children from school? We need to look at those exclusion pathways before they become crises. Some children are separated from the rest of the class from the beginning of their school lives. Through kindness, expediency and current practice some children may only be in class with a support person. Isn't this also exclusion, and if the other children see this, will they believe that exclusion is normal? This book, therefore, is only the start of a much bigger conversation about inclusive practices generally.

About the authors

Lyndal Bond PhD is the Principal Research Officer at the Centre of Excellence in Intervention and Prevention Science. Prior to her appointment at CEIPS Lyndal was the Associate Director at the MRC/CSO Social and Public Health Sciences Unit, Glasgow, UK and Honorary Professor in the Faculty of Medicine at the University of Glasgow. While in the UK she led a programme of research evaluating the effects on health of social interventions. Her research interests include understanding the effects of social interventions on health and health inequalities; researching the implementation and sustainability of complex interventions and evaluating the implementation of evidence-based policy into practice. Her work contributes to the development of health and education policy.

David Broderick PhD has held adolescent-focused research positions with the Murdoch Childrens Research Institute, the Centre for Adolescent Health, and Australian Catholic University. These roles involved a wide range of adolescent-focused topics including school behaviour management, school disengagement, and educational policy. David's recent PhD study examined secondary school student's experiences of school suspension and found that stressors in young people's personal lives commonly shaped experiences of school exclusion. Prior to this, David was employed by Berry Street Victoria working with vulnerable young people who were disengaged from schooling.

Maggie Callingham has a particular interest in ways schools can better engage young people who are marginalized in conventional schooling. This is the focus of her current PhD. Maggie has taught in primary, secondary, community, TAFE, and university contexts. She was principal of an independent primary school. Contact: margaret.callingham@live.vu.edu.au

Janis Carroll-Lind PhD. Earlier in her career Dr Janis Carroll-Lind was a Resource Teacher Special Needs and an Adjustment Class Teacher for students with challenging behaviours. She then lectured at Massey University in inclusive education. Her PhD study was on children's experiences of violence at home and at school. Currently Janis is the

Director of Research and Postgraduate Programmes at Te Tari Puna Ora o Aotearoa/New Zealand Childcare Association. Immediately prior to this she was the Principal Advisor (Education) at the Office of the Children's Commissioner. Contact: Janis.Carroll-Lind@nzca.ac.nz

Terry Carter trained as a teacher in the 1960s and taught in regular classes for 8 years before winning the position of Senior Education Officer at Auckland's Maximum Security Prison in 1973. In 1986 Terry worked as a Visiting Teacher for the Ministry of Education and then later as a Special Education Advisor. Terry is a founding member of the Auckland Regional Behaviour Crisis Response Team, having been a member for 5 years.

Tim Corcoran PhD. Prior to the completion of his PhD in 2008, Tim worked for 10 years in the Queensland public sector. For the majority of this period he was employed as the Townsville District Psychologist for the Queensland Department of Education. His academic career has involved posts in Australia, the UK and Singapore. His research involves critical examination of psychology in learning theory; mental health promotion and early intervention in educational settings; and discourse as socio-political practice. Tim is currently a Senior Research Fellow at The Victoria Institute, Victoria University, Melbourne, and is registered to practise as a General Psychologist with the Australian Health Practitioners Regulation Agency. Contact: tim.corcoran@vu.edu.au

Mike Crosby works for New Zealand's Ministry of Education and has been a member of the Ministry's Behaviour Crisis Response Service for the past 3 years. He has spent 60 years in education as a student, teacher, psychologist and education consultant in New Zealand, Australia, Nauru, Brunei, Qatar and the United Arab Emirates. Contact: mike.crosby@minedu.govt.nz

Sarah E Drew PhD is a Senior Research Fellow at the Centre for Adolescent Health, Royal Children's Hospital and the Department of Paediatrics, University of Melbourne. Sarah is a health sociologist with a background in youth studies and holds a PhD in public health. Her research interests focus on the health service and educational support needs of adolescents and young adults living with chronic illnesses, including cancer. She is particularly interested in complex triadic communication challenges relating to young person-parent-practitioner interactions. Her work contributes to policy development and practice change in health care and education. Sarah will be remembered for her energy and commitment to improving outcomes for young people in the healthcare system. Sarah was passionate about providing a voice to participants in her research and drew upon innovative methods, such as photo journals, to capture their unique lived experiences.

Paul Gibson: Disability Rights Commissioner, The Human Rights' Commission NZ Te Kāhui Tika Tangata. Paul Gibson became Commissioner with responsibilities for disability issues in 2011. Paul is a former president of the Disabled People's Assembly and was involved in the development of the United Nations Convention on the Rights of People with Disabilities (UNCRPD). Mr Gibson is partially blind and uses Braille and assistive technology. Paul has 20 years of experience in the health and disability sector including working for Capital Coast District Health Board as a senior disability adviser. Contact: paulg@hrc.co.nz

Assoc Prof Lynn Gillam PhD is the Clinical Ethicist and Academic Director of the Children's Bioethics Centre at the Royal Children's Hospital Melbourne. She is also Associate Professor in Health Ethics at the University of Melbourne, in the Melbourne School of Population and Global Health. Lynn works in clinical ethics case consultation, ethics education, policy advice and research. Her major interests are in ethically appropriate treatment of children and adolescents in health care and education.

Jessica Heerde PhD is a Post-Doctoral Research Associate at Australian Catholic University. Dr. Heerde is conducting her post-doctoral research on the predictors and outcomes of adolescent health and social behaviours, including marginalized adolescents, to inform prevention and intervention programmes leading to improved outcomes for all young people.

Prof Sheryl Hemphill PhD is Professor of Psychology in the Faculty of Health Sciences, Australian Catholic University. Professor Hemphill is also a foundation leader of a research program in ACU's Learning Sciences Institute Australia. She has conducted research on the development and prevention of externalising behaviours including violence, bullying, and antisocial behaviour in young people for over 20 years. Professor Hemphill has also demonstrated the negative impact of punitive school discipline approaches (e.g., school suspension) on student outcomes. She is a member of the Australian Psychological Society's College of Health Psychologists and registered with the Australian Health Practitioner Regulation Agency Psychology Board. Contact: sheryl.hemphill@acu.edu.au

Michelle Kehoe is a PhD student with Australian Catholic University. Her PhD thesis uses a qualitative approach to explore the use of restorative practices in Victorian primary and secondary school from the teacher and student perspective. Michelle has a particular interest in interventions, especially those that aim to increase student well-being, school engagement and reduce any negative impacts which may result from school suspensions or school bullying. Contact: michelle.kehoe@acu.edu.au

Grant Malins is the Auckland Regional Behaviour Services Manager – Positive Behaviour for Learning. He has led the Behaviour Crisis Response Service since its inception in 2010. Grant has worked in education for 15 years delivering behaviour services in a variety of education settings.

Donald McMenamin PhD; MNZAC has worked as a teacher and school guidance counsellor for 20 years in New Zealand high schools. His Masters and PhD theses are focused on restorative practices in schools and approaches to reducing suspensions and exclusions of young people from school. Donald is a counsellor, supervisor and teacher of narrative therapy. Contact: donaldmcm@gmail.com

Katrina Mohamed is a Gooreng Gooreng woman from Bundaberg, Queensland. Katrina worked in the media industry for 15 years as a journalist, newspaper editor and public relations consultant and then began work with the Shepparton Indigenous community in leadership development and community capacity building. In the McAuley-Champagnat Program (MCP) she develops reciprocal partnerships between MCP and community and corporate bodies, including local Indigenous organizations, to create community connectedness and career pathways for our youth.

About the authors

Barbara J. McMorris, PhD is an associate professor in the School of Nursing at the University of Minnesota, United States. She is also the evaluation team leader for the Healthy Youth Development Prevention Research Centre, located in the Department of Paediatrics, which conducts and disseminates community-engaged research that promotes positive youth development and reduces health disparities among young people. Her research focuses on prevention of health risk behaviours among youth, such as substance use, sexual risk-taking, violence, bullying, and school drop-out. From 2001-06, she was project director for the NIH-funded International Youth Development Study, which fielded adaptations of the Communities that Care student survey to almost 6,000 students in Washington State, US and Victoria, Australia.

Kevin Quin is a psychologist who has been employed by the McAuley-Champagnat Program (MCP) since its earliest days. He assesses students at intake and is available for counselling. He provides advice and educational support to teachers and welfare workers. As a member of the program leadership team he assists in policy development and direction in the daily organization of the program. Kevin is currently completing a PhD at Monash University. Contact: kevin.quin1@gmail.com

Alison Sutherland (nee Hartley), PhD, was born into the underclasses to a violent, criminal father and battered mother. She left school at 15, became a solo mother then married into the working classes. With three young children, Alison commenced her journey along an educational pathway, becoming a secondary school teacher and Head of Commerce. Following the completion of a Masters of Education, she accepted a position as teaching Principal of a Youth Justice School for young, violent offenders. Alison went on to complete a PhD in 2006 entitled 'Classroom to Prison Cell: Young Offenders' Perception of Their School Experience'. Keeping her promise to the young participants to share their stories of why they felt alienated from the school life-world, she wrote a book titled 'Classroom to Prison Cell', published in 2007 by Stead & Daughters Ltd. Alison was employed as a Special Education Advisor for the Ministry of Education Hutt/Wairarapa 'Severe Behaviour Team', and up until her recent retirement, worked as a Resource Teacher of Learning & Behaviour for the Wairarapa cluster.

Alongside her husband, Alison is currently working towards saving New Zealand's unique, critically endangered, Arapawa goat. Contact: Alison@xtra.co.nz

Patty Towl PhD is a researcher and writer in the area of school exclusion. She is a former high school principal and special education needs coordinator who specialises in behavioural and learning needs. She has worked across New Zealand in rural and urban schools, in area and full secondary environments and in diverse cultural situations. Patty has also worked as a New Zealand Aid teacher on a remote island in the Cook Islands. Contact: towl@ihug.co.nz

Index

A

Aboriginal communities *see also* Indigenous Australians 38–9
abuse
   physical 118, 120–1
   school policy 119, 129
   of students by teachers 118
academic achievement *see* student achievement
Achenbach, T M *see also* Young Adult Self-Report (YASR); Youth Self-Report (YSR) 74
Achenbach System of Empirically Based Assessments (ASEBA) 74
adolescent mental health issues 79
advocacy 11–12
   cultural 128
   OCC role 16–7
advocacy groups 35
affective language 138–9, 141–2
Afro-American male students, research study 197
alcohol use 58, 122
American Academy of Pediatrics Committee on School Health 98
antisocial behaviour
   IYDS focus on 94
   questioning motivations for 237–8
   and suspension 58–61, 100, 123, 129–30
   young offenders' perceptions of 122
   and zero tolerance policies 123
antisocial peer groups 52, 121
apprenticeships 130
attention deficit hyperactivity disorder (ADHD) 39, 40, 121

Augimeri, Koegl, Levene and Webster 125
Australia *see also* McAuley-Champagnat; McClelland College: International Youth Development Study; Victoria
   disadvantaged children in 200
   Kimberley uprising 38–9
   National Apology *see also* Sorry Day 187
   Stolen Generation 38–9, 188
   suspension statistics 48–9
   zero tolerance policies 92–3
Australian Research Council 66, 92
   Discovery Projects 111
   funding 94
Australian research projects 53–66, 94–111, 136–7, 197–8, 212
Australians, Indigenous *see* Indigenous Australians
Australians, non-Indigenous 188
Australians 'locked up' 39

B

Becoming a Person 33
Becroft, Judge Andrew 22
behaviour, antisocial *see* antisocial behaviour
Behaviour Crisis Response Service (BCRS) 216–8
   data collection notes 229–33
   educational placements of referred students 2014 **228**
   educational placements of students referred 2010 **229**
   inappropriate behaviours referred **228**

interim management planning **233–5**
intervention plan 224–6
process 218–20
referrals by age **227**
referring facilities 2010-2014 **229**
response criteria 217–8
school staff meeting 218–24
statistics 226–30
behaviour management 92–3
   comparative approaches Australia, US, NZ 51–2
   implications from IYDS 62–5
   in-school approach 209–11
   McAuley-Champagnat model 182–3
   preventive approaches 63–5, 93–4
   restorative practices 138–41
   staff perspectives 102–9
      implications 109–11
   strategy planning 225–6
   student perspectives 101
      implications 109–11
   teachers' perceptions 94
   tokens as tools for 126
   and Youth Self Report 82–4
   zero tolerance approach 51–2, 92–3
behaviour management: IYDS sub-study 94–111
behaviour management *see also* Behaviour Crisis Response Service (BCRS); narrative therapy; restorative practices
Bill of Rights Act 1990 156
Bishop and Berryman (2006) 163
boards of trustees 13
   role in school exclusions 2–3, 17–8, 23–6
Booth and Ainscow (2011) 13–4

Brayton Youth and Family Services 176
bullying
   case study 128
   and disabled students 44
   rationalisation for 122
   reactions to 20–1, 20–2
   school climate and 117
   by teachers 128

C

cadetships 130
Canadian research 198
cannabis use 58
Carruthers, Judge David 22
Children, Young Persons and Their Families Act 1989 15
Children's Commissioner see Office of the Children's Commissioner 15
Children's Commissioner's Act 2003 15
cigarettes *see* tobacco
circles in restorative practice 139–41
code of rights (health system) 45
Collaborative Research Networks (CRN) 212
communication
   documentation issues 171
   home-school 170–1
   in restorative practices approach 138–9
   in stand-downs 159–64, 164–7
      case studies 165–7
communication *see also* parents
communities of practice 155–7
   and stand-downs 156–7, 164–5
Communities that Care survey 54
community
   in narrative therapy 245–6, 252–5
   and student engagement 205–8

community and school partnerships 192, 205
  McClelland College case study 206–9
  and student engagement 199
Connect programme 202, 204–5
  behaviour management and 209–10
  case study 204–5, 206–8
connectedness and student engagement **200**, **202**, 206, 208–9, 210–1
control and student engagement **200**, **201**, 205, 208, 210, 244–51
Convention on the Rights of Persons with Disabilities 32, 36, 43
criminal behaviour *see also* young offenders
  risk factors 115, 123–6
Crown Entity Act 2004 15
cultural advocacy 128, 187
culture, Indigenous Australian 187

D

Danziger, K 81–2
decision-making as narrative therapy process 244–5
Department of Education, Youth and Training 176
Department of Human Services 176
detention *see* suspension, internal
Developmental Psychopathology 74
disability
  and academic achievement 121
  cultural perspectives 41
  and human rights 35, 41–2
  intellectual 32–7
  neurodisability and youth offending 43–4
  terminologies 41–2

disability, students with
  barriers for 16–7, 43
  and bullying 44
  exclusion of 20, 41, 43
  and New Zealand Human Rights Commission 43
  rights to education 32, 42–5
  and stand-downs 158
  and zero tolerance policies 161
disability community, perspectives of 41–2, 44
disadvantaged students
  exclusion of 197–8
  and zero tolerance policies 93
discipline and restorative practices 147–8
diversity and inclusion 14, 41–2
documentation issues 171
Drewery, W 71
drug and alcohol use 58, 122, 160
Drugs and Crime Prevention Committee (Victoria) 22
dyslexia 121

E

Early Assessment Risk List (EARL) 125
education, alternative, registered teacher involvement in 14
education, equal opportunity legislation 13
Education Act 1989 2, 2–3, 13, 18, 43, 154
  equal opportunity legislation 13
  exclusion and expulsion legislation 18
Education Amendment Act 2013 13
Education (Stand-Down, Suspension, Exclusion and Expulsion) Rules 1999 22

educational advocacy *see* advocacy
educational disengagement of
 indigenous Australians   177–8
educational failure and youth crime   22
emotions, relational context of   84–5
equal opportunity in education   13
equity
 for disadvantaged students   212
 and exclusion   197–8
ethnicity
 and external suspensions   49–50, 197
 and youth offending   123–4
euthanasia programmes   35
exclusion
 avoidance strategies   129, 209–10
 boards of trustees role   23–6
 definition, legislation   2–3, 17–8
 as discrimination against disabled students   43
 embedded in schools   257
 and equity   197–8
 hidden *see also* 'kiwi suspension'   129
 language of   71–4
 legislation   18, 154
 Ministry of Education role in   24, 26
 Principal's role in   23–5, 26
 as sociopolitical issue   19, 82–4, 197–8
 structural   45–6
 value and meaning of   82–4
 and youth offending   1, 22
exclusion as behaviour management tool   92–3
exclusion guidelines, information sources   18
exclusion *see also* expulsion, stand-downs, suspension

exclusion statistics   3, 19, 48–9, 51
expulsion
 definitions   3, 17–8
 Ministry of Education obligations   26
 Principal's obligations   26
 slowness of process   102
external suspension *see* suspension, external

F
fairness, procedural see also natural justice   23
 grievance process   126
 perceptions of   119–20
family and student engagement   199
family-school relationships   155, 157–62, 160, 164–8, 167
family-school relationships *see also* parents
Fenning and Rose (2007)   197
food provided at school   127, 186, 190–1, 204

G
Garrett, K   212
Garrin Garrin: A Strategy to Improve Learning Outcomes form Aboriginal Victorians   193
gender and external suspensions   49–50
Gilligan, R   205
Grogan et al (2013)   208

H
Handbook of Research on Student Engagement   198
Hands On Learning programme (HOL)   202, 207
harakeke metaphor   32–3

Harvey and Moosha (1977)   51
Hemphill et al (2006)   27
Hemphill et al (2014)   197–8
Hippisley, Jennifer   175
Holdsworth, Roger   213
How Does School Discipline Affect Student Behaviour, Wellbeing and Educational Progress?   92, 94–111
   extent and process of study   95–6
Human Rights Act 1993   13
human rights and education   13
human rights approach to disability   41–2
Human Rights Commission (HRC), complaints to   43

I

identity stories *see* narrative therapy
IHC   35
inclusion
   and at-risk youth offenders   131–2
   definition   13–5
   of disabled students   42–5
   implications for schools   14
   and *New Zealand Curriculum*   13
Inclusion International   35
Indigenous Australian culture   187, 191
   in welfare context   190
Indigenous Australians
   cultural education of   187
   educational disengagement of   177–8
   learning outcome strategies   193
   and McAuley Champagnat Programme   174–94
   National Apology to *see also* Sorry Day   187
   Shepparton population of   177
   Stolen Generation   188

Individual Learning Plan (ILP)   184–5, 204
ineffective teaching and youth offending   117
intellectual disability
   as learning disability   35
   Robert Martin's story   32–7
   and youth offending   44
Interim Response Fund   21
International Youth Development Study (IYDS)   47, 53–65
   behavioural outcomes after suspensions   58–61
      young adult outcomes 2010/11   58
   conclusions   65–6
   findings   57–61
   implications   61–5
   measures used for analyses   55–7
   as overarching study   94
   overview   94–6
   overview, parameters   53–6
International Youth Development Study (IYDS) behaviour management sub-study   94–111
internships   130
"involuntary minority ethnic status"   123–4
   and stand-downs   159

K

Ka Hikitia - Accelerating Success 2013-2017   14
Kimberley psychopaedic hospital   33–4, 45–6
Kimberley South Africa   37–8, 45–6
Kimberley Western Australia   38–9, 45–6
kiwi as metaphor   40
'kiwi suspensions'   19–20, 27

Kratschmar, Gerhardt   35

L
language
  affective   138–9, 141–2
  cultural contexts   162–3
  of exclusion/inclusion   71, 72, 73–4
  of expulsion   102
  psychological   82
  of punitive approaches   102–3
  and values   81
  of zero tolerance   159–61
learning, Wenger's theory of situated   155–7
learning approach, personalised   203–6, **204–5**
'learning' disability   35
learning plan, individual (IPL)   184–5, 204, 205, 208
legislation
  calls for   43
  Children, Young Persons and Their Families Act 1989   15
  Children's Commissioner's Act 2003   15
  Crown Entity Act 2004   15
  Education Act 1989   2–3, 13, 18, 154
  Education Amendment Act 2013   18
  Education Amendment Act 2013   13
  equal opportunities in education   13
  Group Areas Act   3
  Human Rights Act 1993   13
  Ministerial Order 184   3
  natural justice   156

New Zealand Bill of Rights Act 1990   22, 156
  school exclusion   2–3
literacy   130, 181
  punishment and   128
Liu and Lásló (2007)   159
Local Learning and Employment Network (LLEN)   175
'locked up' Australians   39
Lumos charitable organisation   44

M
Mandela, Nelson (Rolihlahla)   38, 46, 163
Manual for the Child Behaviour Checklist and Revised Child Behaviour Profile   74
Māori
  and European cultural contexts   162–3
  marginalisation of   123
  role models   39–40
Māori students
  and exclusion rates   19
  Ministry of Education strategies for   14
  perceptions of racism   120, 163
  and stand-downs   158, 162–3
marginalisation
  approaches to resolving   258–60
  extent and implications   257–8
  of students with disabilities   17
Margrain and Macfarlane (2011)   27
Martin, Robert   32–7, 46
Māui as excluded child   39–40
McAuley Champagnat Programme
  advisory boards   176–7, 194–5
  case study   **179–81**
  community partnerships   195

development of 175–6
food provided 190–1
foundational principles 182–3
health care 192
Indigenous Australian
    culture 187–9
    student numbers 193
Individual Learning Plan (ILP) 184–5
school staff 191–2
structure of 176–7
student transfer process 184
welfare support 189–90
McClelland Academy Programme (MAP) 202, 207–8
McClelland College 213
    open day flyer **203**, 203–4
McClelland College case study 202–13
    community and school partnerships 206–9
    in-school approach to behaviour management 209–11
    overview 202–3
    personalised learning approach 203–6
McCrae, John 33
meaning and student engagement **200**, **201**, 205, 208
Melbourne, Victoria 136–7
Melbourne Declaration of Educational Goals 64
Mendez and Sanders (1981) 51
Ministerial Order 184 (Victoria) 3
Ministerial Taskforce on Youth Offending 22
Ministry of Education NZ
    equal opportunity policies 13
    and hidden exclusions 129
    National Education Goals 13
    Northern Region statistics 218
    programmes 14, 217
    resources for schools *see also* Behaviour Crisis Response Service 21
    role in exclusions 24, 26
    terminology 160
Ministry of Education NZ *see also* Education Act; Education Ammendment Act
Ministry of Education strategies for Māori and Pasifika students 14
mistreatment *see* abuse; bullying; traumatisation
Modes of Belonging diagram **156**
Morrison, Anthony, Storino and Dillon (2001) 51
Muriranga-whenua as role model 40
Myers, K 162

N

narrative therapy
    case study 238–51
    externalising reputation 239–41
    new reputation building 244–51
    re-telling reputation to peers 241–3
    theory and practice 251–2, 255–6
National Certificate of Educational Achievement (NCEA) 127, 130
National Education Goals 13
National Health and Medical Research Council 66
National Institute of Health 66, 111
National Institute on Drug Abuse 66, 111
natural justice 21, 156
    principles of 22–3
    in stand-downs 169–70

Nazi Germany euthanasia programme 35
neurodisability and youth offending 43–4
New Zealand Bill of Rights Act 1990 22, 156
New Zealand Curriculum and inclusion 13
New Zealand Education Act *see* Education Act
New Zealand Human Rights Commission (HRC), complaints to 43
Nobel Peace Prize 46
Notre Dame College, Shepparton Vic 175
numeracy 128, 186
    punishment and 130

O

Office of the Children's Commissioner for England 43–4
Office of the Childrens' Commissioner (OCC)
    role of 15–7
    school safety report 21–2
    and students' rights 11–12
    Young People's Reference Group 15–16
Ogbu, J U 123
Ombudsman, the 43
Ongoing Resourcing Scheme (ORS) 16
oppositional defiant disorder (ODD) 121
Owen, Alwyn 40

P

paramountcy 21
Parent Legal Information Line for School Issues 18
parents
    attitudes to student achievement 99
    communication, relationships with 64–5, 99, 143–4, 170–1
    issues for Māori and Pasifika 156, 163, 165, 169
    and reflection sheet 143
    and stand-downs 154, 156–7, 158, 164–5
        case studies 165–7
        summary 167–8
    and suspensions 96–8, 106
        role in process 24–7, 130
Pasifika Educational Plan 14
Pasifika students
    and exclusion rates 19
    marginalisation of 123, 158
pastoral care of students 181–2, 185–6
Pearson, N 177, 192–3
peer mentoring 207, 208
peers
    in narrative therapy 241–3, 249–51
    and student engagement 199
peers, antisocial 116–7
    external suspension and 62
    female students and 121
People First 35
Pomeroy, E (2000) 97
Positive Behaviour for Learning Action Plan 2010-2014 14, 217
Principals' role in exclusions 23–6, 156, 168–70
professional development 136, 191–2
psychological language 82

punishment, physical *see also* abuse 118
punitive approaches
    alternatives to 105–6
    language of 102–3
    staff attitudes to 102–6
    and traumatisation of students 118

Q
questionnaires, value of 86

R
racism 37–8, 38–9, 118
    perceived 120, 163
reflections as restorative practice 142–3
Research Centre for Children, Youth and Families 74
research studies *see* International Youth Development Study; restorative practice (RP); Youth Self-Report (YSR)
Responsive Schools 21
restorative justice *see also* restorative practice 93
    definitions 136
    student perspectives 100–1
restorative practice (RP)
    challenges in 146–7
    communication and dialogue 138–9
    conferences 145
    continuum 137, 137–8
    and discipline 147–8
    implications for schools 149–50
    reflections as 142–3
    research study 136–8, 150–1
    school-based 63–4, 106–7, 136
    student perspectives 135

Return to School Plan 3
Rolihlahla (Nelson Mandela) 38
Rowling, J K 44
Rumble, Mark 176

S
safety issues 108, 110–11, 128
    and stand-downs 158
school attendance 17, 115–9
school-based
    interventions 125–32
    restorative practices 136–51
school climate
    effects on students 94, 117
    and suspensions 197–8
    and youth offending 114
school exclusion *see also* exclusion, expulsion, suspension, stand-down 2–3
school-family relationships 155, 157–62, 160, 164–8
    case study 165–7
school membership 155–7
    Modes of Belonging **156**
school policy 64–5
    abuse of 119, 129
    proactive 64–5
school staff
    attitudes to punitive approaches 102–6
    BCRS meeting procedures 218–26
    behaviour management perspectives 102–9
    McAuley Champagnat Programme 191–2
    and restorative practice 144–5
    safety of 108–9, 110–1
    welfare workers on 181–2
'school-to-prison pipeline' 49, 123–4
school transitions 17, 116, 126

school uniforms 127, 147, 204, 205, 211
schools
   and parents 99, 143–4, 170–1
      documentation issues 170–1
   and restorative practice 149–50
   roles and responsibilities 199, 212
   roles and responsibilities of 27–8, 131–2, 156
schools, low-decile, and stand-downs 158
Schools and the Right to Discipline 17
schools providing food 127, 186, 190–1, 204
schools *see also* student engagement
Shepparton, Victoria 175–6, 192
situated learning, Wenger's theory of 155–7
social outcomes predicted by suspensions 58–60
Socio-Economic Indexes for Areas (SEIFA) 99
socioeconomic factors
   and educational outcomes 64, 98–9, 117
   linked to exclusions 19, 49–50, 161–2, 197–8
   and youth offending 123–4
Sorry Day 187, 188–9
South Africa 37–8, 45–6
Special Education, 2000 13
'special education' *see also* disability 44
special needs students *see* disability
sporting achievement and youth offending 121
St Vincent de Paul organisation 192
staff *see* school staff; teachers
Stage, S A (1997) 51
stand-down 2–3, 17, 153–5

at-risk factors 158, 161–2
communication over 159–64
and communities of practice 156–7
Māori students and 162–3
parents' expectations 158
parents' role in 165–7
principals' role in 168–70
as punitive approach 159–61
statistics
   exclusion 3, 19, 48–9, 51
   youth offending 115
statistics *see also* International Youth Development Study, findings
'Stolen Generation,' Australia 38–9, 188
Structured Assessment of Violence Risk in Youth (SAVRY) 125
student
   expectations of teachers 117
   perceptions of antisocial behaviour 122
   perceptions of teachers 44–5, 120–1
   perspectives 96–101, 135
   safety 128
Student Absence Learning Plan 3
student achievement
   and disability 121
   expectations of teachers 117
   ineffective teaching and 117
   proactive approaches 127–8, 127–31
      token system 126–7
   proactive approaches *see also* McAuley-Champagnat Programme; McClelland College Programme;
   suspension as risk factor 50, 58–61
   and youth offending 121

student behaviour
　external suspension as negative factor in　49–50
　proactive approach to　64–5
　referred to BCRS　**228**
　relational context of　84–5
　variable school reactions to　19–20
student behaviour *see also* behaviour management
student engagement
　definitions　198–9
　elements in　200–2
　overview　197–200
　programmes　202
　school role in　211–2
student exclusion *see* exclusion
student identity re-authoring concept　236–8
student perspectives　44, 96, 99–100, 101, 135
student–teacher relationships　117–8, 122, 128, 146, 150, 170
students
　mistreatment of *see also* abuse　118
　as negative role models　131
　pastoral care of　181–2, 185–6
　　health care　192
　positive attributes of　166–7
　responsibilities of　28
　and restorative practice　140–1, 144–5, 146
　rights of　11–12, 125
　　code of rights　45
　support for　130
　　case studies　179–81, 252–5
students, excluded *see also* exclusion　197–8
students, female, and antisocial peers　121, 179
students with disabilities *see* disability

substance use　1, 94
Success for All – Every School, Every Child　13
Sullivan, J S (1989)　51
suspension　3, 17, 24–7
　behavioural outcomes　58–61, 96, 123
　in-school case study　209–11
　informal *see also* 'kiwi suspension'　26
　parent attitudes to　96–8
　student perspectives on　96, 99–100
suspension, external　47–52
　and antisocial peer groups　52, 61
　as predictor of negative outcomes　48, 50, 58–60, 61
　rates in Year 10 Victorian students　**58**
　statistics　48–9, 57–60
　　outcomes　49–50
　v internal　99–100
suspension, internal　52–3
　and disadvantaged students　51
　and negative outcomes　58–60, 61
　positive approaches to　129–30
　as punitive approach　106
　rates in Year 10 Victorian students　**58**
　statistics　51, 57–60
　v external　99–100
suspension *see also* exclusion; International Youth Development Study
Systematic Screening for Behaviour Disorders　125

T

tagging　122
te Riele, Kitty　213

teacher-student relationships 107–8,
    117–8, 120–1, 128, 146, 150, 170
  cultural factors 120
teachers
  abuse of students by 118
  ineffective 117
  restorative practice challenges for
    146–7
  safety of 108–9
  students' perceptions of 44–5,
    120–1
teachers'
  identification of potential offenders
    124–5
  perceptions of behaviour
    management 94, 102–9
  responsibilities to students 28,
    107–8, 125
teachers *see also* school staff
teaching techniques 128
  proactive 139–41
terminology, para-legal 160
terminology of disability 41–2
Theriot et al (2010) 197
tobacco use 58, 122
  among students 127
  relational context of 85
tokens as behavioural management
  tool 126–7
Torres Strait Islanders 188
Towl, P (2012) 157, 158
Towl, P (2014) 237
transitions *see* school transitions
Traumatic Incident Team 21
traumatisation of students 118
Treaty of Waitangi and equal rights
  39–41
'tsunami effect' and youth offending
  see also 'school-to-prison pipeline'
  123–5

U
unemployment and educational failure
  22
United Kingdom
  comparative statistics 49
  research 44
  zero tolerance policies 92–3
United Nations Committee on
  the Rights of Persons with
  Disabilities 36
United Nations Convention on
  the Rights of Persons with
  Disabilities 36, 41
United Nations Convention on the
  Rights of the Child 1989 13
United Nations Universal Declaration
  of Human Rights 1948 13
United States
  comparative statistics 22, 48
  research in 74, 194, 197
  zero tolerance policies 51–2, 92–3
University of Vermont 74

V
vandalism 122
victimisation, perceptions of 122–4
Victoria, Australia
  Drugs and Crime Prevention
    Committee (Victoria) 22
  International Youth Developmentv
    Study 2002 94
  research study in 136–7
Victoria Institute for Education,
  Diversity and Lifelong Learning
  213
Victorian Aboriginal Education
  Incorporated Association 177
Victorian Certificate of Applied
  Learning (VCAL) 185, 186, 190

Victorian Department of Education
  and Early Childhood
  Development   193, 213
violence in schools *see also* abuse;
  bullying   21–2
  BCRS referrals   **228**

W

Walter, Ruby   111
Washington State US
  International Youth Development
  Study 2002   94
welfare workers in schools *see also*
  pastoral care   189–90
Wellington Community Law Centre
  17, 18
Wenger, E   154, 155–7
whakataukī   28, 31–2
Whelan, Dr David   192
White, Michael   243
White, Peter   175–6
White Card   186
Wierenga, Ani   200–2, 213
Wierenga's framework   **200**, 200–2

Y

Young Adult Self Report (YASR)   74
young offenders
  and academic achievement   117, 121
  and exclusion   1
  identifying potential   124–5
    screening tools   125
  and neurodisability   43–4
  perceptions of   119–22, 122–4
  protective factors   121
  risk factors   115, 117, 123–4
  school-based interventions   125–32
  school role in   22, 115–9
    'school-to-prison pipeline'   50

schools' responsibility   131–2
and sporting achievement   121
statistics   115
'tsunami effect'   123–5
Yousafzai, Malala   46
Youth Guarantee Programme   14
Youth Offending, Ministerial
  Taskforce on   22
youth offending *see* young offenders
Youth Self-Report (YSR)   72, 73–6
  Achenbach, T M directive on   82
  competence scales questioned
    77–9
  components and subscales   75
  conclusion   85–6
  as developmental psychology tool
    75–6
  research study   76–81
  syndrome scales   79–81, **80**
Youth Self-Report (YSR) *see also*
  Achenbach, T M

Z

zero tolerance policies   21–2, 92–3, 119
  and antisocial behaviour   123
  embedded in NZ school culture
    163–4
  language of   159–61
  and stand-downs   158
  in United States schools   51–2, 92–3

www.ingramcontent.com/pod-product-compliance
Lightning Source LLC
Chambersburg PA
CBHW080801300426
44114CB00020B/2787